Nasha Fitter is a teacher, entrepreneur and expert on communications and soft-skills training. She is the founder of Fitter Solutions, a Mumbai-based training firm that has groomed thousands of young Indians for jobs in companies like Wipro, ICICI Bank and Hindustan Lever. She has developed a unique curriculum and teaching methodology focusing on the special issues that Indian workers face as they seek to succeed in a global economy.

A leader in her field, she has spoken publicly about the education needs of aspirational young Indians and contributed regular writings to publications like Rediff.com and the *Times of India*.

An MBA graduate of the Harvard Business School, Nasha has also worked as an investment banker on Wall Street and for an NGO that seeks to narrow the digital divide in India. She is currently working at Microsoft Corporation in Redmond, Washington, where she focuses on efforts to improve education in emerging markets like India.

YOU'RE HIRED!

HOW TO GET THAT JOB AND KEEP IT TOO

Nasha Fitter

PENGUIN BOOKS

PENGUIN BOOKS
Published by the Penguin Group
Penguin Books India Pvt. Ltd, 11 Community Centre, Panchsheel Park,
New Delhi 110 017, India
Penguin Group (USA) Inc., 375 Hudson Street, New York, New York 10014, USA
Penguin Group (Canada), 90 Eglinton Avenue East, Suite 700, Toronto, Ontario,
M4P 2Y3, Canada (a division of Pearson Penguin Canada Inc.)
Penguin Books Ltd, 80 Strand, London WC2R 0RL, England
Penguin Ireland, 25 St Stephen's Green, Dublin 2, Ireland (a division of Penguin
Books Ltd)
Penguin Group (Australia), 250 Camberwell Road, Camberwell, Victoria 3124,
Australia (a division of Pearson Australia Group Pty Ltd)
Penguin Group (NZ), 67 Apollo Drive, Rosedale, North Shore 0632,
New Zealand (a division of Pearson New Zealand Ltd)
Penguin Group (South Africa) (Pty) Ltd, 24 Sturdee Avenue, Rosebank,
Johannesburg 2196, South Africa

Penguin Books Ltd, Registered Offices: 80 Strand, London WC2R 0RL, England

First published by Penguin Books India 2009

10 9 8 7 6 5 4 3 2 1

While every effort has been made to verify the authenticity of the information contained in this book, the publisher and the author are in no way liable for the use of the information contained in this book.

ISBN 9780143100577

For sale in the Indian Subcontinent only

Typeset in GillSans by Eleven Arts, New Delh
Printed at Gopsons Papers Ltd, Noida

To my mother,
for always reminding me to stay grounded.

To my father,
for always pushing me to fly.

Contents

Acknowledgements

Other people I would like to thank:

I could not have completed this book without the support of all my friends and family. I would like to give a special thanks to my very close friend AG for pushing me to write this book, for always believing in my abilities, and his constant love and support in all my endeavors.

I would also like to thank my Rediff.com readers and students who volunteered to read drafts of my book in focus groups, and provided me with invaluable feedback. I would especially like to thank Shabbir Shaikh and Suren Mylavarapu for believing so strongly in this book and for going above and beyond my expectations to help make it a success.

This book would not be possible without the passion of my editor Meru Gokhale, who I thank for all her wonderful ideas and for always thinking outside the box.

And last, I would like to thank Amita Jadhav and Shantala Sriramaiah for reading early drafts, spending hours editing, and providing me with the comments and ideas that have truly shaped this book.

Introduction

Is this book for you?

- Have you tried to get a job but been rejected because your English or communication skills were not good enough?
- Do you want to apply for a job and need to learn how to impress recruiters and interviewers?
- Do you have strong technical skills but feel you must improve your soft skills to achieve your dreams?
- Do you want to study or work abroad but want to first improve the way you speak, act and dress?
- Do you find it hard to communicate with and converse easily with foreigners?
- Do you worry that as India is becoming more global you will be left behind if you don't improve your English and other communication skills?

If you said yes to any of the above questions, this book is for you.

This book is an all-in-one solution for Indians who want to improve their English communication and job placement skills to succeed in the global economy.

How is this book different?

This is not a difficult book with unnecessary amounts of information. It is designed to help you speak and write better English in the shortest time possible. I have tried to simplify the complicated grammar rules of the English language and focus on the unique communication problems we face in India and other parts of South Asia.

Instead, this book promises to be:

- Everything you need—English grammar, pronunciation, interpersonal communication, personality building, job placement advice, tips for handling interviews, professional dressing and overall business etiquette.
- Easy and organized—this step-by-step book is logically organized and not confusing. Even if you are not good at learning languages, you will find this book easy to follow.
- Customized for Indians—almost all the exercises include real emails, resumés and conversations from different workplaces in India. This will allow you as a reader to easily relate to this book.
- Result oriented—the book focuses on the most common communication problems in India. Rather than try and teach you all the rules of grammar in one go, which can be intimidating and counterproductive to learning, I have concentrated on the most important rules that you *need* to know to communicate confidently at the workplace. Thus, you will be able to quickly improve your English and other soft skills.
- Entertaining—this book makes learning fun! While subjects like English grammar can be boring, this book tries to keep you entertained while you learn!

How was this book created?

This is not just another English grammar or communication book. It is special. This book comes from the years of research and data collection I did while training hundreds of people in English grammar and soft skills in India.

To make this book effective and customized, I analysed my students' writings, emails and spoken English to find the most common mistakes made in India. Then, using simplified English grammar and other communication rules, I have explained these mistakes and given alternatives. For example, the title of chapter 5 is 'Hi, myself Jyoti.'

This is a common way of introducing oneself in India, but it is wrong due to the incorrect use of pronouns. The correct way to make an introduction is 'Hi, my name is Jyoti.' The chapter explains this mistake as well as other actual, pronoun-related errors. Role-play dialogues and stories are used to explain these rules, which makes the book more entertaining and also more like real life.

Each chapter has been read by focus groups of people between the ages of 18 and 30, to make sure each lesson is absolutely effective. These focus groups helped me to guarantee that this book is perfectly customized and focuses only on the mistakes made in India. If you follow this book properly, you should rapidly see a significant improvement in your communication skills.

Why was this book created?

I wrote this book after four years of running a training company in India and being the BPO specialist adviser on Rediff.com. After working with hundreds of students, I realized that many young people cannot afford to go to fancy communication training schools, or don't have the time. Even those who are able to attend a training program need further practice. However, it is very hard to practise communication by oneself without a proper guide.

When I went to bookstores to find the perfect communication guide for Indians, I couldn't even find one. The English grammar books written in the USA and the UK were too complicated and not customized for Indians. On the other hand, I found that most books written in India were not effective or written in an easy-to-use way. Also, I couldn't find any books that had everything from English grammar to pronunciation to job placement advice to business etiquette.

This book seeks to be the solution. It is an all-in-one guide to help you speak better English, prepare for interviews, and dress and act professionally.

How to use this book

This book is split into four sections:

1. English grammar
2. Pronunciation
3. Interpersonal skills and personality building
4. Job placement skills and professional etiquette

If you are looking for a complete way to improve your communication skills, you should follow the four sections listed above in order. Mark out chapters that are most difficult for you and go back and review them.

However, if you feel you only need to improve in certain areas, it is also perfectly okay to read sections or chapters individually. Even reading a few chapters in this book will help you!

Section 1—English grammar

Each chapter in Section 1 covers a different English grammar topic. It is best if you read all the chapters in order, as they have been designed in a certain way. However, if you feel that you only need to improve in a few areas, it is perfectly okay to just read individual chapters. Browse the chapter titles and see what topics you need to spend the most time on. As a note, how to write emails to company recruiters is also covered in this section.

Section 2—Pronunciation

This section focuses mostly on consonant sound neutralization, although there is one chapter on vowel sounds as well. You can read all the chapters in order, or pick the ones that present the sounds you have the most trouble with. Regardless, make sure you start with the introductory chapter, as it gives you the definitions you will need for the rest of this section.

Section 3—Interpersonal skills and personality building
This section will help you improve your interpersonal communication skills. It's best to read the chapters in order, but not compulsory. You can also focus on the areas you most want to improve.

Section 4—Interview skills and professional etiquette
Chapters in this section can be read individually or in a different order based on your needs. They deal with etiquette and give tips on how to perform at interviews.

SECTION I

Practical English grammar

To get a good job in today's competitive work environment, you have to be an effective communicator. Effective communication has many aspects, but the foundation is English grammar. Bad grammar is one of the main reasons why HR managers reject candidates looking for jobs. An HR manager at a leading BPO said in an interview, 'Ninety per cent of people who apply for positions where they need to interact with people, either over the phone or in person, are turned away due to poor communication skills—mostly grammar related.' If you don't speak and write well, you will not come across as professional in today's global corporate world, no matter how qualified you are.

Yet, despite knowing the importance of good grammar, many people find the subject just too boring and tedious. Don't worry, there is a solution! In an easy, practical and logical way, I will help you go from making the types of mistakes found in Email 1 below, to speaking and writing with the fluency found in Email 3.

Email 1

Dear Mam/Sir

This is with regard to ur company posting for software engineer. Myself Dhiraj and i m having post-graduate in computer science and i is very interested in position. Few years back I join similar company in Bangalore. I applied to your Company last year but I didn't got the job . . . . so, currently looking to see if there are new opportunity bcoz i am very much interested. I am having few skill that is well suited for your company. What exactly you looking out for? please go thru my cv.

Please revert back on the same.

Thanking you.
Dhiraj

This is an email that an HR manager in Mumbai received from a prospective candidate. It is full of errors, and the candidate was not asked to come for the interview because his email was so badly written. Take a look at the email below. The mistakes have been corrected and are in bold.

Email 2

Dear **Ma'am/Sir,**

This is with regard to **your** company**'s** posting for **a** software engineer. **My name is** Dhiraj and **I have a** postgraduate **degree** in computer science. **I am** very interested in **the** position. A few years **ago** I **joined a** similar company in Bangalore. I applied to your **c**ompany last year but I didn't **get** the job**.** **I am** currently looking to see if there are new **opportunities because I** am **very interested**. I **have skills** that **are** well suited to your company. What exactly **are** you **looking for**? **P**lease go **through** my **CV**.

Please get back to me.

Thanks,
Dhiraj

This email no longer contains grammatical errors, but it still doesn't sound professional. Take a look at how we can transform this email to be even better:

Email 3

```
Dear Sir or Madam:

My name is Dhiraj Shah and I obtained your contact
information from your company's website. I am
interested in applying for the software engineering
position that was posted. Currently, I am an engineer
in a Bangalore-based firm and have over two years
of experience in this area. Please find attached
to this email a copy of my CV that details my past
work experience.

I will follow up with you during the week to confirm
you have received this email. I look forward to
speaking with you.

Regards,
Dhiraj Shah
981-122-3456
```

This is a professional, effective email. This section will teach you how to write and speak in this manner. This section does not focus on complicated grammar terms. Instead, common grammatical errors made by Indian speakers have been targeted. All the examples in this section have been taken from actual emails, letters and CVs.

Before you begin this section, remember that some parts may appear more difficult than others. If you don't completely understand everything the first time you read it, be patient, do all the exercises, and you will quickly notice your language skills improving.

This section includes the following chapters:

1. Why don't employers call me after I send them my CV?
   The truth behind constructing sentences

2. How can I make my CV and emails more professional?
   Using nouns properly
3. Is it 'India' or 'the India'? Is it 'USA' or 'the USA'?
   Using articles correctly (Part 1): Before proper and specific nouns
4. Am I 'a' graduate, 'an' graduate or just 'graduate'?
   Using articles correctly (Part 2): Before general nouns
5. Hi, myself Jyoti.
   All kinds of pronouns
6. Is she better, more better, the best, or the most bestest?
   Using comparatives and superlatives
7. Why can't my subject and verb get along?
   Verbs (Part 1): Subject–verb agreement
8. Should I say 'I understand you' or 'I am understanding you'?
   Verbs (Part 2): Present simple versus present continuous tenses
9. She liked me in the past but hates me in the present!
   Verbs (Part 3): Present simple versus past simple tenses
10. It's easiest to keep the past simple
    Verbs (Part 4): Past simple versus other past tenses
11. 'Will I get the job?', 'Will I be getting the job?' or 'Am I going to get the job?'
    Verbs (Part 5): Future tenses
12. I am asking the question correctly, no?
    Asking questions
13. What is your good name? What is your bad name?
    Indianisms (Part 1): Grammatical errors and slang
14. Is it 'Dear Miss Nasha', 'Dear Ms Nasha' or 'Dear Ms Fitter'?
    Indianisms (Part 2): SMS slang, punctuation and writing professional emails

CHAPTER 1

Why don't employers call me after I send them my CV?

The truth behind constructing sentences

Have you ever applied for a job but were not called in for the interview? Do you wonder why? We found that most employers do not return calls because the emails they receive are poorly written. This is mostly due to bad sentence construction. Take a look to see if you have ever written an email that includes some of these common mistakes:

Common Error 1:

✗ To work for your company in Pune.

- This sentence does not express a complete thought. It does not give all the information needed to figure out what the applicant is trying to say.
- When you look at the sentence above you are left thinking, 'What position does he want?'

To make this sentence clear, the writer needs to include more information:

✓ I am applying for the position of an agent in your company in Pune.

Common Error 2:

✗ Going to the interview is Karishma.

- This sentence demonstrates a very common problem—mixed-up word order.

The sentence should read:

✓ Karishma is going to the interview.

Common Error 3:

✗ For interviews, I want to know how to face the extempore rounds because I am only weak in that round so will you please help me out in this.

- There is too much information crammed into a single sentence. This is called a run-on sentence.

The sentence can be rewritten as two separate sentences:

✓ I want to know how to face extempore rounds in interviews, as I am weak in those rounds. Will you please help me?

What will I learn in this chapter?

1.1 How to construct grammatically correct sentences.
1.2 The parts of a complete sentence.
1.3 How to recognize incomplete sentences.
1.4 How to recognize sentences that have a mixed-up word order.
1.5 How to stop making sentences that are long, boring and hard to follow.

1.1 HOW TO CONSTRUCT GRAMMATICALLY CORRECT SENTENCES

In Hindi, the word order of sentences is different from English. For example: *Namish cricket khelta hai.*

The Hindi verb *khelta hai* is placed at the end of the sentence. Literally translated into English, this sentence would read: Namish cricket *plays*.

In English, though, this sentence should be: Namish *plays* cricket.

Here, the subject is 'Namish', the verb 'plays' and the object 'cricket'.

Notice that we placed the verb 'plays' before the object 'cricket'. In English, the verb always comes *before* the object. In Hindi, the verb always comes *after* the object. This difference is one of the main reasons why many of us make mistakes when constructing sentences in English.

Remember this easy formula to form a complete sentence in English:

Subject + Verb + Object = Complete sentence

- Subject: the subject is what the sentence is about.
- Verb: in English, the verb follows the subject and it does the 'work' in the sentence.
- Object: usually found at the end of a sentence, the object is the 'receiver' of the subject's action. It may also be a word that explains the subject or the verb better.

If you follow the subject + verb + object sequence shown above, your sentences will always be clear enough for anyone to understand. For example:

1. **I** *work* for a <u>call centre</u>.
2. **Kersi** *is* an <u>engineer</u>.
3. **Sunil** *likes* <u>mangoes</u>.

When you read each of the sentences shown above, you do not need any additional information to understand what is being said. This is because all the parts required to create a complete sentence are in place.

Each sentence contains a subject:

1. **I**
2. **Kersi**
3. **Sunil**

Each sentence contains a verb:

1. *work*
2. *is*
3. *likes*

Each sentence contains an object:

1. <u>call centre</u>.
2. <u>engineer</u>.
3. <u>mangoes</u>.

Always keeping to the above sequence will help you construct proper sentences. When you forget one of the elements of the sequence, you end up with incomplete sentences called 'fragments'.

1.2 THE PARTS OF A COMPLETE SENTENCE

As we just learned, each part of a complete sentence—subject, verb and object—is crucial towards helping us be grammatically correct and professional. This does not mean, though, that we can never have sentences without one of these parts. In some cases, short sentences can contain just a subject and a verb and no object. For example: 'I ran.'

We don't need to include the object of this sentence—*where* the person is running or *why* the person is running—because these details could be obvious elsewhere in the paragraph in which the sentence occurs.

Other short sentences can contain just a verb and an object, but no subject. For example: 'Go home.'

We don't include *who* the subject is that needs to go home, because again, this detail was probably obvious elsewhere in the paragraph in which the sentence occured.

Usually, sentences *must* contain a subject, a verb and an object. Many of us leave out one of these parts because we take it for granted that the other person will know what we are talking about. This is not a good assumption to make, as we often end up creating fragments which do not have all the necessary parts that make up sentences.

For example:

Fragment	Problem
For a call centre.	What about the call centre?
Kersi is.	What exactly is Kersi?
Likes mangoes.	Who likes mangoes?

! To avoid sentence fragments, look at your sentences and ask yourself whether you have remembered to include a subject, verb and object.

You might be worried that you will not remember the definitions of words like 'subject' and 'verb'. But hang in there; you will soon see the hard work pay off.

1.3 HOW TO RECOGNIZE INCOMPLETE SENTENCES

Let's learn what subjects, verbs and objects really mean, and how we can easily identify them in sentences. This will help us construct complete sentences and speak correct English.

Subject

- The subject of a sentence is a person (Sonali), a place (India) or a thing (table).
- Pronouns can be used to take the place of subject nouns (I, she, he, it, we, they, you).
- The subject performs the action in the sentence.
- The subject is generally found at or near the beginning of the sentence.

Exercise 1.1

Read the following sentences and underline the subject in each case. Check your answers in the answer key before moving on.

1. I am a software developer.
2. Sahil is at home.
3. Mr Gupta has four children.
4. The monkey ate my sandwich.
5. The Indian team won the cricket match.

Verb

Verbs are of mostly two types—action verbs and linking verbs.

- Most verbs are known as 'action verbs', and do all the 'work' in the sentence. (Examples of action verbs include to clean, to feed, to eat, to run).

- Other verbs are known as 'linking verbs', and they hold the sentence together. They connect the subject and the object. (Examples of linking verbs include am, is, are, has, have.)

Exercise 1.2

Identify the verb in each of the sentences given below. Check your answers before moving on.

1. I am a software developer.
2. Sahil is at home.
3. Mr Gupta has four children.
4. The monkey ate my sandwich.
5. The Indian team won the cricket match.

Object

- If the sentence contains an action verb, the word which receives the action of the verb is called the object.
- If the sentence contains a linking verb, the object tends to describe the subject, or give more information about the subject.
- The object can be better remembered as the target or focus of the verb's attention.

Exercise 1.3

Identify the object in each of the sentences below. Check your answers before moving on.

1. I am a software developer.
2. Sahil is at home.
3. Mr Gupta has four children.
4. The monkey ate my sandwich.
5. The Indian team won the cricket match.

! Don't forget to check your answers before moving on.

You now know the three important parts every sentence should have. In the exercises given below, you will use what you have learned to see if you can recognize complete and incomplete sentences.

Exercise 1.4

Read the following sentences. Write 'correct' next to the ones you think are proper, complete sentences. Write 'fragment' next to the ones you think are incomplete. Identify whether the subject, verb or object is missing from each fragment. Check your answers before moving on.

1. What does it take to excel at being a customer support executive?
2. I am working as a data entry operator.
3. Currently working in a company in Bangalore.
4. The basic criteria for a job in a call centre.
5. My English is fairly bad.
6. Even lacking confidence in myself.

Exercise 1.5

Now use the fragments you found in Exercise 1.4 (above) to make complete sentences.

! Don't forget to check your answers before moving on.

1.4 HOW TO RECOGNIZE SENTENCES THAT HAVE A MIXED-UP WORD ORDER

You have now learnt how to identify verbs, subjects and objects in sentences. By now, it is also clear that these elements are needed to construct complete sentences.

Word order in any language is very important. Sometimes, if you change the order of the words, you change the meaning dramatically. For example:

- I ate the carrot.
- The carrot ate I.

These two sentences express *very* different ideas. To make ourselves understood, we must be careful with the word order of sentences.

It is very important to recognize where words should fit in a sentence if you want to speak clear and understandable English. If you are having trouble making sentences, remember the following word order:

Subject + Verb + Object = Complete sentence

The following exercises will help you recognize proper word order.

Exercise 1.6

Identify the subject and the verb in each of the sentences given below. Rewrite the sentences so that they are grammatically correct. Check your answers before moving on.

1. Going to the gym today is Rahul.
2. Pamper herself to Pooja is going to the beauty parlour.
3. Such a boring game is tennis.
4. For her phone number at work I asked a girl.
5. Call the police I suggest you.

! Don't forget to check your answers before moving on.

You should now have a good understanding of subjects, verbs and objects, and the order they should be in.

The *number* of subjects, verbs and objects you put in a sentence also matters. If you have too many, the sentence becomes a run-on sentence. A run-on sentence is difficult to understand because it is long and confusing, and therefore looks unprofessional.

1.5 HOW TO STOP MAKING SENTENCES THAT ARE LONG, BORING AND HARD TO FOLLOW

Sentences that have more than one subject and verb combination are called run-on sentences.

There are two ways to fix run-on sentences:

- Write them out as two or more short sentences.
- Include commas and the words 'and' or 'but'.

Writing run-ons as shorter sentences

Remember Common Error 3 from the beginning of the chapter?

✗ For interviews, I want to know how to face the extempore rounds because I am only weak in that round so will you please help me out in this.

Here, the speaker is expressing several different thoughts which are too confusing when put in the same sentence. It is better to stick to one or two subject–verb combinations in a single sentence. The same sentence has been rewritten below, and the subject–verb combinations are in bold.

✓ **I want** to know how to face extempore rounds in interviews, as **I am** weak in those rounds. Will **you** please **help** me?

This one long sentence has been broken up into two shorter ones. Each sentence has its own subject–verb combination.

! Remember, a single, well-written sentence is far better than a long, complicated one which is difficult to understand.

Breaking run-ons up with commas, 'and' and 'but'

It is also possible to connect two complete sentences and make a longer one. We do this using connecting words like 'and' and 'but'. When using these connecting words, it helps to place a comma before the 'and' or 'but'. Using a comma is not always necessary though, and depends on your personal preference. Take a look at the two separate sentences given below. The subject–verb combinations have been circled.

First part of sentence	Second part of sentence
1. I am very good at dealing with customers.	2. I can't seem to get promoted in my company.
1. She is always telling everyone to do a better job.	2. I think that her presence is very motivating.

These separate complete sentences can be combined by using a comma followed by 'and' or 'but'.

1. I am very good at dealing with customers**, but** I can't seem to get promoted in my company.
2. She is always telling everyone to do a better job**, and** I think that her presence is very motivating.

Note how there are two subject–verb combinations in each of the above sentences. However, these are not run-on sentences due to the way they have been connected.

Exercise 1.7

Read the sentences given below and rewrite them correctly. Check your answers before moving on. Some variations are okay; make sure that your answers are similar to the ones provided in the answer key.

1. My English is quite good but I don't get the chance to practise speaking English so can you tell me how I can improve.
2. I want to improve my grammar and English so what should I do.
3. I have a Bachelor's degree in computer applications I have good typing skills also a good command of English are these things desirable for a job with a multinational.
4. I am interested in getting a job with a software company and I am a graduate in computer science and I have had a few interviews with BPOs but did not get a job.
5. I want to work in a BPO can you please tell me how I should prepare myself for an interview.

To sum up:

- A good sentence needs a subject, verb and object in the right order. If these elements are absent, you end up with a fragment.
- Sentences should have only one subject–verb combination. Otherwise, you might end up with a run-on sentence.

Exercise 1.8

Read the following sentences and rewrite them correctly. Some variations are okay; make sure your answers are similar to the answer key. Check your answers before moving on.

1. Steps to improve my communication skills.
2. How can I prepare myself for a marketing interview and what

are the qualifications I need to be hired and I am also familiar with MS Office.

3. I am working as a project leader in a software company.
4. Where she is?
5. I am a software developer and working for a medium-sized software company.
6. While capturing data for HCA today morning.
7. This is a good job where I am a sales executive and I have to make calls to convince people from the textile industry to be members of our portal.

! Don't forget to check your answers before moving on.

APPLYING WHAT YOU HAVE LEARNED

1. There are three parts to a proper sentence (spoken or written)—the subject, verb and object.
2. Sentences that don't contain one of these three parts are incomplete, and are called fragments.
   ✗ Hoping to get a job in a BPO.
   ✓ **I hope** to get a job in a BPO.
3. You also must follow the subject + verb + object order.
   ✗ Hoping to go she is.
   ✓ **She is** hoping to go.
4. Sentences that have too many subject–verb combinations in them are called run-on sentences. They are long, complicated, hard to follow and unprofessional.
   ✗ For this job I just wanted to know the procedure for applying because I am very interested so could you please let me know as soon as possible.
   ✓ **I** am very interested in this job. **I** would like to know the procedure for applying. Could **you** please let me know the procedure as soon as possible?

This chapter was meant to give you an overview. After you read through the rest of this section, come back and review this chapter.

CHAPTER 2

How can I make my CV and emails more professional?

Using nouns properly

In the previous chapter we learned how to put together grammatically correct, complete sentences. Emails containing well-structured sentences look professional. However, good sentence structure is not enough. To make sure your emails are polished and error-free, you have to be careful not to:

1. Capitalize nouns incorrectly.
2. Pluralize nouns incorrectly.
3. Create long, wordy sentences.

See if you make any of the following common errors.

> Common Error 1:
> ✗ I am looking for stores outside India that sell Ethnic Indian Products.
> ✗ How can I improve my English Language skills?
> • Although the first word of a sentence should always be capitalized, only proper nouns (names of people, names of countries, names of products) are capitalized in the middle of sentences.

The sentences above can be written correctly as follows:

✓ I am looking for stores outside India that sell **e**thnic Indian **p**roducts.

✓ How can I improve my English **l**anguage skills?

Common Error 2:
✗ I work for a company that manufactures medical equipments.
✗ What are the qualification required for the job?
- These two sentences have very similar problems. In the first sentence, 'equipments' should be singular and thus should not have an 's' at the end.
- In the second sentence, 'qualification' should be plural and thus should have an 's' at the end.

The sentences should read:
✓ I work for a company that manufactures medical **equipment**.
✓ What are the **qualifications** required for the job?

Common Error 3:
✗ The files of the company are hard to find.
- This sentence is wordier than it needs to be. By converting the noun 'company' into its possessive form, we can shorten this sentence.

The sentence should read:
✓ The company's files are hard to find.

The above examples relate to errors made in understanding nouns. This chapter will help you eliminate these errors from your writing and speech. It will also give you the foundation you need to understand the next chapter on articles.

What will I learn in this chapter?
2.1 What is a noun?
2.2 How to make nouns plural.
2.3 Possessive nouns can make sentences concise.
2.4 Making nouns plural and possessive.
2.5 Recap.

2.1 WHAT IS A NOUN?

A noun is a person, place, thing or idea.

There are three types of nouns:

1. *Common nouns* are ordinary things that can be seen, touched or heard. For example: house, dog, sky, desk.
2. *Abstract nouns* name ideas, emotions or qualities that cannot be seen. For example: love, joy, grief.
3. *Proper nouns* are the names of people, places or things. For example: India, Kareena, Pepsi.

! Proper nouns are always capitalized. Common and abstract nouns are capitalized only when they begin sentences.

Exercise 2.1

Classify the nouns given below as 'common', 'abstract' or 'proper'. (Identify which nouns that have to be capitalized in the middle of sentences.) Check your answers before moving on.

1. computer
2. ocean
3. love
4. director
5. man
6. marriage
7. death
8. fatima
9. book
10. spain
11. president
12. sadness
13. mumbai
14. tree

Exercise 2.2

Read the list of proper nouns given below. Using the example as a guide, think of the common nouns that describe what each proper noun is. For example:

Proper nouns	Common nouns
Shah Rukh Khan	actor

Check your answers before moving on.

Proper nouns	Common nouns
1. India	
2. New Delhi	
3. Pepsi	
4. Microsoft	
5. Marine Drive	
6. *Times of India*	

Exercise 2.3

Read the email given below. Some proper nouns have not been correctly capitalized. Some common and abstract nouns have been incorrectly capitalized. Correct these errors. Check your answers before moving on.

```
Dear ketan,

Yesterday I went to an Anniversary Party for my Mother and Father. It was a real blast. We held it at the starwood hall in andheri. My brother brought a DJ and he played all kinds of good Music. The President of the hall also came to the Party. Wish you could have been there.

Regards,
joshi
```

! Don't forget to check your answers before moving on.

2.2 HOW TO MAKE NOUNS PLURAL

A singular noun names just one person, place or thing. A plural noun tells you that there are two or more of the same thing. Proper and abstract nouns do not have plurals.

- Can you have two Suns? Of course not!
- Can you have two griefs? No, you can *grieve* twice, but you cannot have 'two griefs'.

Common nouns are the only nouns that can be pluralized. Let's read the following dialogue between Raj and his interviewer, Mr Mehta.

```
Mr Mehta: Do you think your skills would be useful
for our company?

Raj: Yes, because my skill are aligned with the
company's goals.
```

Mr Mehta has asked if Raj's skills are the same ones the company is looking for. However, Raj made a mistake while answering—he did not use the plural form of skill. The correct sentence should read:

✓ Raj: Yes, because my **skills** are aligned with the company's goals.

Whenever you refer to two or more of the same thing, you must make the noun plural. The rules for pluralizing common nouns are as follows:

1. Most words in English can be made plural simply by adding 's' to the end.
   - 1 house → 2 houses
   - 1 cat → 2 cats
2. When a word ends in the letters 's', 'z', 'x', 'ch', or 'sh', an 'es' is added to the end of a word.
   - 1 dress → 2 dresses
   - 1 batch → 2 batches
3. If a noun ends in a consonant followed by the letter 'y', you must change the 'y' to an 'i' and add 'es'.
   - 1 story → 2 stories
4. If a noun ends with the letter 'f', you should change the 'f' to a 'v' and then add 'es' to the end.
   - 1 half → 2 halves

The table below summarizes all of these rules:

Singular word	For plural word
Most words	Add 's'
Ending in s, z, x, ch, sh	Add 'es'
Ending in consonant + y	Drop 'y', add 'ies'
Ending in f	Drop 'f', add 'ves'

There are two more rules we need to keep in mind while making nouns plural. These rules are slightly different from the ones given above.

5. Some nouns in English remain exactly the same whether they are singular or plural.
   - 1 deer → 2 deer
   - 1 aircraft → 2 aircraft
6. A few nouns change their spelling completely depending on whether they are singular or plural. Unfortunately, there is no rule for these changes and they are unpredictable. The more English you read, the more you will start to remember these irregularities automatically.
   - 1 foot → 2 feet
   - 1 mouse → 2 mice

Tips to remember:
Plurals are never made by adding an apostrophe followed by an s ('s).

✗ There are many dog**'s** at her house.
✓ There are many do**gs** at her house.

Words like 'some', 'few' and 'many' always tell you that the noun that follows should be plural.

✗ I see a few car.
✓ I see a few car**s**.
✗ I want some flower.
✓ I want some flower**s**.

Some nouns can be singular even though they refer to more than one person or thing. These are known as *collective nouns*. For example, take the noun 'audience'. An audience can consist of many people. Yet, because we are referring to *one* collection of people, the noun 'audience' is considered singular. Examples of collective nouns include:

- A **group** of people. (The group consists of many people, yet we are referring to *one* collective group.)
- A **committee** of engineers. (The committee consists of many engineers, yet we are referring to *one* collective committee.)
- A **team** of sportsmen. (The team consists of many sportsmen, yet we are referring to *one* collective team.)

If we make a collective noun plural (for instance, if we change 'audience' to 'audienc**es**',) we are indicating *different* collections of people. For example:

- Two **groups** of people. (Now we are referring to *two different* groups.)
- Two c**ommittees** of engineers. (Now we are referring to *two different* committees.)
- Two **teams** of sportsmen. (Now we are referring to *two different* teams.)

Thus, for pluralizing nouns:

Formula 1:
Proper and abstract nouns → No pluralizing required

Formula 2:
Most common nouns → Add 's', 'es', 'ies' or 'ves' to the end
Other common nouns → Change form entirely or do not change at all

Exercise 2.4

Write down the plural forms of the singular nouns given below. Some nouns in the list may be irregular. Check your answers before moving on.

1. File
2. BPO
3. Company
4. Equipment
5. Tooth
6. Key
7. City
8. Tree
9. Wolf
10. Lunch
11. Child
12. Feedback

Exercise 2.5

Some of the nouns in the sentences below are incorrect—either they are singular when they should be plural, or they have been pluralized incorrectly. Correct the mistakes. Check your answers before moving on.

1. Do you have any idea for me?
2. I have a degrees in computer applications.
3. They are very successful persons in their company.
4. What are the qualification I need for the job?
5. One of my friend asked me why I am joining a call centre instead of the corporate industry.
6. What should the answer to this question and other related question be?
7. Thank you for the advices you gave me.
8. My voice sounds totally different on call and my colleagues make fun of it.
9. The childrens have come with the other peoples.
10. He had given me great helps when I installed my softwares.

! Don't forget to check your answers before moving on.

By now you should have a much better idea of when to capitalize nouns and when to pluralize them. Let us now learn how possessive nouns can help us reduce the length of our sentences.

2.3 POSSESSIVE NOUNS CAN MAKE SENTENCES CONCISE

Sometimes we need to refer to who or what owns something. To do this, we use the 'possessive' form of a noun. Zabina's diary entry will illustrate this concept better.

```
Dear Diary,

Today is a very sad day. The computer of my sister
was stolen from the house of my father. The lock
on the door was not secure enough.
```

What is wrong with Zabina's diary entry? Grammatically, it is acceptable. Professionally, it is a big mess! The sentences are longer and wordier than they need to be. Zabina has forgotten the rules for singular possessive nouns. Possessive nouns help us make our sentences smaller.

Singular possessives

- A possessive noun indicates ownership.
- We make the singular possessive form by adding an apostrophe (') followed by 's' to the end of a noun.
- Possessives make sentences clearer and more concise.

Example:
The pen my brother owns.
Brother → Noun
Pen → The thing he owns

To make this sentence more concise, we say: My **brother's** pen. Here, the noun 'brother' has been converted into a possessive noun.

If we rewrite the above diary entry using this new rule, it will look like this:

Dear Diary,

Today is a very sad day. My **sister's** computer was stolen from my **father's** house. The **door's** lock was not secure enough.

If you count the number of words in both diary entries, you will notice that the first one has twenty-eight words and the second one has only twenty-two. We have cut out six words in just two lines by using possessive nouns!

For possessive nouns:	
Singular possessive noun →	Add an apostrophe (') followed by 's' to the end.

! Remember, you can only use an apostrophe when indicating possession. You must never use it to make nouns plural.

✗ There are many **dog's** at her house. (What the sentence is trying to say is that there is more than one dog, for which the plural form—dogs—must be used.)

✓ The **dog's** collar is new. (Here we are talking about the dog's possession: its collar.)

Also, remember that you must add an apostrophe (') and 's' *even* if the noun ends in the letter 's'.

✗ Das' shoes are very nice.

✓ **Das's** shoes are very nice.

Exercise 2.6

Using the above example as a guide, write the possessive form of the nouns given below. Check your answers before moving on.

1. The file of the company.
2. The desk of the boss.
3. The table of my mother.
4. The wedding of her sister.
5. The computer of Karishma.

Exercise 2.7

Read the following possessive phrases. Correct the ones which contain errors. Check your answers before moving on.

1. The drivers phone.
2. The company's transportation.
3. The world's highest mountains.
4. Indias achievements.
5. The population of India.

Plural possessives

Zabina's family has had awful luck. The day after her sister's computer was stolen, her family had another robbery. Read Zabina's diary entry to learn more.

```
Dear Diary,

Another horrible thing has happened. The car of
my parents was stolen. The landlord of our building
really sympathized with us.
```

We know from the above lesson that this diary entry is much too wordy. Zabina has forgotten to convert her nouns into the possessive form again! However, in this diary entry Zabina has to convert *plural* nouns (like 'parents'), into the possessive form.

How do we do this? Let's go over the rules for making plural nouns possessive.

- If a plural noun ends in 's', add *only* an apostrophe *after* the final 's'.
- If a plural noun does not end in 's', add an apostrophe and then add an 's' to the end of the word (same as the rule for singular possessives).

Use this chart to better understand the difference between singular and plural possessives.

Singular noun	Singular possessive	Plural noun	Plural possessive
Toy	Toy's	Toys	Toys'
Child	Child's	Children	Children's

Examples

1. A toy belonging to many children
   Children → Plural noun
   Toy → The thing they own
   To make this more concise, we say: The **children's** toy.

- Since the plural noun (children) does not end in 's', we add an apostrophe and then add an 's' to the end (the same rule as listed for singular possessive nouns).

2. A nest belonging to many birds
   Birds → Plural noun
   Nest → Thing they own
   To make this more concise, we say: The **birds'** nest.

- Since this plural noun (birds) ends in an 's', we simply add an apostrophe after the word.

We can now correct Zabina's diary entry:

```
Dear Diary,

Another horrible thing has happened. My parents'
car was stolen. Our building's landlord really
sympathized with us.
```

For plural possessive nouns
- If ending in 's' → Add an apostrophe (') to the end
- If not → Add an apostrophe (') and then an 's' to the end (same as for singular possessives)

By this point, we have covered a lot of rules. Don't worry if things are a bit blurry. The following exercises will help clarify your doubts.

Exercise 2.8

Write the correct form of the plural possessive for each of the phrases given below. Check your answers before moving on.

1. The lifestyle of Indians.
2. The interviews of the call centres.
3. The qualifications of the candidates.
4. The computers of the employees.
5. The files of the companies.

6. The books of the women
7. The votes of the people

2.4 MAKING NOUNS PLURAL AND POSSESSIVE

In the following examples, pay attention to two things:

1. How singular nouns have been made plural.
2. How both singular and plural nouns have been made into their possessive form.

Singular	Plural
1. The person's car. (One person.)	The people's car. (More than one person.)
2. The boy's car. (One boy.)	The boys' car. (More than one boy.)
3. The wolf's meat. (One wolf.)	The wolves' meat. (More than one wolf.)
4. The city's streets. (One city.)	The cities' streets. (More than one city.)

Exercise 2.9

In this exercise, write the correct plural form of the noun, the correct singular possessive and the correct plural possessive in the blanks provided. Check your answers before moving on.

1. Singular noun: girl
   a. Plural noun: ______
   b. Singular possessive: The ______ lipstick.
   c. Plural possessive: The ______ hairbrushes.
2. Singular noun: person
   a. Plural noun: ______
   b. Singular possessive: The ______ resumé.
   c. Plural possessive: The ______ resumés.
3. Singular noun: foot
   a. Plural noun: ______

b. Singular possessive: Her left ______ fungus problem.
c. Plural possessive: Her _______ fungus problem.

! Make sure you have done the exercises and checked your answers before moving on.

2.5 A QUICK RECAP OF THE FORMULAE IN THIS CHAPTER

Formulae for making nouns plural

Formula 1:
Proper and abstract nouns → No pluralizing required

Formula 2:
Most common nouns → Add 's', 'es', 'ies' or 'ves' to the end
Other common nouns → Change form entirely or do not change at all

Formulae for making nouns possessive

Formula 3:
Singular possessive noun → Add an apostrophe (') followed by 's' to the end

Formula 4:
Plural possessive noun
If ending in 's' → Add an apostrophe (') to the end
If not → Add an apostrophe (') and then an 's' to the end (same as for singular possessives)

Other tips

1. Capitalize only proper nouns in the middle of sentences.
   ✗ He is the **P**resident of **a**merica.
   ✓ He is the **p**resident of **A**merica.
2. Words like 'some', 'few' and 'many' tell you that the noun that follows these words should be plural.
   ✗ There are **some book** on the table.
   ✓ There are **some books** on the table.

Exercise 2.10

Read the sentences given below. Look at the nouns in each sentence and correct the errors, if any. Check your answers before moving on.

1. It is one of the most beautiful monument in the world.
2. The persons were waiting at the bus station.
3. Those women's are very noisy when they engage in small talks.
4. I put the files on Pareshs desk.
5. The food of that restaurant is very good.
6. Those companies workers are very well paid.
7. I cleared the first and second round but could not get through the last round.
8. I am a postgraduate in M.Sc. computer Science and I had given a few interview in BPO.
9. I cannot pronounce word correctly.
10. Please give me some suggestion regarding these.
11. My positions is Business development manager.
12. I have these problem.
13. I like all Abhishek Bachchan movie.
14. It is a small valley surrounded by hills on all side.
15. I have read many biography. However, the most important one is Nehru biography.
16. I love flowers. Every time I see flower's I stop and smell them.
17. I have a lot of problem in my life.
18. She should realize that she is going to be someone wife.

! Make sure you have done the exercises and checked your answers before moving on.

Good work! You have finished the chapter on nouns. The lessons you learned in this chapter will help you master the next two chapters on articles.

APPLYING WHAT YOU HAVE LEARNED

1. Only proper nouns (people's names, names of countries, names of products) are capitalized in the middle of sentences.

   ✗ I saw the President of America.

   ✓ I saw the **p**resident of America.

2. Only common nouns (some exceptions exist) can be made plural. We do this by adding an 's', 'es', 'ies' or 'ves' to the end of nouns.
   - I toy → 2 toy**s**
   - I class → 2 class**es**
   - I pony → 2 pon**ies**
   - I calf → 2 cal**ves**
3. Some common nouns don't change at all when made plural. Others change form completely.
   - I species → 2 species
   - I person → 2 people
4. In order to make our sentences shorter and less wordy, we can use possessive nouns. For singular nouns, we add an **'s** to the end of the noun.

   ✗ The car of my father.

   ✓ My father**'s** car.
5. The same rule applies for making plural nouns possessive.

   ✗ The toys of my children.

   ✓ My children**'s** toys.

6 For plural nouns which end in 's', we simply add an apostrophe (') to the end of the noun.

   ✗ The car of my brothers.

   ✓ My brothers**'** car.

CHAPTER 3

Is it 'India' or 'the India'? Is it 'USA' or 'the USA'?

Using articles correctly (Part 1): Before proper and specific nouns

In the previous chapter, we discussed the different types of nouns, and by now you should be familiar with the differences between proper, common and abstract nouns. In this chapter you will learn how to use articles: 'the', 'a' and 'an'. One major reason why English speakers in India have trouble with articles is that articles are not used in Hindi.

Read this email which was received from a Rediff.com reader. All the articles have been circled while all the nouns have been marked in bold.

> I am working as (a) **customer support executive** in (an) **I.S.P.** in **Kerala**. I am (a) **graduate** in **biology** and also (a) **postgraduate** in **computer applications**. I want to know whether I can get (a) **job** in (a) **BPO** which tallies with my **experience**. What does it take to excel at being (a) **customer support executive**?

You will notice that all the circled articles fall before a noun. Without articles, English sentences sound rough, unsophisticated, and most importantly, grammatically incorrect.

In the above email, notice that certain types of nouns don't need an article. Most of us make mistakes because we don't know which nouns need an article and which don't. We also forget which articles to use. Let's look at some of the most common errors—see if you can relate to any of them.

Common Error 1:

✗ I am going to the Wipro to work.
✗ The India is my home country.
- These two sentences share the same error. They contain articles where they are not needed. Certain types of nouns do not need any articles before them.

The correct sentences are:

✓ I am going to Wipro to work.
✓ India is my home country.

Common Error 2:

✗ My attitude towards the life is to be happy.
✗ I hope a complaint I made will be answered quickly.
- These sentences both contain mix-ups associated with using the article 'the'. The first sentence contains the article 'the' where it is not needed. The second sentence is missing the article 'the' where it is needed.

The correct sentences are:

✓ My attitude towards life is to be happy.
✓ I hope **the** complaint I made will be answered quickly.

The above examples deal with two common errors in adding articles before proper nouns and common and abstract nouns that are *specific*. Don't worry about these grammar terms; by the end of the chapter they will be clear to you.

What will I learn in this chapter?

3.1 Which articles to place before proper nouns.
3.2 How to use the article 'the' before common and abstract nouns that are *specific*.
3.3 Recap.

Before we start

The words 'a', 'an' and 'the' are articles. They come before nouns or noun phrases in a sentence. A noun phrase includes the descriptive word right before the noun. For example:

- I see **a car**.
  '**a**' is the article before the noun '**car**'.
- I see **a red car**.
  '**a**' is the article before the noun phrase '**red car**'. '**Red**' is describing the noun '**car**'.

When we have descriptive words before nouns, the article comes before the descriptive word.

3.1 WHICH ARTICLES TO PLACE BEFORE PROPER NOUNS

We are going to learn about articles through a conversation between Arjun and his father. Arjun comes from a family of five which includes his father, mother and two brothers. Both of Arjun's brothers are engineers. Arjun is in the tenth standard and is talking to his father about what he wants to do with his future.

Father:	*Beta*, have you given any thought to what FYJC you are interested in attending?
Arjun:	Yes Papa, I have. I have decided I want to become an actor. I don't want to go to college. I will move to **the Mumbai** and try my luck!
Father:	*Beta*, I don't mind that you want to be an actor. But there is no such thing as **'the Mumbai'**. Mumbai is a singular proper noun. We do not use the article 'the' before singular proper nouns.
Arjun:	Ok Papa, I won't make that mistake again.

✗ The Mumbai

✓ Mumbai

Father:	What about when you get married? Do you think your wife will be happy if you are an actor?
Arjun:	Of course! In fact, she will be an actress herself! All my friends will say, '**Sharmas** are so famous.'
Father:	That is very nice, *beta*. Except that you must say **'the Sharmas'**—you need to add the article 'the' in front of 'Sharmas'.
Arjun:	But why? You told me that we should not use the article 'the' before proper nouns!
Father:	No, Arjun, I said you should not use the article 'the' before *singular* proper nouns. 'Sharmas' is plural—it includes both you and your wife. Before plural proper nouns, we must add the article 'the'.

✗ Sharmas
✓ The Sharmas

Thus, **formula I:**
For a proper noun
If singular → Use no article
If plural → Use 'the' before the proper noun

There are two exceptions to this rule.

1. Landmarks
   - *The* Air India building
   - *The* Taj Mahal
2. Oceans and Seas
   - *The* Red Sea
   - *The* Indian Ocean

Look at some examples of this formula:

Singular (needs no article)	Plural (needs 'the')
1. I saw **Amitabh Bachchan** on TV. ➤ 'Amitabh Bachchan' is one person—singular.	I saw *the* **Bachchan family** on TV. ➤ '*The* Bachchan family' is more than one person—plural.
2. **Lake Victoria** is very pretty. ➤ 'Lake Victoria' is one lake—singular.	*The* **Great Lakes** are very pretty. ➤ 'The Great Lakes' include more than one lake—plural.
3. **India** is my favourite country. ➤ 'India' is one country—singular.	*The* **United Kingdom** is a nice place to visit. ➤ 'The United Kingdom' refers to a group: England, Scotland, Wales and Northern Ireland—plural.

Exercise 3.1

Read the following sentences. Delete the article 'the' if it has been placed incorrectly. Add the article 'the' if it is missing. Check your answers before moving on.

1. USA is a nice place. The America is a really good place to study.
2. I am going home with the Jagpreet.
3. Himalayas are beautiful.
4. When I was on vacation I went sailing on Caribbean Sea.
5. I saw a movie about the Mount Everest.

3.2 HOW TO USE THE ARTICLE 'THE' BEFORE COMMON AND ABSTRACT NOUNS THAT ARE SPECIFIC

You have now learnt when to use articles before proper nouns. This leaves us with common and abstract nouns. Common and abstract nouns share the same rules when it comes to figuring out which article is to be placed before them. Thus, for the remainder of this chapter, and for the next one, we will clump common and abstract nouns together and simply refer to them 'nouns'. Therefore, anything that is not a proper noun will be referred to in these two chapters simply as a 'noun'. Let us continue the conversation between Arjun and his father.

Father:	You know Arjun, you don't have to become an actor just to be different from your brothers. There are other things you can do to be special. For instance, you can become a doctor.
Arjun:	That's true, Papa! Then I will be known as 'a doctor in the family'!
Father:	Wrong, Arjun. Since you are the *only* doctor in the family, you will always be known as '*the* doctor in the family'. We use the article 'the' if the noun is specific.
Arjun:	What does it mean for a noun to be 'specific'?
Father:	That's a good question Arjun. You will understand more about this from the dialogue between me and my friend Pradeep.

✓ Pradeep: You must be so proud of Arjun.

✓ Father: 'Yes, he is *the* doctor in our family.'

Father: You can see from the above dialogue that both Pradeep and I are thinking of the same person. We both know that you—Arjun—are the doctor I am referring to. This makes the noun 'doctor' *specific*. So we say '*the* doctor'. Now look at my next conversation with Pradeep.

✓ Pradeep: Since Arjun is not available, can you refer me to *a* doctor?

✓ Father: Yes, Dr Suresh is *a* very good doctor.

Father: Here, both my friend and I are thinking of different doctors while we are speaking. This makes the noun 'doctor' general, or unspecific. So, we say '*a* doctor'.

Only use 'the' before a noun when it is clear to the other person exactly who or what you are referring to.

Formula 2:

For a specific noun → Add 'the' before the specific noun

Look at the examples below.

Specific—'the'	Unspecific—'a', 'an' or no article
1. *The* **animals** we saw in the jungle were fierce. ➤ We are referring to certain animals we saw in the jungle.	1. **Animals** are fierce. ➤ We are talking about animals in general.
2. Why do we have to go to *the* **same park** everyday? ➤ We are referring to a specific park.	2. Every day we go to *a* **different park**. ➤ We are talking about all kinds of parks and not one specifically.
3. *The* **interview** I had at *the* **agency** was bad. ➤ We are not referring to all interviews—but to a specific interview given at one agency.	3. I had *an* **interview** at *an* **agency**. ➤ It is unclear exactly which interview or which agency the speaker is referring to.

4. I am *the* **English teacher** at my school. ➤ This means the speaker is the only English teacher at the school (thus specific).	4. I am *an* **English teacher** at my school. ➤ This means the speaker is one of many English teachers at the school (thus unspecific)

Based on what you have learnt, try exercise 3.2.

Exercise 3.2

Figure out whether you need the article 'the' in the space provided before the circled nouns. Check your answers in the answer key before moving on.

Jay is looking for a car and visits a car dealership.

Jay:	I want to buy ___ (car).
Car Dealer:	What type of car are you looking for?
Jay:	I am looking for ___ (red Maruti).
Car Dealer:	Great! Take a look at this one here. What do you think of ___ (car)?
Jay:	I like it a lot!

Exercise 3.3

Figure out if you need the article 'the' in the space provided before the circled nouns. Check your answers before moving on.

Person 1:	Would you like to buy ____ cake?

Person 2:	Yes, I like ____ chocolate cake. It looks yummy!

! Make sure you have completed the above exercises and checked your answers before moving on.

By now you should be more comfortable using articles before proper nouns and other nouns that are specific. Don't worry if you don't feel completely confident yet. The recap and exercises will help you along.

3.3 A QUICK RECAP OF THE FORMULAE IN THIS CHAPTER

Formula 1

For a proper noun:

- If singular → No article is needed
- If plural → Use 'the' before the proper non

Formula 2

- For a specific noun → add 'the'

Exercise 3.4

Read the passage given below. Underline all proper nouns. Circle all specific nouns. Check your answers before moving on.

> Reporting to the CEO of the company is difficult. Sonia had a big responsibility with her new job. She would be in charge of the purchasing and inventory departments and she would have to ensure that all clients get the best service possible. Also, she would have to lead the Maharashtrian team during the company's meetings.

Exercise 3.5

Read the passage given below. Identify all the 'the' articles that have been incorrectly placed. Explain why the placement is incorrect. Check your answers before moving on.

> My attitude towards the life is that I want to help the mankind. I believe that the rural India is not well governed. The roads are not good and the money is not spent well. The both things need lots of attention. I hope that the help will come quickly to the poor people there.

Exercise 3.6

Read the sentences given below. Put the article 'the' before nouns wherever it is missing. Check your answers before moving on.

1. She is involved in murder case.
2. Government should take care of areas surrounding Taj because this year is its 350th anniversary.
3. They will be taking me out to see city where they live.
4. I appeared for an interview at company's headquarters.
5. I'm going to hospital where *nani* is.
6. If you had seen me with another girl at theatre you would have been angry.

! Make sure you have done the exercises and checked your answers before reading further.

APPLYING WHAT YOU HAVE LEARNED

1. In English, we must place articles—'the', 'a' or 'an'—before most nouns and noun phrases.
2. Proper nouns do not need articles unless they are plural. If plural, use the article 'the'.
   - Amitabh Bachchan (no article needed).
   - *The* **Bachchans** (plural—more than one Bachchan).
3. When common and abstract nouns are *specific*, we need to add the article 'the' before them.
   - It is *the* **hottest day** of the year today. (Not all days are the hottest, just the specific one mentioned.)
   - It is *a* **hot day**. (We are talking about one of many similar hot days, so we don't use the article 'the'.)

We have learnt in this chapter that if a common or abstract noun is specific, we need to add the article 'the' before it. You might be wondering, 'But what if a noun is unspecific? What happens then?' The next chapter will help you learn about articles before unspecific nouns.

CHAPTER 4

Am I 'a' graduate, 'an' graduate or just 'graduate'?

Using articles correctly (Part 2): Before general nouns

In the previous chapter, we began learning about articles. We learned that we should place the article 'the' before some proper nouns, and all common and abstract nouns that are specific.

If a noun is neither proper nor specific, it falls into the unspecific or 'general' category. Before general nouns, we use the articles 'a' or 'an', or simply don't use an article at all. This chapter will help you learn which articles to use before general nouns.

Examples of common errors made while placing articles before general nouns are given below. See if you make any of these mistakes.

Common Error 1:

✗ Yoga is effective way for person to stay fit.

- In this sentence, the speaker has forgotten to add articles where they are needed.

The correct sentence is:

✓ Yoga is **an** effective way for **a** person to stay fit.

Common Error 2:

✗ I attended a interview today.

✗ I went to an park with him.

- These two sentences contain the same error—the wrong articles have been used in the right places.

The correct sentences are:
✓ I attended **an** interview today.
✓ I went to **a** park with him.

Common Error 3:
✗ I really had a fun today.
✗ I love eating a spicy food.
- In these sentences, we have made the mistake of using articles where not required. Certain general nouns never require articles to be placed before them.

The correct sentences are:
✓ I really had fun today.
✓ I love eating spicy food.

The above examples deal with mistakes made while placing articles before general nouns. Remember, in this chapter, we will only learn about article placement before general nouns. The previous chapter dealt with the use of articles before proper and specific nouns.

What will I learn in this chapter?

4.1 Which articles to use before singular and plural nouns.
4.2 Which articles to use before nouns that are neither singular nor plural.
4.3 The difference between the articles 'a' and 'an'.
4.4 Recap.

To refresh your memory, remember that there are three types of nouns: *proper*, *common* and *abstract*. Common and abstract nouns share the same rules when it comes to article placement. As we learnt in the previous chapter, if they are specific we simply add the article 'the' before them. If common and abstract nouns are not specific, they are classified as being unspecific, or 'general'. Before general nouns, we do one of the following:

- Add the article 'a' or 'an'.
- Add no article at all.

Let's learn about the use of these two options.

4.1 WHICH ARTICLES TO USE BEFORE SINGULAR AND PLURAL NOUNS

In the previous chapter we read a conversation between Arjun and his father. A recap: Arjun comes from a family of five which includes his father, mother and two brothers. Arjun's brothers are both engineers. Arjun is in the tenth standard and is talking to his father about what he wants to do with his future. Let's learn some more about articles through this conversation.

Arjun: Papa, I am still confused about what to do with my future. I am just boy who is confused.

Father: Arjun, it is perfectly okay to feel confused. But it is not okay to forget to place your articles before your nouns! You cannot say, 'I am just boy who is confused.' Instead, you must say, 'I am just **a** boy who is confused.'

Arjun: But why, Papa?

Father: Well, we already know that the noun 'boy' is unspecific, or general, based on what we have learned. If a general noun is singular, you must place either 'a' or 'an' before the noun. In your sentence, 'boy' is singular.

Remember the following rule:

- We use 'a' or 'an' before general nouns if it is singular.

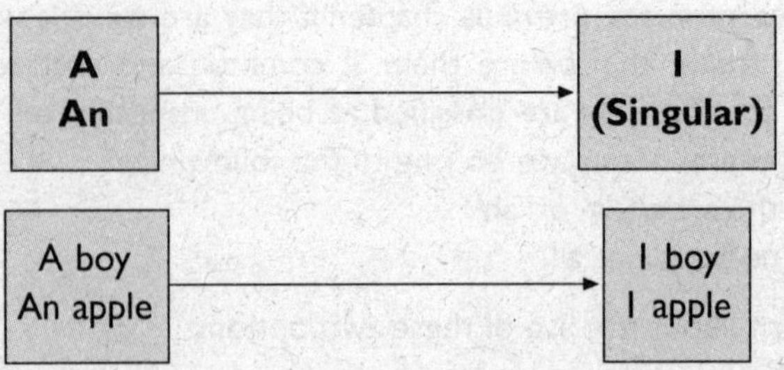

Singular	Plural
I see a boy.	I see boys. I see some boys.
I bought an apple	I bought apples. I bought many apples.

Formula 3
For a general noun:
If singular → 'a' or 'an'
If plural → no article or words like 'some' or 'many'

! Formulae 1 and 2 on articles have been covered in the previous chapter. Let us now continue with the conversation between Arjun and his father.

Arjun: I did not know that 'a' and 'an' are used for the singular. So instead of saying, 'I see *one* boy,' I should say, 'I see *a* boy.'
Father: That's right, Arjun!
Arjun: Also, I can't say, 'I see a boys.'
Father: That's right Arjun, but why?
Arjun: Because 'boys' is plural and I can only use 'a' or 'an' when I am talking about one, singular boy.
Father: You got it, Arjun!

Look at some more examples:

Singular nouns require 'a' or 'an'	Plural nouns require 'some', 'many' or no article
1. I really had *a* good time today. ➤ Because we are talking about one good time, we use 'a'.	1. I had good times there. ➤ Because 'good times' is plural (has an 's' at the end), we don't use the article 'a'.

Singular nouns require 'a' or 'an'	Plural nouns require 'some', 'many' or no article
2. Can I have *a* glass of water? ➤ Because we are talking about one glass of water, we use 'a'.	2. Can I have some glasses of water? ➤ Because 'glasses' is plural (has an 'es' at the end), we don't use the article 'a'.

! Remember, instead of using the word 'one' before singular nouns, use 'a' or 'an'.

Exercise 4.1

Work out whether the articles in bold in the following sentences are correct. If not, explain why. Check your answers before moving on.

1. I am looking for **a** sports shoes.
2. She was **a** happy girl.
3. My favourite hobby is planting **a** flowers in the garden.
4. I gave her **a** bouquet of flowers for her birthday.
5. I saw **a** glass on the table.
6. There was **a** stack of newspapers on the ground.

Exercise 4.2

Rewrite the following sentences correctly. Check your answers before moving on.

1. I saw one park when I was driving.
2. Her hair is wet and she wants some towel.
3. I saw tiger when I went to Kanha National Park.
4. I am working as software engineer in the company.
5. I want to work in BPO.

! Make sure you have done the above exercises and checked your answers before moving on.

You have now learned that if a general noun is singular (boy), you need to place the article 'a' or 'an' before the noun. Also, you have learned that if a general noun is plural (boy**s**), you don't need to place an article before the noun. But what about nouns that are neither singular nor plural? Continue reading to learn more!

4.2 WHICH ARTICLES TO USE BEOFRE NOUNS THAT ARE NEITHER SINGULAR NOR PLURAL

Arjun: Papa, I think I like the idea of studying medicine. I think it will be a fun.

Father: Yes *beta*, I am happy to hear that. However, it is wrong to say, 'be a fun'. You should instead say, 'be fun'—there is no need for an article before the noun 'fun'.

Arjun: But why Papa? 'Fun' is not specific, right? It is a general noun and it seems to be singular. I thought I should use either 'a' or 'an' before it.

Father: Wrong, Arjun. The noun 'fun' is not a singular noun. It is not a plural noun either. It is a special type of general noun.

Arjun: What are these special types of nouns called?

Father: They are called non-countable nouns.

Arjun: Non-countable! That sounds so confusing!

Father: Don't worry Arjun, it is very easy.

Nouns like 'boy' and 'apple' are countable nouns. Countable means that the nouns can be pluralized (made to be more than one).

Singular → boy and apple Plural → boys and apples

Because the nouns 'boy' and 'apple' can be made plural, they are called countable nouns. Now let's take nouns like 'love' and 'air'. Do you love your family? Can you count love in numeric terms? Can you show on paper the difference between singular and plural love? The answer is no. The noun 'love' cannot be counted or made plural.

✗ I have one love for my family.
✗ I have two loves for my family.
✓ I have love for my family.

What about the noun 'courage'? Can you show the difference between singular 'courage' and plural 'courage'? Again, the answer is no. The noun 'courage' also cannot be counted or made plural.

✗ The soldier has one courage.
✗ The soldier has two courages.
✓ The soldier has courage.

Abstract nouns are not the only type of nouns that can't be counted. For example, let's take the common noun 'sand'. Sand is not abstract. You can see it, but you can't count it. 'Sand' is whole and vast, and cannot be split numerically or counted.

✗ The beach has one sand.
✗ The beach has two sands.
✓ The beach has sand.

Remember that the articles 'a' and 'an' are used for singular nouns. If you can't count a noun, then don't put 'a' or 'an' before it. When a general noun can't be counted, it is neither singular nor plural; it is simply 'non-countable'. We don't need to place articles before non-countable nouns.

Arjun: I understand, Papa. If I can't count the noun, I don't need an article! Because I can't count the noun 'fun', I just say, 'I think it will be fun' instead of, 'I think it will be **a** fun.'

Father: That's right, Arjun!

Thus, formula 4

For general nouns

If non-countable (neither singular nor plural) → Use no article or words like 'some'.

This formula can be illustrated with the help of the following example:

Non-countable nouns need no article	Countable nouns use 'a' or 'an' if singular
1. Is there water in the glass? 'Water' as a substance cannot be counted. There is no such thing as 'one water' or 'two waters'. 'Water' is neither singular nor plural, it is non-countable. Thus, you cannot place an article before this noun.	2. Can I have *a* glass of water? You can count the number of glasses of water you have—'one glass of water' or 'two glasses of water'. Thus if you are talking about 'one glass of water', you need to place the article 'a' before it.

Exercise 4.3

Try and work out if the following nouns are countable or non-countable. Check your answers before moving on.

1. Table
2. Detail
3. Hour
4. Air
5. Mankind
6. Holiday
7. Information
8. Love

Let's do a recap of what we have learned so far in this chapter:

> **For general nouns**
> If singular → 'a' or 'an'.
> If plural → no article, or words like 'some' and 'many'.
> If non-countable (neither singular nor plural) → no article.

Exercise 4.4

Rewrite the following sentences correctly. Check your answers before moving on.

1. I need a advice from you.
2. What should I wear when I go for a interviews?
3. I am student in my final year of college and want to sit for the CAT.
4. Every morning when I wake up, I give them a water.
5. She had a information on the issue.
6. She had party for her sister.
7. I am not good at a math.
8. They need to do a work in the office.
9. She needs to get a shirts ironed.
10. I want to specialize in a marketing.

So far we have learned that if we can count the noun and it is singular, we should use the articles 'a' or 'an' before it. But how do we decide which of the two to use? Read the following section to learn how.

4.3 'A' VERSUS 'AN'

Arjun: You know Papa, I have been thinking about what you said about my becoming a doctor. I just don't think I want to.

Father: Then what do you want to do Arjun?

Arjun: Well, I think that there is nothing wrong with following my brothers. I think I want to become a engineer.

Father: That is great news! I am very happy. But Arjun, '**a** engineer' is incorrect.

Arjun: Why Papa? Engineer is unspecific so I don't have to use 'the'. Also I can count it and it is singular, so I definitely need an article.

Father: You are right, Arjun. Except that you need to say '**an** engineer'. You need to use the article 'an' instead of 'a'.

Arjun: I just can't seem to get it right!

Father: Don't worry, you are almost done, Arjun! Just remember this simple rule: 'a' is used before consonant sounds, and 'an' is used before nowel sounds.

'A' is used before consonant sounds	'An' is used before vowel sounds
1. A **b**oy ➤ 'Boy' starts with 'b' which is a consonant sound.	1. An **a**pple ➤ 'Apple' starts with 'a' which is a vowel sound.
2. A **c**ar ➤ 'Car' starts with 'c' which is a consonant sound.	2. An **e**lephant ➤ 'Elephant' starts with 'e' which is a vowel sound.
3. A **u**ser ➤ When we say 'user' it actually sounds like we	3. An **h**our ➤ When we say 'hour' it actually sounds like we

'A' is used before consonant sounds	**'An' is used before vowel sounds**
are saying '**y**u-zer'. We add the consonant sound 'y' to the beginning of the word. So, even though 'user' starts with the vowel letter 'u', because it *sounds* like the consonant sound 'y', we use the article 'a'.	are saying '**o**ur'—we don't pronounce the 'h' sound. So, even though 'hour' starts with the consonant letter 'h', because it sounds like the vowel sound 'o', we use the article 'an'.

! In case you have forgotten—the vowels in the English language are: **a**, **e**, **i**, **o**, **u**. The remaining twenty-one letters in the alphabet are called consonants.

When an adjective—a word that describes a noun—comes before a noun, we must choose 'a' or 'an' based on the sound of the *adjective*.

1. *A* **b**oy came to the room.
   An **a**ttractive boy came to the room.

Notice that the article changed when we inserted the adjective 'attractive' before 'boy'.

2. It's *an* **e**lephant.
   It's *a* **b**eautiful elephant.

Notice the article changed when we inserted the adjective 'beautiful' before 'elephant'.

! If there is an adjective before a noun, the article always complies with how the adjective sounds—not the noun.

✗ It is *a* enormous box.
✓ It is *an* enormous box.

Arjun: I understand now, Papa. This is not hard. So it is 'an engineer' because engineer starts with the vowel sound 'e'.

Papa: That's right Arjun!

Thus, **formula 5**

For a general noun:

- If singular and starting with a consonant sound, use the article 'a'.
- → If starting with a vowel sound use the article 'an'.

Exercise 4.5

Insert 'a' or 'an' before the following words. Check your answers before moving on.

1. Call centre
2. International call centre
3. Software programme
4. BPO
5. Multinational
6. Process
7. Application process
8. Interview
9. Human resource manager
10. HR manager

Exercise 4.6

Fill in the blanks with 'a' or 'an'. Check your answers before moving on.

1. Mr Patel is ____________ unrealistic person.
2. Teresa is ____________ bright woman.
3. Phil has __________ eraser.

4. Ali is ____________ adventurous man.
5. Jatin is _________ irresponsible boy.
6. I don't think I need _________ pen for the meeting.
7. Can you believe she didn't take __________ gift for the birthday girl?
8. I think he is such __________ arrogant person!

Exercise 4.7

Choose the correct word from the options given below. The word should match the article before it. Check your answers before moving on.

1. This is a **unique/unusual** painting.
2. My mother has a **green/orange** purse.
3. We want to live in a **area/quiet area**.
4. They are going to join an **club/exciting club**.
5. What a **attractive/beautiful** dress that is!
6. I am about an **minute/hour** away from finishing.
7. The book has an **interesting/very interesting** theory.
8. I feel like eating a **appetizer/meal**.

! Make sure you have done the above exercises and checked your answers before reading further.

4.4 A QUICK RECAP OF THE FORMULAE IN THIS CHAPTER

Thanks to Arjun and his father, you have learned the rules relating to articles. Let's do a quick recap of the rules we learned in this chapter and the previous one:

Formula 1: for a proper noun:
→ If singular use no article.
→ If plural use 'the'.

Formula 2: for a specific noun:
→ Use 'the'.

Formulae 3 and 4 for a general noun
→ If singular and starting with a consonant sound use 'a'.
→ If singular and starting with a vowel sound use 'an'.
→ If plural, use no article or words like 'some' and 'many'.
→ If non-countable (neither singular nor plural), use no article or words like 'some'.

This is a complete chart that shows you how to choose the correct articles. You may have to go over this chapter and the previous one a few times to fully understand articles.

It might be difficult for you to remember this chart when writing or speaking. To make it easier, memorize the three easy rules given below. Try and read as many newspapers, magazines and books as you can, and start observing how articles tend to follow these rules. These rules don't include everything, but will get rid of most of your mistakes.

3 easy rules for figuring out which article to use

1. For a proper noun, you usually don't need an article.
   → I saw Karishma Kapoor on television.
2. For all other nouns, use 'the' if it is specific.
   → Karishma Kapoor is **the** best actress in India.
3. If the noun is not specific, use 'a' or 'an' if it is singular.
   → I want to be **an** actress too!

Keep these rules in mind while doing the following exercises. Remember that the use of articles will become very easy if you learn these rules and start reading. Reading magazines, books and newspapers every day is very important for your English skills to develop, and you will be surprised at how fast you are improving.

Exercise 4.8

Rewrite the following sentences using 'a', 'an' or 'the' correctly. Explain each mistake and check your answers before moving on.

1. I was eyeing a food on the table.
2. I saw a beautiful girl. A beautiful girl told me her name was Manjeet.

3. Sophia is looking for a interesting book.
4. I want to make some few points.
5. I want to find some solution to the problem.
6. I have a very latest model.
7. Let's have some drink.
8. She didn't have any affair.
9. You've got a wrong information.

Exercise 4.9

The following sentences are either missing articles or contain articles that have been used incorrectly. Fix these errors. Check your answers before moving on.

1. I am just graduate in commerce.
2. It has a audio recording capacity of five hours.
3. The India is a beautiful country.
4. Please provide me with details of tuition classes.
5. She is an hardworking secretary.
6. There is the paint on the floor. Please wipe it.
7. Q: Is he a manager?
   A: He is not exactly manager.
8. She is putting on negative attitude.
9. I have job at Hindustan Lever.
10. I'm nature-loving person.
11. I sit in front of computer all day.
12. I am working for an BPO as an business development associate.
13. What is the difference between call centre and BPO? I am interested in joining the BPO.
14. I am working as project leader in software company.
15. I am a student at NIIT in Delhi and I am currently doing a research in BPO.
16. The city is located in the north-eastern part of the India.
17. Can you do me one favour?
18. I keep asking a genuine questions but no one answers me.

Exercise 4.10

The following email is missing the correct articles. First, read the entire email so you get a feel of the situation. Then add the correct articles where necessary. Check your answers before moving on.

```
Dear Kartik,

We need forty items for a back order analysis.
Contrary to earlier discussion, we have decided
to carry out back order analysis for all forty
items. Earlier mail from Mr Gupta has already
intimated the change.

After internal discussion, we have divided these
forty items between four of us.

In case you feel that we need to change anything
about above matter, please let us know.

Thanks,
Sharique
```

! Make sure you have done these exercises and checked your answers before moving on.

APPLYING WHAT YOU HAVE LEARNED

1. In English, we must place articles before most nouns and noun phrases.
2. If a noun is not a proper, common or an abstract noun that is *specific*, it falls into the general noun category. Before general nouns, we need to add the articles 'a' or 'an', or use no article at all.
3. We use the articles 'a' or 'an' if a general noun is singular.
   ✗ I saw **boy** at the park. (One boy was at the park.)
   ✓ I saw **a boy** at the park.

4. Choose the article 'a' if the first letter of the noun has a consonant sound, and the article 'an' if the first letter has a vowel sound
   ✓ A **b**oy
   ✓ A **t**able
   ✓ *An* **a**pple
   ✓ *An* **e**lephant
5. If a general noun is plural, we can use words like 'some' or 'many', or use no article at all. We cannot use the articles 'a' or 'an' for plural nouns.
   ✗ I saw **a** boy**s** at the park. (More than 1 boy.)
   ✓ I saw boy**s** at the park.
   ✓ I saw **some** boy**s** at the park.
   ✓ I saw **many** boy**s** at the park.
6. If a general noun is neither singular nor plural, we cannot count it. For such non-countable nouns, we use no article at all.
   ✗ There is **a** water in the ocean. (No such thing as one water or two waters.)
   ✓ There is water in the ocean.

If you are feeling confused at this point, go back and read chapters 2, 3 and 4. To perfect your understanding of nouns and articles, you may have to read the chapters more than once.

CHAPTER 5

Hi, myself Jyoti.

All kinds of pronouns

Jyoti is running around the house trying to get ready. Her mother yells, 'Eat something before you go!'

'I don't have time!' Jyoti shouts back.

She grabs her things and runs out of the door. Today is a big day for Jyoti—she has finally been called for an interview with a company she has been interested in for a long time. She feels her stomach turn upside down with nervousness and, as she jumps on to a crowded Mumbai train, she offers a quick prayer hoping that her interview goes well.

She makes it into the company's building just in time and is told by the receptionist to go into the HR manager's office. Jyoti takes a deep breath and opens the door to the office. The HR manager smiles and gets up. He extends his hand to greet her and as Jyoti extends hers, she says, 'Hi, myself Jyoti.'

The HR manager frowns. He is not happy.

What went wrong? Well, as many of you may know, first impressions are very important. A big part of the first impression we make on someone we meet for the first time is the way we introduce ourselves. This is where Jyoti failed. Her introduction—'myself Jyoti'—is grammatically incorrect.

Many of us make this mistake and other similar ones too. See if you can relate to any of the following errors dealing with the incorrect use of pronouns.

Common Error 1:

✗ 'Myself, Jyoti'.

- 'Myself' is usually used as a reflexive pronoun and cannot be used in this sentence.

✓ **My name is** Jyoti.

Common Error 2:

✗ I live in Mumbai itself.

- We sometimes overuse words like 'myself' and 'itself' in order to add more stress to what we are saying. In this sentence the word 'itself' is unnecessary, and actually ends up being grammatically incorrect.

✓ I live in Mumbai.

Common Error 3:

✗ Themselves were discussing the problem.

✗ Me is very happy about the news.

- In these two sentences, the wrong types of pronouns have been used.

✓ **They** were discussing the problem.

✓ **I am** very happy about the news.

Common Error 4:

✗ I am an engineer and am going to represent my company.

✗ They told that I should go home.

- In both these sentences, pronouns are missing.

✓ I am an engineer and **I** am going to represent my company.

✓ They told **me** that I should go home.

Common Error 5:

✗ At the end of the day the choice is your.

- In this sentence, the possessive pronoun 'yours' is missing an 's'.

✓ At the end of the day the choice is **yours**.

What will I learn in this chapter?

5.1 WHAT IS A PRONOUN?

Read the following paragraph:

> Jyoti does not get the job because Jyoti's English skills are weak. Jyoti practises Jyoti's English and then goes for another interview. Jyoti does well in this interview and Jyoti gets the job. Jyoti is really excited and runs to tell Jyoti's family. Jyoti's family is very happy for Jyoti.

When we use the same noun (Jyoti) over and over again, the paragraph becomes repetitive and clumsy. Pronouns are used instead of nouns and make the paragraph sound better. Just like nouns, pronouns identify people, places, things and ideas.

Read the next paragraph and notice how the pronouns (in bold) have replaced of the word 'Jyoti'.

> Jyoti does not get the job because **her** English skills are weak. **She** practises **her** English and then goes for another interview. Jyoti does well in this interview and **she** gets the job. **She** is really excited and runs to tell **her** family. Jyoti's family is very happy for **her**.

This time we replaced some of the 'Jyoti' nouns with the pronouns 'she' and 'her'.

In Hindi, some examples of pronouns are: *main, tu, tum, aap, hum* and *woh*. One major difference between Hindi pronouns and English pronouns is that in Hindi you change the verb following the pronoun to indicate gender:

- *Main gayee* (I went, where the I is female).
- *Main gaya* (I went, where the I is male).
- *Voh gayee* (She went).
- *Voh gaya* (He went).

In English, we don't change the verb depending on the gender ('went' remains the same regardless of 'he' or 'she'). Thus, when using most English pronouns (I, me, you, we, they, us), there is no way to tell the gender at all. It is only when we use pronouns like she, he, her, him, etc. do we learn what gender the speaker is referring to.

There are several types of pronouns that we can use and will cover in this chapter: subject ('she'), object ('her'), reflexive/intensive ('herself') and possessive ('hers').

! Remember, all pronouns take the places of nouns.

5.2 SUBJECT AND OBJECT PRONOUNS

From chapter 1, you may remember that a sentence is formed in the following way:

Subject + Verb + Object = Complete sentence

Subject pronouns replace the subject noun of the sentence ('she' will replace 'Jyoti') and follow the same rules.

Subject pronouns	Verb + Object
I	looked at Jason.
He/She/It	danced with me.
You	smiled at him.
We	loved Tom.
They	heard you.

Object pronouns are the focus of the verb in a sentence.

Subject + Verb	**+ Object Pronouns**
Jason looked	at **me.**
I liked	**him/her/it.**
She called	**you.**
Tom loved	**us.**
You heard	**them.**

5.3 UNDERSTANDING SUBJECT AND OBJECT PRONOUNS

Let us perfect our understanding of subject and object pronouns by following Jyoti through an interview.

```
HR manager:    Jyoti, where did you go to college?
Jyoti:         Me went to Delhi University.
```

Jyoti has made a big mistake. She used the object pronoun 'me' when she should have used the subject pronoun 'I'. Let's go over the first rule for subject pronouns:

Rule 1: Subject pronouns come before verbs and objects. Subjects indicate who or what does the action.

In Jyoti's response, we must ask ourselves *what* the main action or verb is. In this sentence it is the verb 'went'. Now, *who* is doing the main action? In other words, *who* went to Delhi University? Jyoti did. Because Jyoti is the one *doing* the action, Jyoti is the subject of the sentence. From the chart above, we see that we must use 'I' (not 'me'), for subject pronouns. Jyoti should have said:

✓ **Jyoti:** **I** went to Delhi University.

Let's look at another example of this rule:

✗ Yesterday, **her** was talking to Tina.
✓ Yesterday, **she** was talking to Tina.

- 'Talking' is the main verb, or action in this sentence. The pronoun refers to the person doing the talking, and thus we cannot use the object pronoun 'her'. We must use the subject pronoun 'she'.

Continue reading Jyoti's interview:

HR manager:	Jyoti, your CV shows that you received an award from your university. What was it for?
Jyoti:	The principal of our college presented an award to my group members and **I** after we finished a project for the Government of India.

Jyoti has made another mistake. She has used the subject pronoun 'I' when she should have used the object pronoun 'me'. Let's go over the rule for object pronouns:

Rule 2: Object pronouns usually come after subjects and verbs. Objects are the receivers of any action caused by subjects.

In Jyoti's response we must ask ourselves what the main action or verb is. In this sentence it is the verb 'presented'. Now, *who* is doing the action of presenting the award? The principal of the college. Thus, the principal is the subject of this sentence. If the principal is the subject, that would make Jyoti and her group members the objects. They are the ones *receiving* the action. From our chart, we see that we must use 'me' (not 'I') for objects. Jyoti should have said:

✓ The principal of our college presented the award to my group members and **me** after we finished a project for the Government of India.

Let's look at another example of this rule:

✗ She handed the award to **they**.
✓ She handed the award to **them**.

- 'Handed' is the main verb, or action in this sentence. 'She' is the subject of the sentence. The people who received the award are the objects in this sentence and thus we cannot refer to them using the subject pronoun 'they'. We must use the object pronoun 'them' in this case.

Tips on figuring out subject and object pronouns

When there are several subjects in a sentence, you can sometimes get confused about whether to use a subject or an object pronoun. The easiest way to figure this out is to break the sentence down:

1. Sheila and____are going home.
   Should the pronoun in the blank be **'I'** or **'me'**? If you break down the sentence you get one of the following:
   ✓ **I** am going home.
   ✗ **Me** am going home.
   Now, it's easy to see that the correct answer is **'I'**. ('I' is one of the subjects of the verb 'going'.)
2. She will give you and____the prize.
   Should the pronoun in the blank be **'he'** or **'him'**? If you break down the sentence you get one of the following:
   ✗ She will give **he** the prize.
   ✓ She will give **him** the prize.
   Now, it's easy to see that the correct answer is 'him'. ('Him' is one of the objects of the verb 'give'.)
3. They only invited my brother and____to the party.
   Should the pronoun in the blank be **'I'** or **'me'**? If you break down the sentence you get one of the following:
   ✗ They only invited **I** to the party.
   ✓ They only invited **me** to the party.
   Now, it is easy to see that the correct answer is **'me'**. ('Me' is one of the objects of the verb 'invited'.)

Now you have learned about subject and object pronouns. Work on the following exercises and you will soon be proficient in subject and object pronouns.

Exercise 5.1

Mark the correct answer in the sentences below. Check your answers before moving on.

1. **I/me** will give her the message.
2. If you see **she/her**, please give **she/her** the message.
3. It was **I/me** on the phone.
4. My mother asked my sister and **I/me** to finish getting ready.
5. Samir, Tarun and **I/me** went to the movies.
6. **I/me** told **they/them** that the show was over.
7. **They/them** were unhappy with **she/her** work.
8. Will **we/us** apply for the job?

Exercise 5.2

The following sentences have errors relating to subject and object pronouns. Correct the mistakes. Check your answers before moving on.

1. Me am the eldest.
2. I want to work in a call centre because it will have better prospects.
3. My younger brother and me started a small software developing centre in Bangalore.
4. Please give Dev and I your address.
5. Krish ordered filet of fish. They were delicious.
6. Kemaya and me want to join the debate club.
7. I asked they to finish the gardening. They refused.
8. She assisted me once, so now I will help she.

! Make sure you have done the exercises and checked your answers before moving on.

5.4 HOW TO AVOID MISSING SUBJECT OR OBJECT PRONOUNS IN LONGER SENTENCES

Often we don't just mix up our subject and object pronouns, we forget to include them altogether! The three common mistakes made in this area are:

- Forgetting to include a subject pronoun.
- Forgetting to restate the subject pronoun in longer sentences that include 'and' or 'but'.
- Forgetting to include an object pronoun.

No subject pronoun at all

Read the sentence given below and see if you can figure out where the missing subject pronoun should go:

✗ During the test, forgot the answers to all the questions.

The missing pronoun must come before the word 'forgot'. 'Forgot' is the main verb in this sentence. But who is the person who forgot? Who is the subject of this action? We don't know because the subject pronoun is missing. The sentence could also read:

✓ During the test, **I** forgot the answers to all the questions.

(You could insert the pronouns 'he', 'she', 'we' or 'they' and the sentence would still be correct.)

Even if 'who' is doing the action is obvious, you still must state the subject pronoun.

Missing subject pronouns in long sentences

Read the sentence given below and see if you can figure out where the missing subject pronoun should go:

✗ My name is Tasha and am going to appear in the exam.

The missing pronoun must come after the word 'and'. Although we have already stated once who the subject is (Tasha), we need to restate this subject after the word 'and'. The sentence should read:

✓ My name is Tasha and **I** am going to appear in the exam.

Let's look at another example. See if you can find where the missing subject pronoun should go:

✗ I want to go to the party but don't feel very good.

Here, the missing pronoun falls right after the word 'but'. Although we have already stated the subject 'I' at the beginning of the sentence, we need to restate this subject after the word 'but'. The sentence should read:

✓ I want to go to the party but **I** don't feel very good.

When a sentence includes the words 'and' and 'but', it can usually be split into more than one sentence. Let's take a look at the two examples we used above:

First part of the sentence	Second part of the sentence
My name is Tasha.	I am going to appear in the exam.
I want to go to the party.	I don't feel very good.

Do you see how the words 'and' and 'but' connect these two separate sentences? When these words are used as connectors, both the sentences being connected need to include subjects and objects. Keep in mind that this rule does not apply if 'and' and 'but' do not connect two separate sentences:

I like chocolate, candy **and** ice cream.

Here, the word 'and' is not connecting two separate sentences, so the rule does not apply. There are exceptions, but you are better off always including a subject pronoun after an 'and' or a 'but'.

No object pronoun at all

Read the sentence below and see if you can figure out where the missing object pronoun should go:

✗ They told that this is not a good company.

The missing pronoun must come after the word 'told'. 'Told' is the main verb in this sentence. But who was being told? Who is the object of this action? We don't know because the object pronoun is missing. The sentence should read:

✓ They told **me** that this is not a good company.

You can insert the pronouns 'her', 'him', 'them' or 'us' and the sentence would be correct. Even if 'who' the action is being done to is obvious, you must state the object pronoun.

Exercise 5.3

The following sentences contain missing subject and object pronouns. Based on what you just learned, add in the missing pronouns where needed. Check your answers before moving on.

1. During the discussion I had with the client, introduced our products and other relevant information.
2. Last week on Wednesday when I went to the site, spoke to Mr Shah regarding the disadvantages of water-based adhesives.
3. I am a final year student and going to write the CAT this year.
4. I am Christie and have completed my MBA.
5. We are rejecting this order and are sending back to you. We will send accounts representative to your office to collect our money.
6. They are telling that this is not a safe career because may collapse at anytime and I should not get into it.
7. I collect flowers from various places and plant in my garden.
8. Dear Mr Srinivasan,

   I spoke to Mr Patil yesterday about the merchandise we need. He informed that presently they have quantity in stock but may be required in the next month depending on the job schedule. He asked to contact Mr Mulki this week for further discussion. He further informed that the quality may not be as good as the last stock. I told him wanted to inspect myself.

! Make sure you have completed the exercises and checked your answers before moving on.

5.5 REFLEXIVE AND INTENSIVE PRONOUNS

Pronouns such as myself, yourself, herself, etc. are reflexive or intensive pronouns. We can use these pronouns in two ways:

1. As a reflex (reflexive).
2. To make things more intense (intensive).

Let's first learn about reflexive pronouns.

Reflexive pronouns

Look at this picture, in which Jyoti is looking at the mirror.

What action is Jyoti performing in this picture? She is looking. And who is she looking at? She is looking at Jyoti. The *subject* Jyoti is looking at the *object* Jyoti. When this happens, the action is *reflected* from the subject back onto the same subject.

Rule 3: Reflexive pronouns are used when a subject creates an action that reflects back onto the same subject. In this situation, both subject and object are the same.

The chart given below shows how various reflexive pronouns are formed.

Subject	Verb	Object (Reflexive pronoun marked in bold.)
I	looked	at **myself**
He/She/It	looked	at **himself/herself/itself**
You	looked	at **yourself/yourselves**
We	looked	at **ourselves**
They	looked	at **themselves**

So in the picture you just saw, Jyoti is looking at **herself**.

In the beginning of this chapter Jyoti introduced herself to an HR manager as 'Myself, Jyoti.' You will notice that there is no action or verb stated in this sentence. If there is no action, the subject Jyoti cannot reflect anything back on herself. Since there is no action and nothing is being reflected back, it is not grammatically correct to use the reflexive pronoun 'myself' in this sentence.

Tips for introductions

The best way to make an introduction is:

✓ My name is Jyoti.

! 'Myself, Jyoti' should *never* be used as an introduction. 'I am Jyoti' is grammatically correct, but it is not a globally accepted introduction. It is abrupt and will sound curt to most people.

Intensive pronouns

Sometimes we use pronouns such as myself, herself, itself, etc. when we want to intensify a noun. In these cases, the pronoun is actually not needed. For example:

✗ Kavita **herself** closed the door.

Here, we are emphasizing that Kavita alone—and no one else—closed the door. But if we hadn't included the word 'herself', the meaning would have remained the same.

Rule 4: Intensive pronouns are used after nouns in order to intensify them. Remember, without them, the meaning of the sentence remains the same.

Intensive pronouns should be used only rarely, and only when it is especially important to intensify a noun. Take a look at the following dialogue:

HR manager:	Jyoti, where do you live?
Jyoti:	I live in Borivali **itself**.

Jyoti has made a very common mistake. There is no need to intensify the noun 'Borivali' here. When answering questions about where you live or places you have visited, it is better not to place the word 'itself' at the end of the sentence. Jyoti should have simply answered:

✓ I live in Borivali.

Exercise 5.4

Reflexive/intensive pronouns are incorrectly used in some of the sentences given below. Correct those sentences. Check your answers before moving on.

1. I live in Nagpur itself.
2. She hurt herself on the door.
3. I will call him today itself.
4. He accidentally bit himself.
5. I did it yesterday itself.
6. Myself Piyush.
7. The desk closed in on itself.
8. They drove themselves there.

Exercise 5.5

The sentences below contain pronoun mix-ups. Some mix-ups are between reflexive and intensive pronouns and subject and object pronouns. Other mix-ups occur when the wrong reflexive or intensive pronoun is used. Correct these sentences. Check your answers before moving on.

1. It belongs to myself.
2. Themselves were discussing the assignment.
3. Roxanne was giving itself a manicure.
4. It is up to ourself to win the game.
5. I have to train and teach people all the qualities and skills which I have developed in me as a leader.
6. It's no one else's fault, they brought the punishment on themself.
7. It was given to herself.
8. The pizza had many toppings on itself.

! Make sure you have done the exercises and checked your answers before moving on.

5.6 POSSESSIVE PRONOUNS

There are two forms of possessive pronouns—possessive adjectives and possessive pronouns. These words may seem long and complicated, but don't worry, looks are deceptive! This section is easy, so don't get intimidated by difficult-sounding grammar terms.

Both possessive adjectives and possessive pronouns are used to show things we own, or possess. *Possessive adjectives* are used with nouns. For example:

✓ It's **my car**.

In this sentence, 'my' is the pronoun that goes together with the noun 'car'. Because 'my' describes whose car it is, we call it a possessive adjective.

Rule 5: Possessive adjectives are pronouns that go together with nouns. They come before a noun and describe who possesses that noun.

Possessive pronouns simply take the place of a possessive adjective and its noun. Let's take the above example and show its possessive pronoun:

Possessive adjective	Possessive pronoun
It's **my car**.	It's **mine.**

Rule 6: Possessive pronouns are pronouns that take the place of a possessive adjective *and* its noun.

The chart given below lists the different kinds of possessive adjectives and their complementing possessive pronouns.

Possessive adjective	Noun	Possessive pronoun
It is **my**	computer.	It is **mine.**
It is **our**	school.	It is **ours.**
It is **your**	file.	It is **yours.**
It is **his/her**	dog.	It is **his/hers.**
It is **their**	house.	It is **theirs.**

There are two common mistakes with possessive adjectives and pronouns that you should try to avoid:

1. Don't use 'one' after possessive pronouns.
   ✗ Her car is like yours **one**.
   ✓ Her car is like yours.
2. There is no need to repeat the noun if we are using a possessive pronoun.
   ✗ My car is like **your car**.
   ✓ My car is like **yours**.

Exercise 5.6

Fill in the blanks with the correct possessive adjective and possessive pronoun. Check your answers before moving on.

1. For a man: This is ____ car. It is ____.
2. For a woman: This is ____ purse. It is _____.

3. For a friend and his family: This is _____ home. It is ______.
4. For me: This is ____ book. It is ______.
5. For me and my friends: These are _____ toffees. They are _____.
6. For you: This is _____ gift. It is ______.

Exercise 5.7

The following sentences have mistakes relating to possessive adjectives and possessive pronouns. Correct the sentences. Check your answers before moving on.

1. Our house is larger than her house.
2. It's yours file.
3. Her drawing is like your one.
4. That company does not treat it's employees well.
5. The money is not mine, it is your.
6. The black cat is my cat.
7. The baby drank it's milk.
8. It is hims car you are looking at.

5.7 A QUICK RECAP OF THE RULES IN THIS CHAPTER

Pronouns are words used to replace nouns. Let's look at all the rules we have learned that relate to pronouns.

Rule 1: Subject pronouns come before verbs and objects. Subjects indicate who or what does the action.

✓ **I** danced with Kunal.
✓ **She** looks beautiful.

Rule 2: Object pronouns usually come after verbs and subjects. Objects are the *receivers* of any action caused by the subject.

✓ My mother yelled at **me**.
✓ I threw the ball to **him**.

Rule 3: Reflexive pronouns can be used when a subject creates an action that *reflects back* on the same subject. Here, both subject and object are the same.

✓ I accidentally burnt **myself**.
✓ We are very mad at **ourselves** for losing the championship game.

Rule 4: Intensive pronouns are used after nouns in order to intensify them. If removed, the meaning of the sentence should remain the same. Intensive pronouns should be used rarely.

✓ The business was started by Jessica **herself**.
✓ They **themselves** finished the entire project.

Rule 5: Possessive adjectives are pronouns that are used with nouns. These pronouns come before a noun and describe who possesses the noun.

✓ It is **my** computer.
✓ That is **their** apartment.

Rule 6: Possessive pronouns are pronouns that replace a possessive adjective *and* its noun.

✓ The computer is **mine**.
✓ The apartment is **theirs**.

Exercise 5.8

Fill in the blanks with the correct pronouns. Check your answers before moving on.

Jyoti:	Namita, did you take my brown skirt from _________ closet? I need it and I can't find _________.
Namita:	No, I didn't take _________ skirt! You always blame _________ when you can't find something.
Jyoti:	Well, usually when I can't find something it is because _________ took it! You always take my things when you can't find _________ own things.
Namita:	Instead of blaming me, you should ask Tina. Tina and _________ sister always take _________ things without asking.

```
Jyoti:      Yes, ________ always do that. I am
            tired of ___ carelessness with
            my things!
Namita:     Jyoti, don't get so angry. ________
            all make mistakes.
```

Exercise 5.9

Pronouns have been incorrectly used in the following sentences. Correct the sentences and check your answers before moving on.

1. Hi, I am Raj.
2. Recently, I have appeared for four job interviews and failed to get any one of the jobs. The problem is I get very nervous and subsequently unable to pronounce words correctly. I can pronounce the same words correctly with the friends.
3. Hi, myself Gopika.
4. My mother and myself are yoga teachers.
5. Mine question is will you help me?

APPLYING WHAT YOU HAVE LEARNED

1. There are different types of pronouns that you need to be aware of:
   - Subject—I, you, she, he, it, we, they.
   - Object—me, you, her, him, it, us, them.
   - Reflexive/intensive—myself, yourself, herself, himself, itself, ourselves, themselves.
   - Possessive adjectives—my, your, her, his, its, our, their.
   - Possessive pronouns—mine, yours, hers, his, ours, theirs.
2. Subject pronouns replace subject nouns. They are the ones *doing* the action.

   ✗ **Him** played sports all day.

   ✓ **He** played sports all day.
3. Object pronouns replace nouns. They are the ones *receiving* the action.

✗ Nalini danced with Jenny and **she**.

✓ Nalini danced with Jenny and **her**.

4. Reflexive pronouns can only be used when the receiver of the action is the subject itself.

   ✗ **Myself**, Nishita.

   ✓ Nishita hit **herself**.

5. Intensive pronouns should be used very rarely, to make things stand out in exceptional cases.

   ✗ I live in Mangalore **itself**.

   ✓ I saw Amitabh Bachchan **himself** at the restaurant.

6. Possessive adjectives must be followed by nouns. Possessive pronouns take the place of possessive adjectives and their nouns.

   ✗ It is **mine car**.

   ✓ It is **my car**. (Possessive adjective followed by the noun 'car'.)

   ✓ It is **mine**. (Possessive pronoun taking the place of 'my car'.)

CHAPTER 6

Is she better, more better, the best, or the most bestest?

Using comparatives and superlatives

Radha, Avantika and Lavita are sisters. They constantly compare themselves to each other—who is prettier, smarter, nicer, who draws better, cooks better, etc.

Their mother cannot understand why her daughters are always fighting over who is better than the other. Also, since she is an English teacher, she gets extremely upset because they are always grammatically incorrect while comparing each other.

Let's look at some of the comparisons the three sisters make and try to understand why their mother is upset with their grammar. See if you make some of these common grammatical errors.

Common Error 1:

✗ Radha: I am clever than Avantika at mathematics.

- Here, the word 'clever' is the adjective that is being used to compare Radha to Avantika.
- When adjectives are used to compare two or more things they change form. They become comparatives or superlatives. The adjective 'clever' needs to change form for this sentence to be grammatically correct.

Radha should say:

✓ I am **cleverer** than Avantika at mathematics.

Common Error 2:

✗ Avantika: I am more helpful of my three sisters

- Here, Avantika has used the comparative 'more helpful' instead of the superlative 'most helpful'.

Avantika should have said:

✓ I am the **most helpful** of my three sisters

Common Error 3:

✗ Lavita: I am the most beautifulest out of the sisters.
Radha: No, you are not! I am surely more beautifuler than you.

- Lavita and Radha have both made a very common mistake. It is incorrect to use 'most' before an adjective while suffixing 'est' to it (in this case, 'beautiful').
- It is also incorrect to use 'more' before an adjective and suffix 'er' to it (in this case, 'beautiful').

They should have said:

✓ Lavita: I am the **most beautiful** of the sisters.
✓ Radha: No you are not! I am surely **more beautiful** than you.

Common Error 4:

✗ Avantika: I think that Radha eats more to Lavita.

- When we compare two things, we need to use the word 'than' rather than 'to'.

Avantika should have said:

✓ I think that Radha eats **more than** Lavita.

All the above examples deal with common errors made with comparatives and superlatives. You may have noticed yourself making some of these mistakes. In this chapter I will help you understand how to compare things and eliminate such errors from your speech and writing.

What will I learn in this chapter?

! At this point, the terms 'comparatives' and 'superlatives' may sound very complicated. However, you will soon see that these terms are actually very simple. The lessons below are easy to follow, and by the end of this chapter you will feel confident in this area of English grammar.

6.1 WHAT ARE COMPARATIVES?

'Comparative' is just another way of saying 'compare one thing to another'. Comparative sentences are simply:

Thing (or things) → being compared to → thing (or things)

Read the following dialogues between Radha, Lavita and Avantika and take notice of the comparatives:

1. Radha: **I** am *better than* **Lavita**.
   Radha → being compared to → Lavita
   We are comparing one person to another person.
2. Lavita: **My** badminton team is *better than* Radha's badminton team.
   Lavita's team → being compared to → Radha's team
   We are comparing one team to one other team.
3. Avantika: **I** am *smarter than* both **Radha and Lavita**.
   Avantika → being compared to → Radha and Lavita
   We are comparing one person to two other people.

4. Radha: **Lavita and Avantika** are *worse than* **me** at tennis.
   Lavita and Avantika → being compared to → Radha
   We are comparing two people to one other person.

All the above examples should show you that every time you compare something to something else, you form a 'comparative'.

6.2 WHAT ARE SUPERLATIVES?

We just learned that we use comparatives when comparing one thing to another. However, when we want to show that one thing is not just better, but the best, we need superlatives. Superlatives make one thing stand out in a group. Remember the word *superlative* as 'super' or 'the best'. Superlative sentences look like this:

Thing (or things) → being the best out of → things

Read the following dialogue between Radha, Lavita and Avantika and take notice of the superlatives:

1. Radha: **I** am *the best of* my three sisters.
   Radha → being the best out of → the three sisters
   We are making one person stand out in a group of people.

2. Avantika: **My** tennis team is *the best of* all the teams.
   Avantika's team → being the best of → all the teams
   We are making one team stand out in a group of teams.

You should now see that whenever we make one thing stand out in a group, we use superlatives.

You now know the basics behind comparatives and superlatives. Read on to learn how to form them.

6.3 HOW TO FORM A COMPARATIVE

Radha and Avantika are both baking cakes. As usual, they are competing to bake the better cake. Let's read their dialogue:

1. Radha: Avantika, my cake **is bigger** than yours.

We know that this is a comparative because we are comparing one thing to another—in this case, Radha's cake to Avantika's. Let us use the adjective 'big' to compare two cakes. Here, 'big' is the base adjective. To convert it into the comparative form, we need to apply the following formula:

> **Formula 1:** If the adjective is a one-syllable word, add **'er'** to the adjective and **'than'** after it.

! What is a syllable?

Syllables are sound beats. For example, 'walk' contains one syllable. but, 'walk-ing' contains two syllables.

'Big' is a one-syllable word, so, 'big' becomes 'bigg**er than**'. Avantika is now very upset. Radha's cake *is* in fact bigger than hers. So, she replies:

2. Avantika: So what! My cake is **tastier than** yours.

To compare her cake to Radha's, Avantika has used the base adjective 'tasty'.

> **Formula 2:** If the adjective is a two-syllable word ending with 'y', add **'ier'** to the adjective and **'than'** after it.

'Tasty' is a two-syllable word ending in 'y', so, 'tasty' becomes 'tast**ier than**'.

Radha thought about this. Avantika's cake was very sweet and it really was tastier than hers. However, Radha had spent a lot of time decorating the cake with icing. Avantika's cake had no decorations at all.

3. Radha: Fine, your cake is tastier. But my cake is **more special**! Also, it is **more beautiful** than yours!

Radha has used the base adjectives 'special' and 'beautiful' to compare her cake to Avantika's. You may have noticed that Radha did not say:

✗ Radha: But my cake is **specialer** than yours! Also, it is **beautifuler** than yours!

We just learned that you should add either an 'er' to the adjective or change 'y' to 'ier' and add 'than' after it. But these rules do not work with the adjectives 'special' and 'beautiful'. Special is a two-syllable word not ending in 'y', and beautiful is a three-syllable word. There is one last formula for these types of adjectives.

> **Formula 3:** If the adjective is a two-syllable word not ending in 'y', or has more than two syllables, add '**more**' before the adjective and '**than**' after it.

So, 'special' becomes '**more special than**'.
And 'beautiful' becomes '**more beautiful than**'.

You have now learned all three rules for converting an adjective into the comparative form. A quick recap of the three formulae:

1. If the adjective is a one-syllable word, add '**er**' to the adjective and '**than**' after it.

✓ Fat → Fatt**er than**
✓ Tall → Tall**er than**

2. If the adjective is a two-syllable word ending in 'y', change 'y' to '**ier**' and add '**than**' after the adjective.

✓ Happy → Happ**ier than**
✓ Lucky → Luck**ier than**

3. If the adjective is a two-syllable word not ending in 'y', or has more than two syllables, add '**more**' before the adjective and '**than**' after it.

✓ Tired → **More** tired **than**
✓ Exciting → **More** exciting **than**

6.4 WHY THE PHRASE 'MORE BETTER' IS WRONG

We just learned that there are three ways to form a comparative. Remember that you must choose only one of these formulae at a time. For example, you can't say:

✗ Delhi is more hotter than Mumbai right now.

Here, two things have happened to the adjective 'hot':
1. An 'er' has been added to the end (Formula 1).
2. A 'more' has been added before it (Formula 3).

! This is incorrect. You must choose either Formula 1 or Formula 3, *but never both.*

In the above example, because 'hot' is a one-syllable word, Formula 1 is the correct choice:

✓ Delhi is **hotter than** Mumbai right now.

Notice that the word 'more' has been removed.

! Remember, it is wrong to have both a 'more' and an 'er'—more hotter. Also keep in mind that usually, if it is a short word, you simply add an 'er'. If it is a long word, you add a 'more'.

Exercise 6.1

Put the following words into their correct comparative form based on what you have learned. Check your answers before moving on.

1. Short
2. Busy
3. Pretty
4. Gorgeous
5. Amazing
6. Lazy
7. Wonderful
8. Nice
9. Fat
10. Respectful

Exercise 6.2

Identify what is wrong with each of the following sentences, then correct them. Check your answers before moving on.

1. Why are you more sweeter than your sister?
2. Naan is better to chapatti.

3. Between the two girls, Payal is more tall than Perveen.
4. She is more better than him.
5. My girlfriend is beautifuler than yours.
6. After many years I realized I am more smarter than my wife.
7. My brother thinks that working in a call centre is better to working anywhere else.
8. Geeta is more angry today than she was yesterday.
9. Ali was more hungrier than Shaheen when they went to the restaurant.

! Make sure you have done the exercises and checked your answers before moving on.

Now that you have finished learning about comparatives, read on to understand how to form superlatives.

6.5 HOW TO FORM A SUPERLATIVE

The rules to convert adjectives into superlatives are similar to the ones we learned for comparatives. Let's go through these rules with the help of the dialogues given below:

Radha, Avantika and Lavita are all going for an interview for a sales position in the same company. Let's see who is able to convince the employer that she is the best.

1. Avantika: You should hire me because I am **the smartest** of my three sisters.

We know that this is a superlative, because we can see that one thing is the 'most' out of a group of things—in this case, Avantika's intelligence compared to her other two sisters'. Can you identify the base adjective which compares the three sisters?

'Smart' is the base adjective. To covert it to a superlative form, we need to use the following rule:

Formula 1: If the adjective is a one-syllable word, add '**the**' before the adjective and '**est**' to it.

'Smart' becomes '**the smartest**'.

The employer agrees that Avantika is, in fact, the smartest of the three sisters. But the other two are not giving up so quickly!

2. Radha: I agree, Avantika is the smartest amongst us all. However, for a sales job, being friendly is important, and I am **the friendliest** of the three of us.

Radha has used the base adjective 'friendly' to compare herself to her sisters. Since friendly is a two-syllable word ending in 'y', we need to follow Formula 2:

> **Formula 2:** If the adjective is a two-syllable word ending in 'y', add '**the**' before the adjective and change 'y' to '**iest**'.

So, 'friendly' becomes '**the friendliest**'.

The employer agrees with Radha. Being friendly is very important for the job. He is now convinced that Radha is the best candidate. Just as he decides to choose Radha for the position, Lavita decides to speak up.

3. Lavita: I may not be the smartest or the friendliest, but I am **the most patient** and **the most aggressive**! For a sales job, these qualities are very important.

Lavita has used the base adjectives 'patient' and 'aggressive' to compare herself to her sisters. You may have noticed that Lavita did not say: 'I am the patientest and the aggressivest.'

We have learned that you should have an 'est' or an 'iest' at the end adjective. But this does not work with the adjectives 'patient' and 'aggressive'. 'Patient' is a two-syllable word not ending in 'y', and 'aggressive' is a three-syllable word. There is one last formula for these types of adjectives.

> **Formula 3:** If the adjective is a two-syllable word not ending in 'y', or has more than two syllables, just add '**the most**' before the adjective.

So, 'patient' becomes '**the most patient**'.
And 'aggressive' becomes '**the most aggressive**'.

You have now learned all the three rules for converting an adjective into the superlative form. Look at the recap of the three formulae:

1. If the adjective is a one-syllable word, add '**the**' before the adjective and add an '**est**' to it.
   Fat → **the fattest**
   Tall → **the tallest**
2. If the adjective is a two-syllable word ending in 'y', add '**the**' before the adjective and change 'y' to '**iest**'.
   Happy → **the** happ**iest**
   Lucky → **the** luck**iest**
3. If the adjective is a two-syllable word not ending in 'y', or has more than two syllables, add '**the most**' before the adjective.
   Tired → **the most** tired
   Exciting → **the most** exciting

6.6 WHY THE PHRASE 'MOST BESTEST' IS WRONG

Just as we learned while going over comparatives, it is important never to use more than one formula when converting adjectives into the superlative form. For example, the following sentence is incorrect:

✗ Delhi is the most hottest place in India right now.

In this case, two things have happened to the adjective 'hot':

1. An 'est' has been added after it (Formula 1).
2. A 'most' has been added before it (Formula 3).

! This is incorrect. You must choose either Formula 1 or Formula 3, but never both.

In the above example, because 'hot' is a one-syllable word, Formula 1 is the correct choice.

✓ Delhi is the hottest place in India right now.

Remember, you cannot have both a 'most' and an 'est', i.e., most hottest. Also keep in mind that usually, if it is a short word, you just add an 'est'. If it is a long word, add a 'most'.

Exercise 6.3

Put the following words into their correct superlative form based on what you have just learned. Check your answers before moving on.

1. Short
2. Busy
3. Pretty
4. Gorgeous
5. Amazing
6. Lazy
7. Wonderful
8. Nice
9. Fat
10. Respectful

Exercise 6.4

Correct the following sentences based on what you have learned about superlatives. Check your answers before moving on.

1. I went to Lonavla with my brother and had the most happiest time!
2. She is most interesting of all the friends.
3. My math teacher is the boringest of all.
4. Why are we sitting in the most cool area of the entire theatre?
5. I keep falling in love with the most weirdest girls.
6. The business requires the most large investment.
7. She speaks the fluentest English of all the students in the class.
8. Why are you always trying to get best deal with every shopkeeper?
9. The people who talk the fastest are always the ones hiding the most criticalest details.
10. I want to be best person in the world.

! Make sure you have done the exercises and checked your answers before moving on.

You have now learned all about comparatives and superlatives. Let's do a quick recap:

	Comparative	**Superlative**
One-syllable word (eg. tall)	'-er' + 'than' = tall**er than**	'the' + '-est' = the tall**est**
Two-syllable word ending in 'y' (eg. ugly)	'-ier' + 'than' = ugl**ier than**	'the' + '-iest' = the ugl**iest**
Two-syllable word not ending in 'y', or a word with more than two syllables (eg. intelligent)	'more' + adjective + 'than' = **more** intelligent **than**	'the' + 'most' + adjective = **the most** intelligent

6.7 TWO SIMPLE EXCEPTIONS TO THESE RULES

There are two exceptions to the rules we have learned on forming comparatives and superlatives.

Exception 1: Using the adjective 'good'

- As a comparative: better

✓ She is *better than* him at badminton.

- As a superlative: the best

✓ She is *the best* badminton player in the school.

Exception 2: Using the adjective 'bad'

- As a comparative: worse

✓ He is *worse than* her at badminton.

- As a superlative: the worst

✓ He is *the worst* badminton player in the school.

6.8 HOW COMPARATIVES AND SUPERLATIVES SOMETIMES RESULT IN THE SAME MEANING

There are times where you can use the comparative or the superlative form, and still get the same meaning. For example:

✓ Radha is nicer than both her sisters.
This is a comparative.

✓ Radha is the nicest of all her sisters.
This is a superlative.

Comparatives and superlatives are very similar, and are both essentially used to compare things. Remember that you can *always* use a comparative to get your message across. In certain situations—say when you are comparing one thing to a group—you can *also* use a superlative.

You may be thinking, 'If I can always use a comparative to get my point across, why even bother learning about superlatives?' Well, if you only used comparatives all the time it would be monotonous! Language is supposed to be dynamic and so it is important for us to learn different ways of saying the same thing.

What is important is that you don't mix up the rules between comparatives and superlatives. There are certain keywords that can only be used for one or the other. Look at the chart given below:

Keywords for comparatives	Keywords for superlatives
Than	Out of Among Of/Of all/Of the The (before the adjective)

! This chart does not include all possible keywords, but these are the most common keywords used.

If you are forming a comparative, you must use the keyword 'than'. If you are forming a superlative, you must use one of the other keywords displayed in the box.

! It is incorrect to form a superlative and also use the keyword 'than' in the sentence.

Take a look at the following dialogues, where comparatives have been used with superlative keywords and vice versa:

1. I am the **most beautiful than** my sisters.

This sentence is incorrect because:

- 'most beautiful' is a superlative.
- 'than' is a keyword that can only be used with comparatives (see chart).

We can rewrite this sentence correctly in the following ways:

If forming a comparative	If forming a superlative
I am *more beautiful than* my sisters.	I am *the most beautiful of* my sisters.

2. She is **prettier of the** other sisters.

This sentence is incorrect because:

- 'prettier' is a comparative, and 'of the' is a keyword that can only be used with superlatives (see chart above).

We can rewrite this sentence correctly in the following ways:

If forming a comparative	If forming a superlative
She is *prettier than* her sisters.	She is *the prettiest of all her* sisters.

3. He is **the nicer than** his father.

This sentence is incorrect because:

- 'nicer than' is a comparative
- 'the' is a keyword that can only be used before superlatives (see chart above).

We can rewrite this in the following way:

If forming a comparative	If forming a superlative
He is *nicer than* his father.	This sentence cannot be placed in the superlative form.

! Remember, you can always use a comparative to get your meaning across, but it is only when making certain types of comparisons that you can use a superlative. In this case, we are comparing one person to one other person (his father), and not a group. Thus, we can't use the superlative form.

Exercise 6.5

Read the sentences given below. Figure out whether each sentence contains a comparative or a superlative. Check your answers before moving on.

Example: Akshay is richer than all of them.
Answer: Comparative
Keywords: 'richer than'

1. Your friends are nicer than mine.
2. She is the happiest girl out of them all.
3. Kunju is coming earlier than her sister.
4. Your dog is fatter than hers.
5. My father is the most interesting man I know.

Exercise 6.6

In the sentences given below, choose the correct comparative or superlative form. Underline the keywords that suggest whether the sentence is a comparative or a superlative. Check your answers before moving on.

1. Firoze was **more intelligent/the most intelligent** among his circle of friends.
2. Tina was **taller/the tallest** out of her family.
3. Rohini was **sweeter/sweetest** than her sister.
4. Between Australia and India, India has the **better/the best** cricket team.
5. Kunal rides his bike **faster/the fastest** of all the children in the building.
6. Aarthi likes her brother **the most/more** of her siblings.

Exercise 6.7

Correct the following sentences. Some sentences may have more than one correct answer. Check your answers before moving on.

1. Delhi roads are the broader than Mumbai roads.
2. Why can't Avinash be nicer out of his brothers?
3. Pratima works harder and is a good candidate for the job.
4. She is more better than him.
5. I cleared my final rounds fastest than anyone in my group.
6. My accent is not nicest than hers.
7. I am the elder in the family.
8. I have worked there for three years and I am the better in terms of work quality.
9. When I go for an interview, I always do more worse at extempore rounds.
10. I panic the more than my friends when going for interviews.

! Make sure you have done the exercises and checked your answers before moving on.

You have successfully completed the chapter on comparatives and superlatives. Read the chapter summary to revise.

Understanding syllables

Syllables are sound beats. Think of when you sing a song—you always break up words based on syllables. Let's take a song everyone is familiar with—'Happy Birthday'. Try singing this song and listen to how you break up the different beats of sound:

Hap-py birth-day to you (Six syllables).
Hap-py birth-day to you (Six syllables).
Hap-py birth-day dear A-mit (Seven syllables).
Hap-py birth-day to you (Six syllables).

If counting sound beats is still not clear to you, read the rules given below for how to count syllables.

Rules for counting syllables:

- If a word contains *one* vowel

In this case, the answer is easy—the word has only one syllable. For example:

1. walk
2. drink
3. lynch

These words contain one vowel and have only one syllable.

- If a word has *more than one* vowel

Count how many times a vowel or vowels are separated by consonants. The number of syllables is always one more than this number. For example:

One-syllable words:

1. **Boat**
2. **Laugh**

Even though there is more than one vowel in these words, they are not separated by consonants. Thus these words contain only one syllable each.

Two-syllable words:

1. **Hitting**
2. **People**
3. **Typhoid**

The vowels in the above words are separated once by consonants and so contain two syllables.

Three-syllable words:

1. **O**ctober
2. **Beautiful**
3. **Typical**
4. **Happiness**

The vowels in these words are separated by consonants twice and so contain three syllables.

These rules continue for words containing four, five or six syllables. Remember that each syllable must contain at least one vowel.

Exception

There is one exception to this rule. We don't count syllables when vowels are silent. For example, take the word 'tape':

T**a**pe

Although the two vowels—'a' and 'e' are separated once, this is *not* a two-syllable word. It is a one-syllable word. Why? Try saying the word 'tape'. Notice how you don't actually pronounce the last 'e'—it is silent. Because of this, 'tape' has only one sound beat. Examples of other words like this include:

1. T**y**pe
2. B**i**ke
3. B**a**the
4. M**i**ne

All these words contain one syllable each.

APPLYING WHAT YOU HAVE LEARNED

1. When comparing things and people we can always use comparatives. Sometimes, we can also use superlatives.
2. The way to remember comparatives is: the word should end in 'er', 'ier' or should follow the word 'more'.
   ✓ tall**er** than
   ✓ prett**ier** than
   ✓ **more** beautiful than
3. We must never use both 'er'/'ier' and 'more'. The following are incorrect:
   ✗ **more** tall**er** than
   ✗ **more** prett**ier** than
   ✗ **more** beautiful**er**
4. The way to remember superlatives is: the word should end in an 'est'/'iest', or should follow the word 'most'.
   ✓ the tall**est**
   ✓ the prett**iest**
   ✓ the **most** beautiful

5. We must never use both 'est'/'iest' as well as 'most'. The following combinations are incorrect:
   ✗ **most** tall**est**
   ✗ the **most** pretti**est**
   ✗ the **most** beautiful**est**
6. 'Than' should only be used after comparative form adjectives.
   ✗ He is **tallest than** me.
   ✓ He is **taller than** me.
7. Words like 'among us', 'out of' and 'of the' should only be used after superlative form adjectives.
   ✗ He was the **better among us**.
   ✓ He was the **best among us**.
   ✗ He was the **better of the group**.
   ✓ He was the **best of the group**.

CHAPTER 7

Why can't my subject and verb get along?

Verbs (Part 1): Subject–verb agreement

As we discussed in chapter 1 the formula for a simple sentence is:

Subject + Verb + Object = Complete sentence

When the subject of the sentence does not agree with the verb—meaning when the subject is singular and the verb is plural, or vice versa—the sentence becomes grammatically incorrect.

Look at some common subject–verb disagreements. Do you find yourself making mistakes like this?

Common Error 1:

✗ I have been trying to improve my vocabulary, but my efforts proves futile.

✗ That child are exposed to the sun.

- In the first sentence, the verb 'proves' disagrees with its subject 'efforts'.
- In the second sentence, the verb 'are' disagrees with its subject 'child'.

The correct sentences are:

✓ I have been trying to improve my vocabulary, but my efforts **prove** futile.

✓ That child **is** exposed to the sun.

Common Error 2:

✗ Corporate jobs have long working hours, but pays a lot.
- Here, you have two verbs—'have' and 'pays'—that relate to the *same* subject, 'corporate jobs'.
- The verb 'have' correctly agrees with its subject. Unfortunately, the second verb 'pays', does not.

The correct sentence is:

✓ Corporate jobs have long working hours, but **pay** a lot.

Common Error 3:

✗ It no matter
- The verb is missing.
- 'No' is not a verb.

The correct sentence is:
✓ It **does not** matter.

What will I learn in this chapter?

7.1 Different types of verbs.
7.2 Making subjects and verbs agree.
7.3 Helping or linking verbs.
7.4 Making multiple verbs agree with one subject.
7.5 No sentence should be without a verb.
7.6 Creating sentences with multiple subject/verb combinations.

If you are worried that learning verbs will be too hard, don't worry! The good news is that in both Hindi and English, verbs share a lot in common. For one thing, both languages have a present, past and future tense.

As you go through this chapter and the following ones, you will find that learning about verbs in English is less complicated than learning them in Hindi. In English, verbs don't change depending on whether the subject is feminine or masculine.

Let's start the chapter with a quick recap of the different types of verbs in English.

7.1 DIFFERENT TYPES OF VERBS

The three types of verbs in English are:

1. Action verbs—they 'act' what the subject is doing. (Subjects are circled, verbs are underlined.)
   - We swim together. (We are doing the action of swimming.)
   - Tasha ran home. (Tasha is doing the action of running.)
   - Rakesh caught the ball. (Rakesh is doing the action of catching.)
2. Linking verbs—they link the subject to a description. (Subjects are circled, verbs are underlined.)
   - Diwali is full of lights. ('full of lights' describes Diwali.)
   - Tina became a better person. ('better person' is a description of Tina.)
   - The cake tastes very sweet. ('very sweet' describes the cake.)
3. Helping verbs (Auxiliary verbs)—they 'help' the main verb. Helping verbs come before the main verb. (Subjects are circled, helping verbs are underlined.)
   - I am going to the park. (The main verb here is 'going'.)
   - Does she have to look at me? (The main verb here is 'look'.)
   - I did not want it. (The main verb here is 'want'.)
   - Mummy was laughing. (The main verb here is 'laughing'.)
   - You should call her. (The main verb here is 'call'.)

! In Hindi, the helping verb comes *after* the main verb: 'Main ja raha *hun*.'

Translated literally, this reads: 'I going am.' In English, however, we place the helping word *before* the main verb to say: 'I am going.'

Examples of verbs

Action verbs	Linking verbs	Helping verbs
Walk, drink, eat, like, want, dance, study, work, need, run, cook, draw, jump, laugh	Be (is, am, are, was, were, be, been), have (have, has, had) look, remain, seem, grow, feel, appear, taste, sound	Be (is, am, are, was, were, be, been), have (have, has, had), do (do, does, did), should, shall, can, could, will, would, must

Some linking verbs (like look, feel, taste, etc.) can also be action verbs.

- I <u>looked</u> at the sky. (Action word—'I' am doing the action of looking.)
- I <u>looked</u> tired. (Linking word—'looked' is linking the description 'tired' to the subject 'I'.)

Now that you have refreshed your memory about verbs, let's move on to the rest of the chapter.

7.2 MAKING SUBJECTS AND VERBS AGREE

In this chapter, we will learn about verbs in the present tense.

✗ We likes to go for picnics.

Does the subject 'we' agree with the verb 'likes'? Let's learn the rules for subject and verb agreement:

Subject	Agreeing verb
I	Like
You	Like
He/She/It	Like**s**
We	Like
They	Like

! The verb only changes when the subject is 'he/she/it' by adding an 's' to the end of the verb. If you have forgotten the rules for pronouns like 'he/she/it', refer back to chapter 5.

As we can see from the chart, the subject 'we' does not agree with its verb 'likes'. The sentence should read:

✓ We **like** to go for picnics.

Try another one:
✗ Our dog eat a lot.

The subject 'dog' falls in the 'it' category. Thus, the correct sentence is:
✓ Our dog **eats** a lot.

You may be confused as to how 'dog' falls into the 'it' category. Or you may have doubts about how to place other nouns in their correct categories. When you are creating sentences with nouns, it may help you to replace them mentally with pronouns (I, he, she, it, you and they). This will make it easier to know which form of the verb to use. Examples:

Subject noun	**Subject pronoun**	**Agreeing verb**
I	I	Like
You	You	Like
Jagpreet/Rupali/(The) dog	He/She/It	Like**s**
Tony, Pradeep and I	We	Like
My friends/Rashmi and Jay	They	Like

- 'Rashmi and Jay' are the subject 'they'. The word 'and' means that the subject is always plural.
- When the noun or pronoun subject is plural ('we' or 'they', which means there are more than one), never add an 's' to the following verb.

Exercise 7.1

Figure out whether the subject agrees with the verb in the following sentences. If not, correct the verb. Check your answers before moving on.

1. My friends visits me.
2. Yasmin call for her food.
3. These things belongs to my mother's friend.
4. Jehangir ask us every day if we want to eat with him.
5. I cleans my office all the time.
6. Sushmita Sen has a very nice smile and her height make her different from other heroines.
7. He look like his father.

! Make sure you have done the exercises and checked your answers before moving on.

7.3 HELPING OR LINKING VERBS

✗ She are going to the park.

The verb 'are' (a form of the verb 'be') is a helping and linking verb. The helping/linking verbs 'be', 'have' and 'do' follow subject–verb agreement rules that are different from what we just learnt. Don't worry—these rules are easy and will take you only a moment to learn:

Be	
Subject	**Agreeing verb**
I	Am
He/She/It	Is
You	Are
We	Are
They	Are

Have	
Subject	**Agreeing verb**
I	Have
He/She/It	Has
You	Have
We	Have
They	Have

Do	
Subject	**Agreeing verb**
I	Do
He/She/It	Does
You	Do
We	Do
They	Do

! Remember, 'don't' is short for 'do not', 'doesn't' is short for 'does not', 'isn't' is short for 'is not', etc.

After studying these rules, we can see that the verb 'are' does not agree with its subject 'she'. For the subject and verb to agree, the sentence should read:

✓ She **is** going to the park.

Exercise 7.2

Figure out whether the subject agrees with the verb in the following sentences. If not, correct the verb. Check your answers before moving on.

1. The people has made up their minds.
2. The table are on sale.
3. He don't speak English very well.
4. Even if the actor don't do the best, he is my favourite.
5. My trousers is on the bed.

! Make sure you have done the exercises and checked your answers before moving on.

7.4 MAKING MULTIPLE VERBS AGREE WITH ONE SUBJECT

So far we have learnt that each subject should agree with the verb that follows it. As sentences get more complex, you will notice that one subject can have multiple verbs. It is important that each and every verb in the sentence is in agreement with its subject.

Let's keep this in mind while looking at the next example:
✗ All those who gets selected looks very handsome.

The subject 'all those' falls into the 'they' category. The correct sentence is:
✓ All those who **get** selected look very handsome.

Exercise 7.3

Decide whether the subject agrees with the verb, or verbs in the following sentences. If not, correct the verbs. Check your answers before moving on.

1. She never watch TV in the evenings.
2. She don't know what she are talking about.
3. They goes to the badminton club every day.
4. Rahul forget the way to the office all the time.
5. I am looking for a company that have good opportunities and that are close to my home.
6. The driver know the way to the airport.
7. This activity are very boring.
8. The people has to leave because they is bothering everyone.
9. Good things is hard to find.
10. I love her because she understand and respect my family.

! Make sure you have done the exercises and checked your answers before moving on.

7.5 NO SENTENCE SHOULD BE WITHOUT A VERB!

Every subject needs a verb.

✗ The samosa not very good.

This sentence is missing a key element—the verb. The correct sentence is:
✓ The samosa **is** not very good.

! Remember, 'no' and 'not' are not verbs.

Exercise 7.4

Figure out whether the subjects in the following sentences contain a verb. If not, add the correct verb using the present tense. Check your answers before moving on.

1. I not going to the interview.
2. They no want to give us the forms.
3. The unemployment rate going up.
4. Some good offers also available.
5. She not really want to work in a call centre.

7.6 CREATING SENTENCES WITH MULTIPLE SUBJECT–VERB COMBINATIONS

Some sentences have more than one subject–verb combination. These combinations tend to be connected with words like 'and', 'but' and 'that'. Take a look at the following example. The subjects are circled and the verbs are underlined:

(We) <u>are</u> happy that (she) <u>is</u> coming.

First part of the sentence: (We) <u>are</u> happy

Second part of the sentence: that (she) <u>is</u> coming

'We are happy' is a complete sentence in itself, while 'she is coming' depends on the first part to make sense. Without it, it would be a fragment.

Notice that both parts contain their own subject and verb combinations. The same rules you have learnt in this chapter apply to both parts. Each subject must have at least one verb which agrees with it.

✗ I are so happy that they not going to be there.

In the first part of this sentence, 'I are so happy', the verb 'are' does not agree with its subject 'I'. The correct sentence is,

✓ I **am** so happy.

But 'I' is not the only subject in this sentence. We also have the subject 'they'. Does the subject 'they' agree with its verb? The answer is no. In fact, the subject 'they' does not even have a verb! The correct sentence is:

✓ I **am** so happy that they **are** not going to be there.

Now, complete the following exercises to master what you have just learned.

Exercise 7.5

In the following sentences, verbs are not in agreement with their subjects. There may be more than one incorrect verb in each sentence. Some of the sentences are missing verbs. Correct the mistakes. Check your answers before moving on.

1. What books do Dinesh read?
2. Insurance companies does give people a safety net if something bad happen.
3. The audience are not enjoying the movie because the script are boring.
4. It no matter if the movie are bad.
5. These tourists has to go and gets their tickets.
6. I want to different from others.
7. We just not getting enough sleep.
8. You all was sitting there.
9. I belongs to a traditional family.
10. Some apples was good and some was bad.
11. I is looking for a girl who understands me.
12. She run away because she are such a shy person.
13. I no want that.
14. I want to independent.
15. Some fake companies also there in the market.
16. That right.
17. You seems to be very smart.

Exercise 7.6

Pick the correct verb in the sentences below. Check your answers before moving on.

1. The boss and her staff is/are attending the work get-together.
2. Both Maria and Manoj attend/attends cricket games.
3. Pratima has/have a beautiful baby.
4. The latest information the Congress party received was/were wrong.
5. Sayed and his wife do/does go to parties together.
6. The software engineers wasn't/weren't able to leave work early.
7. Theatre halls that don't has/don't have nice chairs are hard for people to like.
8. My mother likes to cook/cooks every day.

! Make sure you have done the exercises and checked your answers before moving on.

APPLYING WHAT YOU HAVE LEARNED

1. In any sentence, subjects and verbs must agree with each other. Subjects can be in the form of pronouns or nouns.
2. Only when the subject is in the 'he/she/it' form do you need to add an 's' to the end of most verbs.
   - He like**s** her.
   - The dog run**s** fast.
3. If the subject is in any other form (I, you, we, they), the verb must remain untouched.
   - I **love** my mother.
   - We **eat** together.
   - They **believe** in God.
4. Some verbs change altogether to match their subjects. The ones to remember are 'be', 'have' and 'do'.
   - I **am** here/I **have** to go/I **do** love you.
   - She **is** here/She **has** to go/She **does** love you.
   - We **are** here/We **have** to go/We **do** love you.

5. Every sentence must have a verb. 'No' is not a verb.
   ✗ I no have any money.
   ✓ I **do not** have any money.
6. Complex sentences can have multiple verbs relating to the same subject. Or they could have more than one subject and verb combination. Make sure that all verbs relate to their subjects properly.
   ✗ <u>He</u> run and play cricket.
   ✓ <u>He</u> **runs** and **plays** cricket.
   ✗ <u>Anand</u> do read more books than <u>my sisters</u> does.
   ✓ <u>Anand</u> **does** read more books than <u>my sisters</u> **do**.

CHAPTER 8

Should I say 'I understand you' or 'I am understanding you'?

Verbs (Part 2): Present simple versus present continuous tenses

You are at an interview, waiting for the HR manager. You are nervous. You tell yourself, 'Stop being nervous! She's only going to ask me about myself, what I have done before, and my educational qualifications. How hard can that be?'

You are right. In an interview you simply have to talk about yourself. Unfortunately, many of us fail at this very easy task. Why? There are usually two reasons—we are not prepared, or we construct our sentences incorrectly. When constructing sentences, verbs and tenses can be one of the largest problem areas.

In the last chapter we went over ways to make our subjects and verbs agree. In this chapter, we will learn how to differentiate between the present simple tense—'I understand'—and the present continuous tense—'I am understanding'—while going through interview questions. (For tips on how to prepare for interviews, refer to Section 4.) Now read the common errors listed below. Can you relate to any of them?

Common Error 1:

✗ I am having questions to ask you.
✗ I am understanding you.
✗ She does not remembering me.

- These three sentences demonstrate a very common error—the verbs are in the present continuous tense, when they should be in the present simple.

- Some verbs (like 'understand'), should never be used in the continuous tense.
- While using the helping verb 'does', you should place the main verb in the present simple tense.

The correct sentences are:
✓ I **have** questions to ask you.
✓ I **understand** you.
✓ She does not **remember** me.

Common Error 2:

✗ We enjoying ourselves at the disco.
- Here, the verb in the continuous tense ('enjoying') is missing its helping verb 'are'.

The correct sentence is:
✓ We **are** enjoying ourselves at the disco.

Common Error 3:

✗ Right now I am walking and listen to music.
- Since both actions 'walk' and 'listen' are happening at the same time and are ongoing, they should both be in the continuous tense.

The correct sentence is:
✓ Right now I am **walking** and **listening** to music.

What will I learn in this chapter?

8.1 How to form the present simple and continuous tenses.
8.2 Not to use 'do' or 'does' before continuous tense verbs.
8.3 Learning to use the present simple and the continuous tenses.
8.4 Two additional rules for the present continuous tense.
8.5 Recap.

8.1 HOW TO FORM THE PRESENT SIMPLE AND CONTINUOUS TENSES

You should already be fairly familiar with the present simple and present continuous tenses, because both are used in Hindi.

- Present simple: '*Mein kaam karta hoon.*' (I work.)
- Present continuous: '*Mein kaam kar raha hoon.*' (I am working.)

Let's learn how these tenses are formed in English:

Present simple	Present continuous
I walk	I **am** walk**ing**
She/He/It walks	She/He/It **is** walk**ing**
We walk	We **are** walk**ing**
They walk	They **are** walk**ing**
You walk	You **are** walk**ing**

As can be seen, the continuous tense is formed in two ways:

- A form of the helping verb 'to be' (am, is, are) is added before the main verb.
- The main verb has an 'ing' at the end.

The helping verb does not always come right before the main verb.

- He **is** definitely **running** late for the meeting.
- I **am** not really **feeling** good today.

! If you have forgotten the forms of the helping word 'be', see Chapter 7.

8.2 'DO' AND 'DOES'

Remember, you can only use the helping verb 'to be' (am, is, are) before a continuous tense verb. When using the helping verbs 'do' or 'does', you have to keep the main verb that follows in the simple tense (never the continuous).

Correct	Incorrect
✓ I **do remember** you.	✗ I **do remembering** you.
✓ She **does love** you.	✗ She **does loving** you.
✓ I **do not** (don't) **remember** you.	✗ I **do not** (don't) **remembering** you.
✓ She **does not** (doesn't) **love** you.	✗ She **does not** (doesn't) **loving** you.

8.3 LEARNING TO USE THE PRESENT SIMPLE AND CONTINUOUS TENSES

Many of us tend to confuse the present simple and continuous tenses. The chart given below will help you understand the difference between these two tenses at a very basic level.

Present simple	Present continuous
Rule 1: Current, fact-driven situations. ✓ I **work** at Infosys.	**Rule 1:** Ongoing actions that are incomplete. ✓ I **am working** on a project right now.
Rule 2: Habit or regular action in the past, present or future. ✓ I **go** to work every day.	**Rule 2:** Actions planned in the future. ✓ I **am going** to work tomorrow.

The above rules should give you a basic overview of the difference between the present simple and continuous tenses. Now, to work on your understanding of the above rules—read a dialogue between Anand, who is looking for a new job, and a company recruiter.

Using the present simple tense

```
Recruiter: Anand, where do you live?
Anand:     I am living in Mulund, a suburb of Mumbai.
```

Anand has used the continuous form of the verb 'to live' (am living). This is incorrect—he needs to use the present simple tense for current, factual situations (see present simple tense rule 1). Anand **lives** in Mulund—this is current, and it is a fact.

✓ Anand: I **live** in Mulund, a suburb of Mumbai.

Let's look at some more examples of present simple tense rule 1:

Correct	Incorrect
✓ He does not **want** tea right now. ➤ This is a current situation.	✗ He does not **wanting** tea right now. ➤ Because this is a current situation, we can't use the continuous tense.
✓ People **breathe** air. ➤ This is a fact.	✗ People are **breathing** air. ➤ Because this is a fact, avoid using the continuous tense.

Let's continue reading the dialogue between Anand and the company recruiter.

```
Recruiter: What is your favourite hobby?
Anand:     I like to surf the Internet. Every
           evening I am surfing the Internet for
           at least two hours.
```

In the second sentence, Anand has used the present continuous form of the verb 'to surf' (am surfing) incorrectly. When we describe a regular action or a habit, we must use the present simple tense (see present simple tense rule 2). Anand says that he surfs the Internet every evening—making the action regular.

✓ Anand: I like to surf the Internet. Every evening I **surf** the Internet for at least two hours.

Let's look at some more examples of present simple tense rule 2:

Correct	Incorrect
✓ I **eat** chapattis every day. ➤ This is a regular action that happened in the past, continues to happen in the present, and will continue to happen in the future.	✗ I **am eating** chapattis every day. ➤ Because this is a regular action, avoid using the present continuous tense.
✓ She never **remembers** my name. ➤ This is a habit—she didn't remember in the past, doesn't remember in the present, and will continue to not remember in the future.	✗ She **is** never **remembering** my name. ➤ Because this is a habit, avoid using the present continuous tense.

Using the present continuous tense

Now, let's learn when we should use the present continuous tense instead of the present simple.

```
Recruiter:   Where do you work at the moment?
Anand:       I currently work at Excel Advertising,
             a large marketing company.
Recruiter:   Okay. I need to get an idea of what
             you do on a day-to-day basis. What
             projects are you working on?
Anand:       Right now I work on a project with
             Infosys.
```

Anand has incorrectly used the verb 'to work' in the last sentence in the present simple tense. It should have been in the present continuous tense—'I am working.' This is because we use the present continuous tense to show actions that are in progress at the time of speaking, and not yet complete. Since Anand is *still* working on the project with Infosys, it is not complete.

✓ Anand: Right now I **am working** on a project with Infosys.

Let's look at some more examples of this rule:

Correct	Incorrect
✓ I can't meet you because **I am working** right now. ➤ This is an ongoing action.	✗ I can't meet you because I **work** right now. ➤ Because this is an ongoing action that is not yet complete, we can't use the present simple tense.
✓ They **are** sweating while **climbing** the mountain. ➤ This is an ongoing action.	✗ They are sweating while **climb** the mountain. ➤ Because this is an ongoing action that is not yet complete, we can't use the present simple tense.

Let's read some more of Anand's interview with the recruiter.

`Recruiter:`	`Have you told your current employer that you are planning to leave the company?`
`Anand:`	`No, I have not. I` **`go`** `to tell them as soon as I know I have another offer.`

Anand has forgotten that the present continuous can be used for *future actions* as well. Since he plans to tell his company he has a new job *after* he receives an offer (in the future), he could use the present continuous tense (see present continuous tense rule 2).

✓ Anand: No, I have not. I **am going** to tell them as soon as I know I have another offer.

- Anand could have also used the future tense, which we will cover later in this section. For future actions we can use both the present continuous and future tenses.

Let's look at some more examples of present continuous tense Rule 2:

Correct	Incorrect
✓ I **am going** to the doctor later. ➤ This action is planned for the future.	✗ I **go** to the doctor later. ➤ Since this is a future action, you need to use either the continuous or the future tense.
✓ She **is arriving** tomorrow. ➤ This action is planned for the future.	✗ She **arrives** tomorrow. ➤ This is grammatically correct—but the meaning has changed. By using the present simple tense, we have made it a 'fact' that she will arrive tomorrow, rather than a future action.

Exercise 8.1

The following sentences have mistakes relating to the present simple and continuous tenses. Correct them and explain why the sentence is wrong based on the rules you have just learned. Check your answers before moving on.

1. Tigers are living on land.
2. Rehanna watches TV right now.
3. I am eating bread every day.
4. She does looking very nice.
5. Because she is cooking alone, I help her.
6. I am planning on implement the report's recommendations.
7. Q: What are your hobbies?
   A: I am liking to paint.

8. I always watching Amir Khan's movies.
9. I do wanting to go to Delhi.
10. They look at the sky because the airplane show is going on.
11. Akshay go to the park tonight.
12. We are watching the World Cup every day.

! Make sure you have done the exercises and checked your answers before moving on.

You have just learned the basic rules for forming the present simple and continuous tenses, and how to avoid common errors. Let's learn two additional rules for the present continuous tense.

8.4 TWO ADDITIONAL RULES FOR THE PRESENT CONTINUOUS TENSE

There are two more rules to keep in mind when using the present continuous tense. Let's continue reading the dialogue between Anand and the recruiter to learn about these two additional rules.

Recruiter:	Why do you want to leave your current company?
Anand:	Because I currently **working** long hours, and I do not get to see my family.

Here, Anand has forgotten to add a form of the helping verb 'to be' (am, is, are) before the present continuous tense verb 'working'. This is a common mistake. Remember that if the verb is in the present continuous form ('ing') you must add a form of the helping verb 'to be' before it.

✓ Anand: Because I **am** currently **working** long hours, and do not get to see my family.

Present Continuous Tense Rule 3: Remember to place the helping verb 'to be' before the main verb.

Let's look at some more examples of present continuous tense rule 3:

Correct	Incorrect
They **are driving** to the party together.	They **driving** to the party together. ➤ Helping verb 'are' is missing.
She **is looking** very sad.	She **looking** very sad. ➤ Helping verb 'is' is missing.

Very good! We now have one last rule to learn about the present continuous tense. Keep reading Anand's dialogue with the company recruiter.

```
Recruiter:    What type of university degree do
              you hold?
Anand:        I am having a degree in computer
              engineering.
```

Anand has made another common mistake. He has used the verb 'have' in the present continuous form. Certain words, for example, have, like, understand (see the list below) should not be be used in the present continuous tense except in certain contexts. Anand should have kept the verb in the simple tense.

✓ Anand: I **have** a degree in computer engineering.

> Present Continuous Tense Rule 4:
> Some words should not be placed in the present continuous form except in certain contexts (i.e., they can't always be combined with 'is', 'are' or 'am').

Examples of verbs that you should avoid placing in the present continuous tense include (this is not a complete list):

Agree	Belong	Feel
Have	Hear	Know
Like	Love	Mean
Need	Own	Prefer
Recognize	Remember	See
Smell	Taste	Think
Understand	Want	

You may notice that most of the verbs listed above are not action verbs. Most of them are opinions, beliefs, feelings or possessions. Therefore, you should avoid placing them in the present continuous tense except in certain contexts. For example, let's compare the verb 'run' to the verb 'need' ('need' is one of the verbs on the list above).

We can show the *action* of someone running. But, we can't show the action of someone needing. Though 'need' is a verb, it is not an action verb. It is not continuous, not moving. For verbs like 'need' and the others listed above, remember to keep them in the present simple tense.

Let's look at some more examples of present continuous tense rule 4:

Correct	Incorrect
✓ I **understand** you. ➤ Keep this verb in the present simple tense.	✗ I **am understanding** you. ➤ There is no action in 'understanding'. It isn't easily placed in the present continuous tense.
✓ She **knows** it. ➤ Keep this verb in the present simple tense.	✗ She **is knowing** it. ➤ There is no action in 'knowing'. It can't easily be placed in the present continuous tense.
✓ I **like** the music. ➤ Keep this verb in the present simple tense.	✗ I **am liking** the music. ➤ There is no action in 'liking', it is an opinion. It can't easilybe placed in the present continuous tense.
✓ We **have** a red car. ➤ Keep this verb in the present simple tense.	✗ We **are having** a red car. ➤ There is no action in 'having'. It is a fact that they have a red car. Thus, it can't easily be placed in the present continuous tense.

Exception to Present Continuous Tense Rule 4

Yes, there are exceptions to this rule. From the table above, some verbs like 'to think', 'to feel', 'to have', etc. can, in certain situations, be used in the present continuous tense. For example:

Correct	Incorrect (Verbs should be in the present simple tense.)
✓ Zarine **is thinking** hard. ➤ Here, 'thinking' serves as an action verb.	✗ Zarine **is thinking** that you are a nice person. ➤ In this situation, 'thinking' is an opinion. Zarine is simply expressing an opinion and not doing an action. 'Thinks' is correct.
✓ Abhishek **is feeling** sick in his stomach. ➤ Here, 'feeling' is an action verb—imagine Abhishek's stomach churning inside.	✗ Abhishek **is feeling** that the test was hard. ➤ Here, 'feeling' is not an action, but an opinion. Abhishek 'believes' the test was hard. 'Feels' is correct.
✓ Anu **is having** a baby. ➤ Here, 'having' is an action verb—Anu is doing the action of giving birth to her baby.	✗ Anu **is having** a car. ➤ In this situation, 'having' is used as a possession, not an action. 'Has' is correct.
✓ They **are having** a party. ➤ Here, 'having' serves as an action verb as it means the same thing as 'giving' or 'throwing' a party.	✗ They **are having** an important assignment. ➤ Here, 'having' is used as a possession, not as an action. 'Have' is correct.

If exceptions confuse you, just try and avoid using the above listed verbs in the present continuous tense—keep them in the present simple to be safe. As you become more familiar with the English language, these little nuances will start making more sense!

8.5 A QUICK RECAP OF THIS CHAPTER

Present simple tense rules

Rule 1: Use for current, fact-driven situations.
✓ Firoze **likes** fruit with ice cream.
✓ They don't **take** the train when it rains.

Rule 2: Use for habits or regular actions (past, present and future).
✓ Rohini and Brinda **pray** together every day.
✓ Yasmin **exercises** on Mondays and Wednesdays.

Present continuous tense rules

Rule 1: Use for ongoing actions (i.e., in progress at the time of speaking).
✓ Anil can't call me right now because he **is driving**.
✓ I **am making** parathas and won't be done for another hour.

Rule 2: Use for actions planned in the future.
✓ We **are going** to the movies tonight.
✓ Gurjot **is planning** a big party for me tomorrow.

Rule 3: Don't forget to place a form of the helping verb 'to be' (am, is, are) before the main verb.
✗ Rashmi **looking** nice for the wedding.
✓ Rashmi **is looking** nice for the wedding.

Rule 4: Some words cannot always be placed in the continuous tense. This means they cannot have both an ending in 'ing' and a form of the verb 'be' (am, is, are) before them.
✗ I **am knowing** what to do.
✓ I **know** what to do.

If you feel confused, don't worry. Go over exercises 8.2, 8.3, 8.4 and 8.5. Practice will make it easier.

Exercise 8.2

The following sentences have mistakes relating to the usage of the present simple and continuous tenses. Correct them, and explain why each sentence is incorrect based on the rules you have just learned. Check your answers before moving on.

1. I am knowing your girlfriend.
2. She does not remembering my name.
3. I loving my dog.
4. I am having certain questions to ask you.
5. Presently, she depending on others.
6. We partying at my friend's house.
7. I don't like movies which are having little emotion.
8. I am having a day off from work on Saturday.
9. My elder brother working as a software engineer in Dubai.
10. I having strong values and am a romantic at heart.
11. I would like to know if you going to accept this offer.
12. I completed my education at India's premier institute, and now I working with a major company in Bangalore.

Exercise 8.3

Correct the sentences that are wrong. Check your answers before moving on.

1. I am not understanding.
2. They are chewing gum.
3. I am not hearing you.
4. He is not wanting tea.
5. We are liking this music.
6. She is smoking a cigarette.
7. I am knowing your girlfriend.
8. She is not remembering how to do it.
9. I am having my reception on Tuesday.
10. I am loving my dog.
11. They are not needing me.
12. I am seeing your files on my screen.
13. I am concentrating on the assignment.
14. I am meaning that I did it.
15. I am having a small red car.

16. Rekha is not thinking very clearly.
17. I am not owning my apartment.
18. James is driving.
19. I am belonging to a large family.
20. You are eating chicken.
21. We are having offices in five cities.
22. I want to work in a finance company because it is having growth prospects.
23. I was not knowing there would be such high security.
24. I see myself running the organization and manage lots of people.

Exercise 8.4

Circle the correct verbs to complete the dialogue. This exercise covers rules learned in this chapter as well as subject–verb agreements (covered in the previous chapter). Check your answers before moving on.

Customer:	Hi, I **need/am needing** to update my information for your files.
Agent:	Just give me a second, sir. I **look/am looking** for your information.
Customer:	My computer information **is/are** not updated.
Agent:	I will update that for you now. I **need/am needing** the serial number on the back of your computer.
Customer:	It **is/are** 548291. How long will it take you to **update/updating** the system?
Agent:	I also **require/requires** the warranty information.
Customer:	I **don't have/doesn't has** a warranty.
Agent:	I **am seeing/see** from your previous account that you had a warranty before?
Customer:	Yes, I **am believing/believe** so.
Agent:	You **is/are** right. Okay, that is all the information I need.

Exercise 8.5

Tick the answer that is grammatically correct. Check your answers before moving on.

1. Q: Do you speak English well?
   - ❑ Yes, I speak English well.
   - ❑ Yes, I am speaking English well.
2. Q: What are you doing?
   - ❑ I watch a movie.
   - ❑ I am watching a movie.
3. Q: What do you usually do for fun?
   - ❑ I watch movies.
   - ❑ I am watching movies.
4. Q: Where does your brother live?
   - ❑ He lives in Hyderabad.
   - ❑ He is living in Hyderabad.
5. Q: Why isn't she picking up the phone?
   - ❑ Because she sleeps.
   - ❑ Because she is sleeping.
6. Q: Why are you going for another interview?
   - ❑ Because I did not get the last job.
   - ❑ Because I am not getting the last job.
7. Q: Why is your sister always looking stressed?
   - ❑ She is having a very tough job.
   - ❑ She has a very tough job.
8. Q: What are you doing tomorrow?
   - ❑ I am going to play tennis.
   - ❑ I play tennis.
9. Q: Why don't you invite me for the party?
   - ❑ I don't want you there.
   - ❑ I am not wanting you there.
10. Q: When is your family leaving?
    - ❑ They leaving tomorrow.
    - ❑ They are leaving tomorrow.

! Make sure you have done the exercises and checked your answers before moving on.

APPLYING WHAT YOU HAVE LEARNED

1. We form the present continuous tense by adding a form of the verb 'to be' (am, is, are) before the main verb, and by adding an 'ing' to the end of the main verb.
   - Present simple tense—I **run** quickly.
   - Present continuous tense—I **am running** quickly.
   - Present simple tense—We **watch** TV together.
   - Present continuous tense—We **are watching** TV together.
2. While using the helping verb 'to do' or 'does', always keep the main verb following it in the present simple tense.
   ✗ I **do enjoying** it.
   ✓ I **do enjoy** it.
   ✗ She **does looking** fat.
   ✓ She **does look** fat.
3. The present simple tense should be used for current situations, when stating facts, or for recurring events.
   ✗ I **am loving** my mother.
   ✓ I **love** my mother.
   ✗ I **am driving** to work every day.
   ✓ I **drive** to work every day.
4. The present continuous tense should be used for ongoing and future events.
   ✗ Right now I **walk** to school.
   ✓ Right now I **am walking** to school.
   ✗ I **invite** her to the party on Saturday.
   ✓ I **am inviting** her to the party on Saturday.
5. While using the continuous tense, you need to always remember to add a form of the helping verb 'to be' before the main verb.
   ✗ I **going** to the park.
   ✓ I **am** going to the park.
   ✗ The company **growing** fast.
   ✓ The company **is** growing fast.

6. Certain verbs are usually not used in the present continuous form, and should be kept in the simple tense.
   ✗ I am having a TV.
   ✓ I **have** a TV.
   ✗ I am not understanding what she said.
   ✓ I do not **understand** what she said.

CHAPTER 9

She liked me in the past but hates me in the present!

Verbs (Part 3): Present simple versus past simple tenses

In the previous chapter we learnt the difference between 'I understand' and 'I am understanding'—the present simple tense and the present continuous tense. In this chapter we will cover the difference between the present simple tense and the past simple tense.

See if you make any of the common errors listed below:

Common Error 1:

✗ Last week I have a bad cough.

- Here, the speaker is talking about something that happened last week—i.e., in the past. Thus, we need to use the past tense 'had', and not the present tense 'have'.

The correct sentence is:

✓ Last week I **had** a bad cough.

Common Error 2:

✗ Sanjay, you had a diploma in computer engineering, so why do you want to work in a call centre?

- Here, the past tense 'had' is used incorrectly. Sanjay still has his diploma—it has not gone away—thus, we need to use the present tense.
- Remember, we use the present tense for current, factual situations.

The correct sentence is:

✓ Sanjay, you **have** a diploma in computer engineering, so why do you want to work in a call centre?

Common Error 3:

✗ Firoze were unhappy with the results.

- In chapter 7 we learnt that subjects and verbs need to agree. This is true in the past tense as well.
- In this sentence, the past tense verb 'were' does not agree with its subject, 'Firoze.'

The correct sentence is:

✓ Firoze **was** unhappy with the results.

Common Error 4:

✗ I did looked at her and she is pretty.

- If we use the helping verb 'did', we must place the main verb following it in the present simple tense.
- This is the same rule we learnt in the last chapter for the verb 'to do'. (The past tense of 'do' is 'did'.)

The correct sentence is:

✓ I **did look** at her and she is pretty.

What will I learn in this chapter?

9.1 The difference between the present and the past tense.
9.2 How to form the past simple tense.
9.3 When to use the past tense.
9.4 Do not use 'did' before past tense verbs.

9.1 THE DIFFERENCE BETWEEN THE PRESENT AND THE PAST TENSE

Just as in English, in Hindi too there is a difference between the present and past tense.

Present: '*Main bahut nachti hoon.*'
Past: '*Main nachti thi.*'

It would sound funny if we said '*Main kal nachti hoon*', wouldn't it?

Many of us make the mistake of mixing up the present tense with the past tense when we speak in English. And it sounds just as awkward and funny as the above Hindi sentence. The box below states the basic differences between the present and past tenses.

Read the dialogue between Sunil and Tanvi in the box below. Sunil and Tanvi were good friends at one time. But today, they no longer are. Unfortunately, poor Sunil is still 'living in the past' and cannot differentiate between the present and past.

Present simple tense	Past simple tense
Rule 1: Use for current situations or facts Sunil: I **like** Tanvi. ➤ This is a current feeling that Sunil has right now.	**Rule 1: Use for actions that ended in the past** Tanvi: I **liked** Sunil. ➤ Tanvi has *stopped* liking Sunil. Her liking for him is in the past.
Rule 2: Use for habits or regular actions in the present Sunil: I **watch** movies with Tanvi. ➤ According to Sunil, watching movies with Tanvi is a regular occurrence.	**Rule 2: Use for habits or regular actions in the past (could be quick actions or actions that happened over time)** Tanvi: I **watched** movies with Sunil. ➤ According to Tanvi, it is something that happened regularly only in the past. It has stopped now.

9.2 HOW TO FORM THE PAST SIMPLE TENSE

There are three ways to form the past simple tense:

1. For most verbs, just place a 'd' or an 'ed' at the end.
   - I **live** here now → I **lived** here before.
   - I **smoke** a lot → I **smoked** a lot.
2. For some irregular verbs, you need to change the form of the entire verb.

- I **get** good marks → I **got** good marks.
- I **go** on Wednesdays → I **went** last Wednesday.
- He **builds** big houses → He **built** big houses.

3. For other irregular verbs, you don't need to change the verb at all.
   - I **hit** the car today → I **hit** the car yesterday
   - I always **cut** myself → I **cut** myself last week.

Don't worry too much about irregular verbs. As you read more books, magazines or newspapers you will start to recognize them automatically.

! In the past tense, it doesn't matter if the subject is 'I', 'she', 'we', etc. Verbs in the past tense stay the same for all subjects.

✓ I **danced** a lot. /You **danced** a lot. /She **danced** a lot. /We **danced** a lot. /They **danced** a lot.

Helping verbs

Remember the helping verbs 'to be', 'to have' and 'to do'? Just like the present tense, these three verbs follow their own rules in the past tense. Let's learn how to use them in the past tense:

To be

Subject	Present	Past
I	Am	**Was**
He/She/It	Is	**Was**
You	Are	**Were**
We	Are	**Were**
They	Are	**Were**

To have

Subject	Present	Past
I	Have	**Had**
He/She/It	Has	**Had**
You	Have	**Had**
We	Have	**Had**
They	Have	**Had**

To do

Subject	Present	Past
I	Do	**Did**
He/She/It	Does	**Did**
You	Do	**Did**
We	Do	**Did**
They	Do	**Did**

! As you can see, in the past tense, only the helping verb 'to be' changes form for different subjects. The other two stay the same regardless of the subject.

9.3 WHEN TO USE THE PAST TENSE

Sunil desperately wants to be friends with Tanvi again. Read the following dialogue and pay attention to any past versus present tense mistakes.

Sunil:	Tanvi, why don't you like me any more?
Tanvi:	Because we once went to a party and you **are** very mean to me.

Do you notice anything wrong with Tanvi's answer? The party that Tanvi is talking about happened in the past. Thus, all the verbs in the sentence should be placed in the past tense. 'Are' is a present tense verb.

✓ Tanvi: Because we once went to a party and you **were** very mean to me.

Sunil:	I'm sorry about that! What else have I done wrong?
Tanvi:	Remember our first day at college? We **have** a welcome programme. You **was** late and **keep** me waiting.

In this answer, Tanvi has made many mistakes! Let's go through them:

1. Tanvi first says, 'We *have* a welcome programme.' 'Have' is a present tense verb, which would mean that the welcome programme is happening in the present. But this is clearly wrong as Tanvi is talking about their first day of college—an event that happened in the past.
2. Tanvi then says, 'You *was* late.' Here, the tense is correct. But Tanvi has forgotten to make her subject and verb agree!

3. Last, Tanvi says, 'and *keep* me waiting.' Again, Tanvi is talking about past events and should use past tense verbs. 'Keep' is a present tense verb.

✓ Tanvi: Remember our first day of college? We **had** a welcome programme. You **were** late and **kept** me waiting.

Tanvi:	Why do you want to be my friend?
Sunil:	Because I **missed** you every day. I **looked** forward to seeing you and I am sad that I **didn't**.

Here, Sunil has incorrectly placed many of the verbs in the past tense instead of the present!

! You should try and remember what tense to use based on the question asked.

Tanvi asked Sunil why he wants to be her friend *now*. She is asking about a *present* feeling. Thus, Sunil's answer should be in the present tense:

✓ Sunil: Because I **miss** you every day. I **look** forward to seeing you and I am sad that I **don't**.

Exercise 9.1

Based on the questions asked, correct the answers that are incorrect. Check your answers before moving on.

1. Q: Hi, can you help me boot my computer?
   A: One second, I had some urgent work to do first.
2. Q: What did you and your new colleagues do yesterday?
   A: We went to a restaurant to having lunch and all my colleagues introduces themselves.
3. Q: What did you do on your first day at work?
   A: On my first day we have an induction programme. Our programme were at 10 a.m.
4. Q: Why are you here to see me?
   A: I needed your help.

5. Q: Have you worked on my file yet?
   A: Yes, I have make the new entries.
6. Q: Where do you and your family live?
   A: My elder sister, my mother and I lived together in Mumbai.
7. Q: Do you feel better now after going to the doctor?
   A: I felt much better now.

Exercise 9.2

Rewrite the following sentences in the past simple tense. Check your answers before moving on.

1. I forget her name.
2. I know her father and mother.
3. She wears red shoes.
4. I don't see her.
5. She sweeps the floor.
6. She never tells a lie.
7. I don't eat meat.
8. He spends his time working.

Exercise 9.3

Tanvi and Sunil are friends again and are having a conversation over coffee. Tanvi asks Sunil, 'What place do you love the most?' Sunil's answer is given below. He has made errors in using the past and the present tenses. There are also some errors with regard to subject–verb agreement as well as with the continuous tense (covered in the last two chapters). See if you can find all the errors and correct them. Check your answers before moving on.

```
I really love my hometown because it is away from
the city. Whenever I went outside from my home, I
can only seen natural beauty. Also, I really missed
my relatives. It is also very safe there; there is
no problems in going out alone. Now I live in Delhi
and here if I go out at night, people were telling
me that it is not safe. Whenever I have these
problems I missed my hometown.
```

! Make sure you have done the exercises and checked your answers before moving on.

9.4 DO NOT USE DID BEFORE PAST TENSE VERBS

In the last chapter, we learnt a grammar tip for the verb 'do': If you are using the verb 'do' as a helping verb, remember to always keep the main verb following it in the present simple tense.

✗ I *do* **remembering** you.
✓ I *do* **remember** you.
✗ She *does* **loving** you.
✓ She *does* **love** you.

This same rule applies when 'do' is used in its past tense 'did'.

✗ I *did* **remembered** you.
✓ I *did* **remember** you.
✗ She *did* **loving** you.
✓ She *did* **love** you.

! As you can see, when we use the verb 'did', the verb that follows it *must* be kept in the *present simple tense* even if we are talking about a *past* action.

Exercise 9.4

The following sentences all include the verb 'did'. Correct the sentences that have errors.

1. How did you did that?
2. We did not made any food today.
3. We didn't got the error message this time.
4. Did you get that computer replaced?
5. We didn't had that on the monitor.
6. Where did you bought the original computer from?

! Make sure you have done the exercises and checked your answers before moving on.

Exercise 9.5

The following sentences contain past versus present tense mistakes. They are also filled with incorrect subject–verb agreements. Correct these errors.

1. They told me that if I get my diploma quickly they will give me a promotion. So now I preferred to get it quickly.
2. In college I used to be very independent. I never bother about anything in life.
3. I didn't took a typing test.
4. Just as my company change my future, I want to help others.
5. I were eliminated in the fourth round.
6. My friends have interviewed with Tata but they didn't got the job.
7. The boy kick the ball.
8. It was build in memory of love.
9. In the end we was just happy to be home.
10. I have two sisters and both of them get married and are settled.
11. I will call you in case your cheque got bounced.
12. Whenever I get stucked she helps me.
13. Did you clicked on anything?
14. She hitted the ball really hard.

! Make sure you have done the exercises and checked your answers before moving on.

Good work! By now, you have gone through nearly all the basic rules for forming tenses.

APPLYING WHAT YOU HAVE LEARNED

1. If an action happened in the past, or was a regular habit in the past, keep it in the past tense!
2. For most verbs, the past tense is formed by adding a 'd' or an 'ed' to the end.
   - Dance → Danced
   - Look → Looked
3. Some irregular verbs, though, have to be altered completely or not changed at all.

- Speak → Spoke
- Hit → Hit

4. You don't have to worry about subject–verb agreements in the past tense *except* for the verb 'to be'.
   - I looked/She looked/We looked/They looked/You looked—all verbs are the same regardless of the subject.
   - I was/She was/We were/They were/You were—some verbs are different depending on the subject.
5. If using the helping verb 'did', the main verb that follows must be kept in the *present simple tense*.

   ✗ I **did** danc**ed** with her.

   ✓ I **did** dance with her.

CHAPTER 10

It's easiest to keep the past simple

Verbs (Part 4): Past simple versus other past tenses

Manoj is a recent graduate looking for his first job. He decides to write an email to a company recruiter. As he begins writing, he gets stuck. He wants to convey in his email that he studied at Jai Hind College. But he doesn't know which of the following versions to choose from:

1. I *studied* at Jai Hind college. (Past simple.)
2. I *did study* at Jai Hind college. (Past simple.)
3. I *was studying* at Jai Hind college. (Past continuous.)
4. I *have studied* at Jai Hind college. (Present perfect.)
5. I *had studied* at Jai Hind college. (Past perfect.)

The truth is that all five versions are technically acceptable! They are all different types of past tenses and they all have similar meanings. Sometimes, though, only one of the above mentioned past tenses should be used. In the previous chapter we covered the past simple tense (the first two of the above five choices). In this chapter, we will learn about the others.

You may be confused to find the 'present perfect' tense in the above list, but, despite its name, this tense is used for actions completed in the past that still have some effect on the present situation. To make learning this tense simpler, I have included it in the chapter on past tenses. See if you have ever made any of these errors.

Common Error 1:

✗ I was having an office in Chandigarh.

- It is incorrect to use the past continuous tense 'was having' in this sentence. This is a sentence where you should use only the past simple tense.

✓ I **had** an office in Chandigarh.
✓ I **did have** an office in Chandigarh.

Common Error 2:

✗ I gone there.

- This example represents a structural mistake in using the present perfect.

The correct form of the phrase is:
✓ I **have** gone there.

We will learn the following four tenses in this chapter:

1. Past simple—I **worked** *or* I **did work**.
2. Past continuous—I **was working**.
3. Present perfect—I **have worked**.
4. Past perfect—I **had worked**.

What will I learn in this chapter?

10.1 It's easiest to use the past simple tense.
10.2 How to form the past continuous tense.
10.3 When you must use the past continuous tense.
10.4 How to form the present perfect tense.
10.5 When you must use the present perfect tense.
10.6 How to form the past perfect tense.
10.7 When to use the past perfect tense.
10.8 Recap.

10.1 IT'S EASIEST TO USE THE PAST SIMPLE TENSE

That's right. For the most part, when in doubt, if you stick to the past simple tense you will be more or less safe. (See chapter 9 if you have forgotten the rules for the past simple tense.) Take a look at the examples given below:

✓ Past continuous tense—I **was working** at Hindustan Lever last year.
✓ Past simple—I **worked** at Hindustan Lever last year.

- Both these sentences pretty much mean the same thing. You can use both the past simple and the past continuous for actions that happened over some time in the past.

✓ Present perfect tense—I **have worked** really hard on that assignment.
✓ Past perfect—I **had worked** really hard on that assignment.
✓ Past simple—I **worked** really hard on that assignment.

- All these sentences pretty much mean the same thing. You can use all three—the present perfect, the past perfect and the past simple—for actions that ended in the past.

As you can see from the above examples, by using the past simple tense 'worked', you get more or less the same meaning as when using the other tenses. Thus, if you are not completely confident with your English skills yet, stick to using the past simple tense instead of the others. You will usually be correct.

There are some situations, though, when we either have to, or absolutely should not, use one of the other tenses. The rest of this chapter will help you learn about those situations.

10.2 HOW TO FORM THE PAST CONTINUOUS TENSE

Before we learn when to use the past continuous, let's first learn how to form this past tense. In Hindi, the past continuous is formed as: '*Main kaam kar raha tha.*'

In English, we form this tense in the following way:

1. A past tense form of the helping verb 'to be' is added before the main verb.
2. The main verb has an 'ing' at the end.

Pronoun	Past tense of 'to be'	Verb with ending in 'ing'
I	was	walking
She/He/It	was	walking
We	were	walking
They	were	walking
You	were	walking

! If using a verb ending in 'ing', do not forget to add 'was' or 'were' before it.

✗ I sleeping.
✓ I **was** sleeping.

✗ Uncle and Aunty fighting.
✓ Uncle and Aunty **were** fighting.

Compare this tense with the present continuous and past simple tenses (covered in previous chapters):

Present continuous	Past simple	Past continuous
I am walking	I walked	I was walking
She is walking	She walked	She was walking
We are walking	We walked	We were walking
They are walking	They walked	They were walking
You are walking	You walked	You were walking

Remember the rules for the present continuous tense in chapter 8? We learned that you should avoid using some words in the continuous tense. This means you should not have both an ending in 'ing' and a form of the verb 'to be' (is, am, are) before them.

✗ I am knowing you.
✓ I know you.
✗ We are having a car.
✓ We have a car.

The same rule applies for the past continuous. For words that should not be used in the past continuous, just use them in the simple past tense.
✗ I was knowing you.
✓ I knew you.
✗ We were having a car.
✓ We had a car.

If you are unsure about this rule, refer back to chapter 8.

10.3 WHEN YOU MUST USE THE PAST CONTINUOUS TENSE

As mentioned earlier in this chapter, you can use the past continuous tense when referring to actions that happened over time in the past.
✓ I **was running** in the park.
  ➤ Running is an action that happened over time.
✓ They **were watching** a movie at the cinema.
  ➤ Watching a movie is an action that happened over time.

In these situations, we can also use the past simple tense and get the same meaning. Now let's learn when we *must* use the past continuous tense. (When the past simple just won't do!) We'll do this through reading some emails that Manoj has sent to recruiters in order to get a job.

```
Dear HR Manager,

I browsed the Internet when I saw this job posting.
```

Is this sentence correct? Unfortunately for Manoj, it's not. Right now both the verbs 'browsed' and 'saw' are in the past simple tense.

So it is unclear which action happened first. What Manoj is trying to say is:

- First action: I was browsing the Internet.
- Second action: I saw the job posting.

Additionally, these actions are not of the same *length*. As browsing the Internet happened first and is a longer action, it takes more time. It was while browsing the Internet that Manoj saw the job posting. Thus, we can't use the same tense for both actions. The longer action that happened first (browsing the Internet) must be placed in the past continuous tense. The second, shorter action must be placed in the past simple tense. Manoj should have written:

✓ Dear HR Manager,
I **was browsing** the Internet when I **saw** this job posting.

> **Rule 1:** When a longer action is interrupted by a shorter action, you must use the past continuous tense. In this situation, the past simple does not work.

Let's look at some examples of this rule:

Correct	Incorrect
✓ I **was sleeping** when he called. ➤ 'Sleeping' is the longer action that was happening over time. The 'sleeping' was interrupted by the phone call.	✗ I **slept** when he called. ➤ To 'sleep' and to be 'called' are not actions of the same length, and thus can't be in same tense. Also, the actions did not start at the same time—the person was 'sleeping' first.
✓ They **were swimming** when Zubin saw them. ➤ 'Swimming' is the longer action that was	✗ They **swam** when Zubin saw them. ➤ By placing 'swam' in the past simple tense, it seems that

Correct	Incorrect
happening over time. Zubin seeing them is the shorter action that happened while they were still swimming.	they swam after Zubin saw them. We need to use the past continuous tense to show that the 'swimming' was the longer action happening first.

Exercise 10.1

The following sentences have errors relating to both the structure and the use of the past continuous tense. Correct the mistakes while keeping the sentences in the past tense. Check your answers before moving on.

1. She called me while I were watching the news.
2. Last year Tricia working in a call centre.
3. I was having a Maruti car.
4. We were not knowing what to do.
5. That was belonging to me.
6. Pradeep ran when he suddenly fell on the ground.
7. They were having an off day yesterday.
8. I talking last month to the class.
9. Sorry, we were needing you to send your CV yesterday.
10. My senior finally was agreeing to let us go after four hours of overtime.
11. I danced when they cut me off.
12. Are you working last year?
13. I was knowing you were coming.
14. She were helping me with my studies.
15. I was liking her when I met her.

! Make sure you have done the exercises and checked your answers before moving on.

You now know when to use the past continuous tense. Let's move on to learn about other situations where you cannot use the past simple tense.

10.4 HOW TO FORM THE PRESENT PERFECT TENSE

The present perfect tense sounds difficult, but is actually very easy to form. In Hindi, it is: *'Maine kaam kiya hai.'*

In English, we form this tense by following this simple rule:

'Has/have' + past participle of a verb.

Don't worry if you have not heard the term 'past participle' before. It's simple.

! For most verbs, the past participle is the same as the past tense of the verb.

Add 'has/have'	+ Past participle	(Same as past tense)
I have	worked	(worked)
She has	danced	(danced)
We have	lost	(lost)
They have	bought	(bought)
You have	jogged	(jogged)

See! The above past participles are exactly the same as their past tenses.

The past participle is different from the past tense only for a few verbs that are irregular (i.e., verbs that do not follow the same rules).

Add 'has/have'	+ Past participle	(Past tense)
I have	been	(was)
She has	gone	(went)
We have	gotten (USA) or got (UK)	(got)
They have	known	(knew)
You have	seen	(saw)

As you can see from the above chart, some past participles are different from their past tenses. There are just a handful of these. The more regularly you read books, magazine and newspapers, the more you will become familiar with these irregularities. For now, just try to remember the most common ones listed above.

! Remember, you can only use the past participle of a verb if you include a 'has/have' before it.

Incorrect	**Correct—Using present perfect tense**	**Correct—Using past simple tense**
✗ I been there.	✓ I **have been** there.	✓ I **was** there.
✗ She gone home.	✓ She **has gone** home.	✓ She **went** home.
✗ We gotten lunch.	✓ We **have gotten/ got** lunch.	✓ We **got** lunch.
✗ They known it.	✓ They **have known** it.	✓ They **knew** it.
✗ You seen her.	✓ You **have seen** her.	✓ You **saw** her.

So, for irregular verbs, if you can't remember to add a 'has/have', stick to placing them in the past simple tense.

10.5 WHEN YOU MUST USE THE PRESENT PERFECT TENSE

As mentioned earlier in this chapter, you can use the present perfect tense when referring to actions that ended in the past.

✓ I **have gone** to the park.

This action happened and ended in the past.

✓ They **have watched** a movie at the cinema.

This action happened and ended in the past.

However, in these situations, you can also use the past simple tense and get the same meaning. Let's continue reading Manoj's emails and learn when we *must* use the present perfect tense.

Manoj found a job and has now been working for a year. Unfortunately, he is not happy and decides to start emailing HR managers in other companies in order to find a new job.

```
Dear HR manager,

Over the last year I worked at India Telecom as an
engineer.
```

Here, Manoj has used the past simple tense 'worked'—but that sounds like he no longer works at India Telecom. (Remember the rule for the past simple tense? It represents an action that *ended* in the past. If you have forgotten this rule refer to chapter 9). But this is not true; Manoj is still working there.

The present perfect tense has an additional quality that the past simple does not—it allows us to convey that something started in the past, but continues in the present. Manoj should have used the present perfect tense instead to say:

✓ Dear HR Manager,
Over the last year I **have worked** at India Telecom as an engineer.

Rule 2: When an action started in the past, but is still going on in the present, you must use the present perfect tense. In this situation, the past simple does not work.

Look out for these phrases that help us know that an action started in the past but still continues in the present:

- 'Over the'—*Over the* three years that Ashem **has lived** in Pune he **has been** very happy.

Ashem lived in Pune three years ago, and still continues to live in Pune today. He was also happy in the past, and still continues to be happy in the present.

- 'Since'—Tinaz **has worked** as an engineer *since* last year.

Tinaz worked as an engineer one year ago and continues to work as an engineer today.

- 'For'—*For* the last two years I **have enjoyed** being in school.

This person enjoyed being in school two years ago, and continues to enjoy being in school today.

As you can see, we use the present perfect tense for all the above examples. If you are confused about why this tense is called 'present perfect', don't worry. Don't be scared by the terms—just remember that you need to add the words 'have' or 'has' before the past participle of any verb for the present perfect.

Manoj is not doing so well. Because his grammar was weak, the HR manager did not answer his email. Manoj is not one to give up, though, and tries again.

> Dear HR Manager,
>
> I **visited** your office before. I was impressed with your company.

Manoj has again used the past simple tense 'visited' when he should not have. All we know is that Manoj visited the office 'before' 'Before' is not an exact time. When we don't state *exactly when* something happened, it is better to use the present perfect tense:

✓ Dear HR Manager,
I **have visited** your office before. I was impressed with your company.

> **Rule 3:** When you are talking about something you have/haven't done without stating exactly when, you are better off using the present perfect tense.

What is important is to remember that if the exact time *is* stated, you should avoid using the present perfect tense. Stick to the past simple.

✗ I **have cooked** with my mother last night. (Present perfect.)
✓ I **cooked** with my mother last night. (Past simple.)

Take a look at the following examples which will help make this rule clearer for you:

Present perfect	Past simple
1. We **have met** before. ➤ The exact time is not mentioned. 'Before' is vague. So, we use the present perfect tense 'have met'.	1. We **met** yesterday. ➤ 'Yesterday' is an exact time. So, we use the past simple tense instead.
2. **Have** you ever **danced** with her? ➤ The exact time is not mentioned. This question really means 'Is there any time at all in the past that you have danced with her?' So, we use the present perfect tense 'have ... danced'.	2. **Did** you dance with her last night? ➤ 'Last night' is an exact time. So we use the past simple tense 'did' instead.

Manoj is getting smarter. He realizes when he should use the present perfect tense 'have worked' instead of the past simple tense 'worked'. He feels more confident and decides to send out another email.

> Dear HR Manager,
>
> I **have went** to two of your company presentations. I was very impressed and want to know if you have any positions available in your technical department.

Manoj has used the present perfect tense, as he stated the number of times he went to the company presentations (two), but did not state exactly when those times were. Manoj also correctly added the word 'have' to form the present perfect tense. But unfortunately, he has made yet another mistake! As we just learned, we need to add 'have' or 'has' before the past participle of a given verb. Here, Manoj has used the past tense 'went'. He should have written:

✓ Dear HR Manager,
I **have gone** to two of your company presentations. I was very impressed and want to know if you have any positions available in your technical department.

Exercise 10.2

The following sentences have errors relating to the present perfect tense. Correct them by changing only the verbs in the sentences. Check your answers before moving on.

1. I gone through different situations in my life.
2. I never hurt anyone before.
3. I can speak English fluently without fear, but I not yet completed my graduation because of my family circumstances.
4. Last week, I have gone to see my uncle in Nagpur.
5. Everything gone in vain.
6. I worked as a software professional for the last one year.
7. Are you gone crazy?
8. Everyone been to the temple today.
9. My younger sister who have got married in the last year is coming with us.
10. I have called you just yesterday.
11. How long you was in Delhi?
12. My family never went outside of our hometown.
13. I was working for the last four years.

! Make sure you have done the exercises and checked your answers before moving on.

You have now learnt when to use the present perfect tense—for example, 'have worked' instead of the past simple tense 'worked'.

You are almost done with learning the past tenses! Let's move on to the next tense, the past perfect.

10.6 HOW TO FORM THE PAST PERFECT TENSE

In Hindi, the past perfect tense is written as: '*Maine kaam kiya tha.*'

In English, past perfect tense formation is very similar to the formation of the present perfect tense. Instead of adding 'has/have', we simply add 'had' before the past participle of a given verb.

Add 'had'	+ Past participle	Past tense
I had	been*	was
She had	gone*	went
We had	gotten/got*	got
They had	washed	washed
You had	studied	studied

*Just as we learnt for the present perfect tense, past participles are different from past tenses only for irregular verbs.

! Remember, for the present perfect and past perfect tenses, you must use the past participle.

10.7 WHEN TO USE THE PAST PERFECT TENSE

Manoj has still not found another job. He stays positive, though, and sends out one last email.

> Dear HR manager,
>
> Before I **went** to see your presentation, I had read about your company in *Business India.*

Good for Manoj! He finally didn't make any mistakes. You will notice above that Manoj has used the past perfect tense 'had read'. Take a look below at what it would sound like if Manoj used the past simple tense instead:

✓ Dear HR manager,
Before I went to see your presentation, I **read** about your company in *Business India.*

There is no real difference. Other than showing that an action ended in the past (like the past simple tense), the past perfect tense shows that one action happened *before* another action. Most of the time though, we can get the same meaning across with the past simple tense too.

Rule 4: We can use the **past perfect tense** when referring to an action that happened *before* another one.

What is important to remember is that if you *do* choose to use the past perfect tense, you do so correctly!

Exercise 10.3

Make the necessary changes so the sentences below are in the past perfect tense. Check your answers before moving on.

1. I went there before we met.
2. We had not enjoy any luxuries until my father became a manager.
3. I had work as an independent designer prior to joining this firm.
4. Jagpreet had went to Ahmedabad recently, so I called him to learn more about the city.
5. We enjoyed the delicious food my sister had cook.
6. The rain stop before we found our umbrella.
7. When I woke up this morning, my brother already left.
8. I went to the office after I eaten my food.

10.8 A QUICK RECAP OF THE RULES IN THIS CHAPTER

When talking about actions that happened in the past, it is usually easier to use the past simple tense. Sometimes, though, we need to use another tense to get our point across. Let's go over the rules for when it is better to use a tense other than the past simple.

Situations in which you need to use tenses other than the past simple

Rule 1: Past continuous—When a longer action is interrupted by a shorter action, you must use the past continuous tense.

- I **was sleeping** when he called.
- They **were climbing** the hill when the accident happened.

Rule 2: Present perfect—When an action started in the past, but is still going on in the present, you must use the present perfect tense.

- Over the last five months she **has lost** twenty kilos.
- I **have been** here since December.

Rule 3: Present perfect—When you are talking about something you have/haven't done without stating exactly when, it is better to use the present perfect tense.

- They **have gone** there before.
- She **has** never **been** to Calcutta.

Rule 4: Past perfect—Use when referring to an action that happened *before* another one.

- We **had eaten** there first.
- My brother **had won** the tournament before him.

! Remember to use the past participle for the present perfect and past perfect tenses. For some irregular verbs, this while different from the past tense.

Let's lay out a chart so you can see all the different past tenses you have learned:

	Past Simple	Past Continuous	Present Perfect	Past Perfect
I	worked	was working	have worked	had worked
She/He/It	worked	was working	has worked	had worked
We	worked	were working	have worked	had worked
They	worked	were working	have worked	had worked
You	worked	were working	have worked	had worked

The above tenses are very similar and there are only a few rules you need to remember. The exercises below will help you master what you have learned. And always remember—the more books, newspapers and magazines you read, the more you'll learn!

Exercises 10.4

Pick the best response for each question. Check your answers before moving on.

1. Q: Why don't you like your current job?
   - ❑ Because I have been there for over three years and I still was not receiving a raise.
   - ❑ Because I have been there for over three years and I still didn't receive a raise.
   - ❑ Because I have been there for over three years and I still have not received a raise.
   - ❑ Because I have been there for over three years and I still had not received a raise.
2. Q: What did you like most about your university days?
   - ❑ I enjoyed the freedom to make my own choices.
   - ❑ I was enjoying the freedom to make my own choices.
   - ❑ I have enjoyed the freedom to make my own choices.
   - ❑ I had enjoyed the freedom to make my own choices.

3. Q: When did you visit the museum?
   - ❑ I have gone there on Tuesday.
   - ❑ I went there on Tuesday.
   - ❑ I was going there on Tuesday.
   - ❑ I had gone there on Tuesday.
4. Q: What were you doing when you heard the good news?
   - ❑ I worked on a project for my company.
   - ❑ I was working on a project for my company.
   - ❑ I have worked on a project for my company.
   - ❑ I had worked on a project for my company.
5. Q: What did you do before your boss arrived?
   - ❑ I was completing the entire proposal and kept it ready.
   - ❑ I completed the entire proposal and kept it ready.
   - ❑ I have completed the entire proposal and kept it ready.
   - ❑ I had completed the entire proposal and kept it ready.
6. Q: How long have you worked here?
   - ❑ I was working here since last September.
   - ❑ I worked here since last September.
   - ❑ I have worked here since last September.
   - ❑ I had worked here since last September.

Exercises 10.5

Correct the mistakes in the sentences below by changing only the verbs. All sentences should all be in one of the past tenses. For some, there may be more than one possible answer. Check your answers before moving on.

1. Maria has already completing the tenth standard.
2. We waited at the terminal for our bags to arrive when we saw Sapna Aunty.
3. Jehangir has enroll in a university.
4. Tinaz had apply for several jobs.
5. I seen some interesting advertisements.
6. Sanya was talking on the phone when her boss was coming into the office.
7. Gurjot have decided to work in a hospital.

8. They ran along the beach when a bicycle cut across their path.
9. For the last week, she definitely not been in a good mood.
10. The magazine had wrote that our school won the prize.
11. Everyone is ecstatic that Rashid gets a raise and is now our head of finance.
12. The price of oil have fell and this is affecting many people.
13. I shopped at the mall last week when I met Riyaz.

! Make sure you have done the exercises and checked your answers before moving on.

APPLYING WHAT YOU HAVE LEARNED

1. When speaking about actions that occurred in the past, it is easiest to use the past simple tense.
   - I **worked** on the project yesterday.
   - I **did work** on the project yesterday.
2. Sometimes, though, we need to use another form of the past tense to get our meaning across.
   - I **was working** on the project yesterday when the phone rang. (Past continuous.)
   - I **have worked** on the project before. (Present perfect.)
   - I **had worked** on the project first. (Past perfect.)
3. When using the past continuous tense, we must remember to add 'was' or 'were' before the verb ending in 'ing'.

   ✗ She working on it last week.
   ✓ She **was working** on it last week.
   ✗ They working on it last week.
   ✓ They **were working** on it last week.
4. When using the present perfect or past perfect tenses, we must remember to use the past participle of a verb and not the past tense.

   ✗ I have went to the park.
   ✓ I **have gone** to the park. (Present perfect.)
   ✗ I had went to the park.
   ✓ I **had gone** to the park. (Past perfect.)

5. When using the past participle of a verb, we must remember to place 'have', 'has' or 'had' before it.
   ✗ I gone to the park.
   ✓ I **have gone** to the park. (Present perfect.)
   ✓ I **had gone** to the park. (Past perfect.)
   ✗ She gone to the park.
   ✓ She **has gone** to the park. (Present perfect.)
   ✓ She **had gone** to the park. (Past perfect.)

CHAPTER 11

'Will I get the job?', 'Will I be getting the job?' or 'Am I going to get the job?'

Verbs (Part 5): Future tenses

Most of us spend a lot of time talking about the future. We always think about what we are planning to do over the weekend, what job we hope to get in the future, or what we would like to accomplish in our careers some day. It almost seems as if the future is more important to us than the present.

Since we spend so much time thinking and talking about the future, it is important that we do so with correct grammar. Read the common errors shown below and see if you too make some of these mistakes.

Common Error 1:

✗ My name is Vikram and I going to study commerce next year.

- Here, we have forgotten to add the helping verb 'am' before the future tense 'going'.

The correct sentence is:

✓ My name is Vikram and I **am** going to study commerce next year.

Common Error 2:

✗ I will be organize everything.

- In this sentence, the speaker is confused about whether to use the simple future tense or the future continuous tense. He has used bits of both!
- We need to either remove the word 'be' or add an 'ing' to the verb 'to organize.'

This sentence can be correctly written in two ways:

✓ I **will organize** everything.

✓ I **will be organizing** everything.

Common Error 3:

✗ When I will go to the office, I will be very busy.

- If using the word 'when', we must keep the verb following it in the present tense even if the action is happening in the future.

The correct sentence is:

✓ When I **go** to the office, I will be very busy.

Common Error 4:

✗ We would be coming at nine o'clock.

- Try to avoid using the word 'would' before verbs ending in 'ing'.

The correct sentence is:

✓ We will be coming at nine o'clock.

What will I learn in this chapter?

11.1 How to form the future simple tense.
11.2 How to form the future continuous tense.
11.3 Rules for using the future simple and continuous tenses.
11.4 Future simple tense exception—'will' versus 'be going to'.
11.5 Future simple tense exception—'if' statements.
11.6 Understanding future tense rules through dialogues.
11.7 Using the present tense for future actions.
11.8 Grammar tips.
11.9 Rules and lessons.

11.1 HOW TO FORM THE FUTURE SIMPLE TENSE

The future simple tense can be formed in two ways. You should be familiar with both ways, as they are also used in Hindi:

1. '*Main kaam karunga.*' (I will work.)
2. '*Main kaam karne wala hun.*' (I am going to work.)

Let's learn how these tenses are formed in English.

To form 'I will work', use 'will' + the base form of the verb

! The base form of a verb is the simple tense without any changes. For example, 'work' (not works).

	Add 'will'	Base form of verb
I	will	work
She/He/It	will	work
We	will	work
They	will	work
You	will	work

You may notice that for this tense we use the same formula no matter *who* the subject is (I, she, we, etc)—that makes it a whole lot easier!

You can also shorten the word 'will' if you like:

- I + will = I'll
- She/He/It + will = She'll/He'll/It'll
- We + will = We'll
- They + will = They'll
- You + will = You'll

You can use the shortened form of the word 'will' if you prefer. If you don't want to, that's fine too.

	Present tense of verb 'be'	'Going to'	Base form of verb
I	am	going to	work
She/He/It	is	going to	work
We	are	going to	work
They	are	going to	work
You	are	going to	work

! Refer to chapter 7 if you have forgotten how to form the present tense of the verb 'to be'.

Now let's learn the rules for forming the future continuous tense.

11.2 HOW TO FORM THE FUTURE CONTINUOUS TENSE

In Hindi, the future continuous tense is written as:
'Main Kaam kar raha hunga' (I will be working)
In English, to form this tense use 'will be' + verb ending in 'ing'

	Add 'will be'	**Verb ending in 'ing'**
I	will be	working
She/He/It	will be	working
We	will be	working
They	will be	working
You	will be	working

And that's it! Let's compare the future simple tenses to the future continuous tense:

Future simple ('will')	**Future simple ('be going to')**	**Future continuous**
I will work.	I am going to work.	I will be working.
She will cook.	She is going to cook.	She will be cooking.
We will talk.	We are going to talk.	We will be talking.
They will go.	They are going to go.	They will be going.
You will listen.	You are going to listen.	You will be listening.

Be careful not to mix-up the rules between these tenses. If you use 'will be', then the verb following it must end in 'ing':
✗ I will be run.
✓ I will be runn**ing**.

✗ I will be speak.
✓ I will be speak**ing**.

Similarly, if you only use 'will', you need to make sure the verb following is in its base form:
✗ I will runn**ing**.
✓ I will run.
✗ I will speak**ing**.
✓ I will speak.

Exercise 11.1

Using the rules you have learned above on forming future tenses, fill in the blanks with either 'will' or 'will be'. Check your answers before moving on.

1. Mr and Mrs Gopaldas __________ visiting Bombay next year.
2. I ______________ go to the show at 7 p.m. tomorrow.
3. I ______________ do my work when I want!
4. I ______________ interviewing at ten offices this week.
5. The HR manager ______________ call me if they like me after my interview.
6. My parents ______________ watching the cricket match in an hour.
7. Your inputs _______ help us greatly.

! Make sure you have done the exercises and checked your answers before moving on.

11.3 RULES FOR USING THE FUTURE SIMPLE AND CONTINUOUS TENSES

We have just learned that there are three ways of expressing the future tense:

1. 'Will work'. (Future simple.)
2. 'Am going to work'. (Future simple.)
3. 'Will be working'. (Future continuous.)

There are certain situations in which we can use all these three tenses and end up with the same meaning. At other times, though, we must use only one of these three tenses to get our message across. Read the following exceptions to get a basic understanding of these instances.

Future Simple Rules	Future Continuous Rules
➤ Use when speaking about plans and predictions that will happen quickly, or will happen over a period of time in the future (after this moment).	➤ Use when speaking about plans and predictions that will happen over a period of time only in the future, where the time is clearly stated.
• I **will speak** to her later. • I **am going to speak** to her later. ➤ (Future plan.)	• I **will be speaking** to her later. ➤ (Future plan that will happen over time—'speaking' is an action that happens over time.)
• She **will work** tomorrow. • She **is going to work** tomorrow. ➤ (Prediction for the future.)	• **She will be working** tomorrow. ➤ (Prediction for the future that will happen over time—'working' is an action that happens over time.)

As you can see from the table above, the future simple tense can often be used to convey the same meaning as the future continuous tense. Thus, if you are worried about making mistakes, when in doubt use the future simple tense.

If you do decide to use the future continuous tense, make sure the action is in fact *continuous* and happening over time (not a quick action).

11.4 FUTURE SIMPLE TENSE EXCEPTION—'WILL' VERSUS 'BE GOING TO'

Both the future simple tenses ('will' and 'be going to') can be used for almost all the same future actions. There are a couple of exceptions to this rule, though, that you will need to remember:

> **Exception 1: For future plans**
> - Use 'will' if talking about a plan that you decided on at the very moment of speaking.
> - Use 'be going to' if talking about a plan you have thought about or already planned in the *past*.

'Be going to' is the root of 'am going to'. Remember, 'am' is a present tense form of the verb 'to be'.

Let's look at an example of where you should use the word 'will':

Neil: I can't find my calculator!
Akshay: Don't worry, I **am going to let** you use mine.

Akshay's plan to let Neil use his calculator clearly happened during the time of speaking, as Akshay didn't even know Neil needed a calculator until that moment. Because this plan was decided so suddenly and without previous planning, you should use 'will'.

✓ Akshay: Don't worry, I **will let** you use mine.

Let's now look at an example of where you should use 'be going to':

Lanaja: Hey Ami, what are you going to do later tonight?
Ami: I **will go** to a party.

Ami is talking about a plan she has obviously already thought about and made in the past—to attend a specific party. Thus, she should have said:

✓ Ami: I **am going to go** to a party.

Take a look at one last example.

Husband: Hey, we are out of shampoo.
Wife: Okay, I **will buy** more shampoo when I go to the store.

Here, since the wife used the future simple tense 'will', she is implying that she did not have plans to buy more shampoo until now. But, let's say she replied:

✓ Wife: I know, I **am going to buy** more shampoo when I go to the store.

This sentence is also correct. Here, by using 'am going to', the wife is implying that she knew they were out of shampoo and had already planned to go to the store to buy more.

Are there times you could get confused by this exception?

Sometimes, it is not obvious whether we are talking about a sudden plan or a plan made in the past. For example, take a look at these two emails:

Email 1:

Dear Mr Meyer,

I just wanted to let you know that **Pranav is going to drive** to Pune tomorrow to meet you.

Thanks,

Tariq

Email 2:

Dear Mr Meyer

I just wanted to let you know that **Pranav will drive** to Pune tomorrow to meet you.

Thanks,

Tariq

Here, using both future tenses 'be going to' and 'will' works! The reason is that Tariq is not actually talking about a future *plan*; he is talking about a future *prediction*. Tariq is *predicting* that Pranav will drive to Pune tomorrow. For predictions, we can use both 'will' and 'be going to'.

Now, you might be wondering, 'this seems like a plan to me, not a prediction!' The difference between plans and predictions can be so small that at times we really can't tell. To avoid confusion and make your life easier, just remember these points:

- Use 'will' if talking about a very sudden action.
- Otherwise, just use 'be going to'.

11.5 FUTURE SIMPLE TENSE EXCEPTION—USING 'IF' STATEMENTS

Don't worry—this is the last exception you need to remember for the future simple tense!

> **Exception 2: For 'if' statements:**
> When forming 'if' statements, we must use the *present tense* even if we are talking about a future action.

Let's look at some examples of 'if' statements where we can't use the future tense.

1. **If**
   ✗ She will be unhappy **if** she **will not get** the job (Future tense).
   ✓ She will be unhappy **if** she **does not get** the job (present tense).
2. **When**
   ✗ **When** you **will leave** tomorrow, remember to take the bag (Future tense).
   ✓ **When** you **leave** tomorrow, remember to take the bag (Present tense).
3. **Before**
   ✗ I will cook tonight **before** he **is going to get** home. (Future tense.)
   ✓ I will cook tonight **before** he **gets** home. (Present tense.)

4. **After**
   ✗ **After I am going to watch** TV I will call him (Future tense).
   ✓ **After I watch** TV I will call him (Present tense).

As you can see from the above examples, when using an 'if' statement, the verb after the 'if' statement needs to be kept in the present tense even if we are talking about a future action.

11.6 UNDERSTANDING FUTURE TENSE RULES THROUGH DIALOGUES

The above explanations should have given you a basic overview of future tenses. Let's now perfect your understanding by reading a dialogue between Tesha and her teacher.

Teacher:	Tesha, do you think it will rain tomorrow?
Tesha:	Yes, I think **it rains** tomorrow.
Teacher:	Tesha, you have forgotten the rules about the future tense that you learned in class today!
Tesha:	Why? What did I say that was wrong?
Teacher:	I asked you a question about something that is going to happen in the *future*. You answered using the present tense, 'rains'.
Tesha:	Oh I am sorry! I should have said, 'Yes, I think it **will rain** tomorrow.'
Teacher:	Very good Tesha. You can also say 'Yes, I think it is going **to rain** tomorrow' or 'Yes, I think it **will be raining** tomorrow' as we are talking about a future prediction that will happen over time.

Look at these examples of **future tenses**

Correct	Incorrect
✓ I **will go** to the park tomorrow.	✗ I **go** to the park tomorrow. ➤ Because this is a future action we are predicting to happen, we need to use one of the future tenses.
✓ I **am going to go** to the park tomorrow.	
✓ I **will be going** to the park tomorrow. ➤ Since this is a future prediction that will happen over time, all three tenses are acceptable.	

Teacher: Tesha, I need to ask you for a favour. If it rains tomorrow, will you bring me an extra umbrella? I just lost mine.
Tesha: Sure, I **am going to bring** you an umbrella.
Teacher: Thanks Tesha. But you have made another grammatical mistake! Remember, if you are talking about a plan that you decided on at the moment of speaking, you must not use 'am going to'.
Tesha: Oh yes, I forgot! I should only use 'will'. I should have said, 'Sure, I **will bring** you an umbrella.'
Teacher: That's right Tesha.

Let's read another example of **exception 1:**

Correct	Incorrect
✓ Q: I just found out that my brother can't drive me to the party. A: Don't worry, I **will pick** you up.	✗ Q: I just found out that my brother can't drive me to the party. A: Don't worry, I **am going to pick** you up.

➤ *This future plan to help someone was made at the time of speaking, so use 'will'.*	➤ *This future plan to help someone was made at the time of speaking, so avoid using 'am going to'.*

Teacher: Tesha, I am teaching a special class this Sunday to help some of the students before the exam. Would you like to come?

Tesha: Oh, I would love to come, but I can't. I **will go** to a function at my brother's house.

Teacher: Tesha, I think you should cancel going to the function as you just made another grammatical mistake! It is obvious that you had made the plan to go to your brother's function in the past. Remember, for future plans you have made in the past, you can't use the future tense 'will'.

Tesha: You are right! I have to use 'am going to'. I should have said, 'I **am going to** a function at my brother's house.'

Let's read another example of exception 1:

Correct	Incorrect
✓ Q: What are you doing tomorrow? A: I **am going to** the movies with Raj. ➤ *Since this is a future plan that was obviously planned in the past, you can use 'am going to'.*	✗ Q: What are you doing tomorrow? A: I **will go** to the movies with Raj. ➤ *Since this is a future plan that was obviously planned in the past, avoid using 'will'.*

Exercise 11.2

Read the questions given below. Out of the two answers that have been provided, choose the correct one (sometimes both answers will be acceptable). Check your answers before moving on.

1. Q: Why do you like your college?
   A: ❑ Because we will have lots of good teachers.
   ❑ Because we have lots of good teachers.
2. Q: What do you like to do for fun?
   A: ❑ I like to take photographs of people.
   ❑ I will like to take photographs of people.
3. Q: Where will you live when you move to Bombay?
   A: ❑ I live in Bandra.
   ❑ I will live in Bandra.
4. Q: Kishori aunty just called and asked if you could help her carry her bags.
   A: ❑ Yes, I'll help her.
   ❑ Yes, I am going to help her.
5. Q: What are you doing later?
   A: ❑ I play cricket with my friends.
   ❑ I will be playing tennis with my friends.
6. Q: Will you catch the ball if I throw it to you?
   A: ❑ Yes, I'll catch it.
   ❑ Yes, I will be catching it.
7. Q: When will you be meeting Rupali?
   A: ❑ I'll be meeting her tomorrow.
   ❑ I am going to meet her tomorrow.
8. Q: What time have you decided to go to the ceremony?
   A: ❑ I'll go at 4 p.m.
   ❑ I am going to go at 4 p.m.
9. Q: Do you know what floor the interview is on?
   A: ❑ Yes, I'll walk you there.
   ❑ Yes, I am going to walk you there.
10. Q: Do you want to go shopping this afternoon?
    A: ❑ No, sorry I can't. I am going to go to my dance class.
    ❑ No, sorry I can't. I will go to my dance class.

11. Q: When will you go to the park?
    A: ❑ I go in the afternoon.
    ❑ I will go in the afternoon.

! Make sure you have done the exercises and checked your answers before moving on.

Let's continue perfecting your understanding of the future tense by reading the rest of the dialogue between Tesha and her English teacher.

Teacher: Okay Tesha, I will see you tomorrow. Also, please start studying for the exam.

Tesha: Don't worry, **after I will get** back from the function at my brother's house, I will do nothing but study.

Teacher: Tesha, you better study hard because you just made another mistake. Remember, when forming an 'if' statement, the verb following it must remain in the present tense.

Tesha: Yes, that is right. I used the word 'after', which indicates an 'if' statement. I should not have put the verb 'get' in the future tense. I should have said 'Don't worry, **after I get** back from the function at my brother's house, I will do nothing but study.'

Teacher: Very good Tesha. See, you understand all the rules. You just need to reread the lesson on future tenses to perfect your knowledge.

Let's read another example of exception 2:

Correct	Incorrect
✓ **When I get** angry, I yell at everyone! ➤ As we are using the word 'when', we need to place the verb following it in the present tense.	✗ **When I will get** angry, I yell at everyone! ➤ As we are using the word 'when', we should avoid placing the verb following it in the future tense.

11.7 USING THE PRESENT TENSE FOR FUTURE ACTIONS

Yes, there are certain times when you can use both the present simple *and* the present continuous tenses to show a future action. (If you have forgotten these tenses, refer to chapter 8.)

By using the present simple tense, you can make future actions sound like facts. Thus you should generally use this tense when referring to events that were planned for the future at a set time.

✓ I **leave** for Baroda at 3 p.m.
✓ The game **begins** at 4 p.m. tomorrow.

We use the present continuous tense when talking about future plans that are pretty much certain to happen.

✓ I **am working** all day tomorrow.
✓ She **is letting** me take a day off next week.

You can also use the future simple tenses covered in this chapter for all the above examples and get the same meaning:

✓ I **will leave** for Baroda at 3 p.m. / I **am going to leave** for Baroda at 3 p.m.
✓ The game **will begin** at 4 p.m. tomorrow. / The game **is going to begin** at 4 p.m. tomorrow.
✓ I **will work** all day tomorrow. / I **will be working** all day tomorrow.

✓ She **will let** me take a day off next week. / She **is going to let** me take a day off next week.

Don't be too worried about the multiple ways to say the same thing. It would be boring if there were only one way to say something. Remember, though, that if you want to make things easier for yourself, use one of the future simple tenses for future actions.

11.8 GRAMMAR TIPS

There are two common errors that we make while forming the future tense—incorrect use of the future continuous tense, and incorrect use of the word 'would'.

Incorrect use of the future continuous tense

Just like we saw for the present continuous tense, we usually don't place verbs that are not active in the future continuous tense. Let's look at some examples of this rule:

✗ I **will be having** a car next week. (Future continuous tense.)
✓ I **will have** a car next week. (Future simple tense.)
✓ I **am going to have** a car next week. (Future simple tense.)

To 'have' a car next year is not an action that happens over time—it is a fixed event. Thus, you should avoid using the future continuous tense.

✗ She **will not be remembering** me next year. (Future continuous tense.)
✓ She **will not remember** me next year. (Future simple tense.)
✓ She **is not going to remember** me next year. (Future simple tense.)

To 'remember' someone at a particular time next year is not an action that happens over time. Thus, you can't use the future continuous tense.

Incorrect use of the word 'would'

The word 'would' should not be used in the future continuous tense, or before any verb that has an ending in 'ing'. Take a look at the chart below.

Incorrect	Correct—Using future simple	Correct—Using future continuous
✗ I **would be going** to the party.	✓ I **will go** to the party. ✓ I **am going to go** to the party.	✓ I **will be going** to the party.
✗ She **would be running** in the park later.	✓ She **will run** in the park later. ✓ She **is going to run** in the park later.	✓ She **will be running** in the park later.
✗ I **would not be writing** an email to her.	✓ I **will not write an** email to her. ✓ **I am not going to write** an email to her.	✓ **I will not be writing** an email to her.
✗ We **would be coming** to your house at 4 p.m.	✓ We **will come** to your house at 4 p.m. ✓ We **are going to come** to your house at 4 p.m.	✓ We **will be coming** to your house at 4 p.m.

11.9 RULES AND LESSONS

Let's revise all the rules that we just learned in this chapter that deal with future tenses.

Future simple tense

Use when speaking about plans and predictions that will happen quickly, or over a period of time in the future. (After the present moment.)

✓ I **will win** the race.
✓ I **am going to study** all night.

Exception 1: For future plans

Use 'will' if talking about a plan that you decided upon at the very moment of speaking. Use 'be going to' if talking about a plan you have already thought about, or planned *in the past*.
✓ Are you stuck? Don't worry, I **will help** you.
✓ I decided yesterday that I **am going to go** to the party with Jayant.

Exception 2: For 'if' statements:

When forming 'if' statements, we use the *present* tense even if we are talking about a *future* action.
✓ *If* I **win** the race, I will be very happy.
✓ *After* I **send** you my CV, I will call you to follow up.

Future continuous tense

Use when speaking about plans and predictions that will happen over a period of time in the future, where the time is clearly stated.
✓ I **will be swimming** all afternoon.
✓ Tomorrow, they **will be working** on the project together.

Exercise 11.3

The future tense has been incorrectly used in the following sentences. Correct these sentences by changing only the verbs; don't try to change the entire sentence. Check your answers before moving on.

1. I will grateful as I am lacking in self confidence.
2. When I will be improve myself I come and take classes from you.
3. Please provide me with your valuable suggestions which help me improve my English.
4. Don't worry, Suman would be coming to the party!
5. I will be liking her if she gets a haircut.
6. Since we have already forwarded our technical data to them, we visiting their Nasik plant next week.

7. How long you be staying?
8. She would be going there in the evening.
9. We will not be understanding the movie.
10. I will be buying her a thank you gift next week if she gives me the job offer!
11. We would be joining you there.
12. I going to apply for a job in a multinational.
13. I will be take care of the whole process.
14. I am going to call him after I will go there.

! Make sure you have done the exercises and checked your answers before moving on.

APPLYING WHAT YOU HAVE LEARNED

1. The future tense is formed in in three ways:
   - Future simple tense using 'will'—I **will work**.
   - Future simple tense using 'be going to'—I **am going to work**.
   - Future continuous tense using 'will be' + 'ing'—I **will be working**.
2. For spur-of-the-moment plans, simply use 'will'. For premeditated plans, use 'be going to'.
   - Oh, is Sachin waiting for me to call? **I'll call** him now. (Spur-of-the-moment plan—use 'will'.)
   - I know Sachin is waiting for me to call. I **am going to call** him now. (Premeditated plan—use 'be going to'.)
3. Use either 'will' or 'be going to' to talk about future predictions.
   - I think it **will rain** tomorrow. (Using 'will'.)
   - I think it **is going to rain** tomorrow. (using 'be going to'.)
4. Use the future continuous tense 'will be' + 'ing' for both plans and predictions *only* if they happen over time.

   ✗ Throw the ball to me. I **will be catching** it. (This is a quick action.)

   ✓ It **will be raining** tomorrow. (This is a long action.)
5. When writing 'if' statements, we must keep the verb following the 'if' word in the present tense even if we are talking about something in the future.

✗ **If** I **will work** hard, I will make more money.
✓ **If** I **work** hard, I will make more money.

6. Sometimes, we can use the present simple and present continuous tenses for future actions too.
   ✓ She **arrives** at 8 p.m. tomorrow. (Using present simple)
   ✓ We **are going** to the wedding tonight. (Using present continuous)
7. Just like the present continuous tense, avoid using certain verbs in the future continuous tense.
   ✗ I **will be having** my CV for you by tomorrow.
   ✓ I **will have** my CV for you by tomorrow.
8. Avoid placing the word 'would' before verbs ending in 'ing'.
   ✗ We **would** be meeting you at the function
   ✓ We **will** be meeting you at the function.

CHAPTER 12

I am asking the question correctly, no?

Asking questions

Have you ever been frustrated because you feel people don't take you seriously enough? When you email a recruiter for a new job, you don't get called for an interview. When you speak to a customer or a client, they don't seem to understand the point you are making. When you have a conversation with your boss, he or she doesn't seem to agree with what you say. Do you sometimes feel that you are just not being effective enough when you communicate?

In any conversation, asking correct questions is as important as giving correct answers. The types of questions we ask shows how knowledgeable we are on a subject. Good questions make people take us seriously.

However, if we use incorrect grammar while framing questions, it doesn't matter how good the content of the question is. In India, many of us make the mistake of asking questions incorrectly. This is mostly because we don't realize that questions need to follow a special grammatical word order. See if you can identify with any of the common errors listed below.

Common Error 1:

✗ You can give it to me, no?

- You should avoid starting questions with nouns or pronouns (like 'you'). It is important that you always use a 'question word' to begin your questions. Some examples of question words include 'can', 'why' and 'when'.
- It is also incorrect to add 'no' to the end of a question.

This sentence should read:

✓ Can you give it to me?

Common Error 2:

✗ Why she is not happy?

- Here, we have started the sentence correctly with a question word: 'why'. However, the rest of the sentence structure is wrong.
- Questions follow a word order that is different from other sentences.
- We can't place nouns or pronouns (like 'she') after the question word 'why'. Instead, the question word 'why' needs to be followed by a verb.

The question should be correctly written as:

✓ Why **is she** not happy?

Common Error 3:

✗ My question is that when I went for an interview in a call centre, I passed the first and second rounds but did not pass the last round so what should I do now.

- This question is long and confusing. When we read it, we aren't sure exactly what the person asking. We can guess, but we don't know for sure.
- Also, this question isn't just a question—it includes factual statements. Sentences should be concise, and facts should be separated from questions.
- Instead of writing one long sentence with everything crammed together, break things up into shorter sentences.
- Last, when asking a question, you must always start with a question word and end with a question mark.

This question could be asked more clearly as:

✓ When I went for an interview in a call centre, I passed the first and second rounds, but not the last. What do I need to do in the future to pass the final round?

This section will help you avoid some of the common mistakes people make when they ask questions in English. To learn how to create coherent and interesting questions, see Section 3 of this book.

What will I learn in this chapter?

12.1 WHAT ARE QUESTIONS?

We ask questions when we want to gather more information about a particular subject. In English, we must use one of these words when asking a question:

1. **Question words**
   - 5 Ws—Who, What, When, Where, Why
   - How
   - Which
2. **Verbs**
   - 'To be' (am, is, are, were, was, will be), 'to do' (do, does, did), 'to have' (have, has, had) can, could, would, should, may

There are additional verbs like 'must', 'shall' and 'ought' that are not as common. In this chapter, we will not be focussing on these less common verbs.

In order to appear professional, it is very important to start your questions with one of the above words. Let's now learn the structure you need to follow while using these words.

12.2 STARTING QUESTIONS WITH QUESTION WORDS

In chapter 1, we learned how to structure sentences in a specific word order. When we ask questions, we need to follow a different word order. When using question words (the 5 Ws, how and which), we need to follow the following rules:

Formula 1—Word order for the 5 Ws and How:
Question word + verb + subject (noun/pronoun) + main verb/ additional parts

You need not use all the parts of this formula. For example, take the question, 'Who is it?' For this question, we have only used the first three parts of the formula:

Question Word + Verb + Subject
Who + is + it?

The first three parts are mandatory for forming any question. For longer questions, make sure you follow the remaining parts of the formula given above.

Take a look at the chart below which gives examples of sentences formed by the 5 Ws and how.

Question Word	+ Verb	+ Subject	+ Main Verb/ Additional Parts
Who	is	the hero?	
What	aren't (are not)	you	doing right?
When	can	you	come?
Where	should	she	live?
Why	don't (do not)	you	try harder?
How	are	you	coping with your loss?

Some of you may have forgotten the different forms of the helping verbs 'to be', 'to do' and 'to have', and which pronouns should complement each form. We have covered these topics in the chapters on verbs and pronouns. Also, you can use the recap at the end of this chapter as a reference.

Exceptions: which and what

In the chart above, you may have noticed that we don't include the question word 'which'. This is because 'which' uses a slightly different formula:

Formula 2—Word order when using which and what:
Question word + subject noun + verb/main verb + additional parts

The only real difference in this formula is that the subject noun comes directly after the question word. Also, please note that the question word 'what' can follow this rule as well. Take a look at this chart, which gives some examples of Formula 2:

Question word	+ Subject noun	+ Verb	+ Additional parts
Which	car	hit	yours?
What	movie	did	you see?

Remember, 'which' and 'what' are the *only two question words* that can have a noun following them.
✗ **Why car** is it? ('Car' is a noun.)
✓ **Which car** is it?
✓ **What car** is it?

Also, keep in mind that when forming a question 'which and 'what' can only be followed by a noun—*never a pronoun.*
✗ What **she** does at Wipro? ('She' is a pronoun.)
✓ What **mobile phone** does she want?

Exercise 12.1

The following questions are structured incorrectly or are missing words. Fix them. Check your answers before moving on.

1. Why you want to join a call centre?
2. What you looking out for?
3. How she will get time to reply to my mail?
4. When she want to come?
5. What the word 'soft skills' really mean?
6. What could be my answer?
7. What time I should get back to you?
8. Which model you are using?
9. Why she will reply?
10. What you did?
11. What language you are speaking in?

! Make sure you have done the exercises and checked your answers before moving on.

12.3 STARTING QUESTIONS WITH VERBS

When we structure questions using verbs, we follow the exact word order we learned for Formula 1. The only difference is that we don't include a question word:

> **Formula 3—Word order using verbs:**
> Verb + subject (noun/pronoun) + main verb/additional parts

Compare the following:
What **did** you do today? (Using a question word.)
Did you do anything today? (Using a verb.)

You'll notice that both sentences follow the same word order. The only major difference in the second sentence is that we haven't started with the question word 'What'.

Take a look at some examples of questions created with verbs:

USING VERBS

Verb		+ Subject	+ Main Verb/ Additional Parts
'to be'	Am Were Was Are Is Will Will	I you Sonal (she) you Supriya (she) George (he) they	going with you? at school? waiting? happy? your boss? pay for lunch? enjoy the show?
'to do'	Did Did Do Does	you Nandan (he) they Tina (she)	find him? go to the meeting? want to eat? look good?
'to have'	Have Has	you Meenakshi (she)	bought the present? gone home?

Exercise 12.2

Each of the sentences below is missing the initial question verb. Fill in the correct answer using the verbs you just learned. (There may be more than one correct answer for each question.) Check your answers before moving on.

1. ______ Mr Gupta in his office?
2. ______ you get all the data you needed for your project?
3. ______ you going to the interview?
4. ______ she eaten yet?
5. ______ she eat yet?

SOME MORE VERBS

Verb	+ Subject	+ Main verb/ additional parts
Can	she	help me with this project?
Could	you	dance with me?
Would	Ami (she)	be interested?
Should	they	go home now?
May	I	call you later?

Exercise 12.3

Correct the following questions. Check your answers before moving on.

1. You are going to the movies?
2. They didn't enjoy it?
3. I may come in for an interview tomorrow?
4. Is they dancing in the sangeet?
5. She could help me?
6. She will be there, no?
7. Have she gone to get her waxing done?
8. Ketan is not going to be able to help?
9. I can go now, no?
10. Are going to help me?

! Make sure you have done the exercises and checked your answers before moving on.

You might be wondering, 'With so many ways to start a question, which one do I choose?' Most of us do not have trouble using the verbs 'to be', 'to do' and 'to have', as their meanings are more obvious. Usually, we tend to have problems using the 5 Ws, how, which and can, could, would, should and may. Let's go through some examples of when each of these options can be used.

12.4 WHEN TO USE QUESTION WORDS

Each one of the 5 Ws, how and which help you find a different type of answer.

- 'Who' is used to ask about a person. The answer to a 'who' question is a noun or a pronoun.

Question	Answer
Who was that?	That was **my boss**.
Who sent out the report?	**He** sent out the report.

- 'What' is used to ask about a thing, action or an abstract concept. The answer to a 'what' question is usually, but not always, a noun or a verb.

Question	Answer
What is that?	That is **my new car.**
What are you doing?	I am **writing** a report.

- 'When' is used to ask about a general or specific time frame. The answer to a 'when' question is usually a time or a period of time.

Question	Answer
When is the meeting?	The meeting is **tomorrow morning**.
When is the meeting?	The meeting is at **11 a.m.**

- 'Where' is used to ask about a location. The answer to a 'where' question is usually be a noun.

Question	Answer
Where are you going for your vacation?	I am going to **Goa** for my vacation.

- 'Why' is used to find a reason. The answer to a why question will always be an explanation.

Question	Answer
Why did you quit your last job?	I quit my last job **because I wanted more challenging opportunities.**

- 'How' is used when you need to know the way in which something happened. 'How' is used with 'many' or 'much' when you need to know the number of a particular thing.

Question	Answer
How do I get to your office?	You **turn left at the stoplight on Peddar Road** to get to my office.
How many clients do you have?	I have **ten clients**.
How much money should we charge for this project?	We should charge **2000 rupees** for this project.

- 'Which' asks for the one specific thing among many similar people, places, or things a person is talking about.

Question	Answer
Which car is yours?	My car is **the red one**.

Recap of question words

Use this question word	When you need an answer about
Who	A person
What	An action, concept, noun
When	Time (abstract or specific)
Where	A place

Why	An explanation
How	An explanation
How many	A number
How much	A number or quantity
Which	A specific noun

Exercise 12.4

Fill in the blanks with the correct question word. There may be more than one right answer. Check your answers before moving on.

1. ________ is your name?
2. ________ is your interview?
3. ________ did you leave the meeting?
4. ________ project are you working on?
5. ________ do I get a job in a software engineering company?
6. ________ is the new mall?

Exercise 12.5

Read the following sentences. These sentences are answers to questions. Write a possible question for each answer. Note that there may be more than one question that goes with each of the answers below. Check your answers before moving on.

1. My flight is at 9 p.m.
2. I got here by train.
3. I decided to fly Kingfisher Airlines.
4. I left my old job for a better opportunity.
5. Shiraz and Kartik are going to the theatre.

! Make sure you have done the exercises and checked your answers before moving on.

12.5 WHEN TO USE VERBS

The type of question you are asking changes depending on which verb you choose.

- 'Can' and 'could' generally refer to a person's ability to perform the desired action. They can also be used as requests.

Question	Answer
Can you use Microsoft Office?	Yes, I learned how to use it last year.
Could you help me with this project?	No, because I don't have the time.
Could you have done a better job?*	Yes, I could have tried harder.

*If you are referring to something in the past, use could (not can).

- 'May' is a very polite way to request permission to do something. (More polite than 'can'.)

Question	Answer
May I call you for an interview?	Yes, I would like that.
May I use the bathroom?	No, you may not, because the class is in session.

- 'Would' is a polite way to ask someone if they are willing to perform a desired action.

Question	Answer
Would you do me a favour?	No, because I do not believe in doing favours.

- 'Should' is a polite way to ask someone for advice.

Question	Answer
Should I take the test again?	Yes, because I think you need a higher score.

Exercise 12.6

Fill in the blanks with the appropriate verb (Can, Could, Would, Should, May). Check your answers before moving on.

1. _____ you hand me the remote control?
2. I need his advice. _____ I call him again?
3. Thank you for looking at my CV. _____ I meet you sometime to discuss job opportunities?
4. _____ you be interested in tutoring me in math?
5. ____ you hear what I am saying?
6. ______ you read my report for me?
7. ______ I see the minutes from the last meeting?
8. ______ you do the work if you needed to?

! Make sure you have done the exercises and checked your answers before moving on.

12.6 A QUICK RECAP OF THE RULES IN THIS CHAPTER

We have gone through the different ways to ask questions in this chapter. Read the following summary to recap what you have learnt.

Rules for structuring questions

Formula 1—Word order when using the 5 Ws and 'how' (question words):

Question word + verb + Subject (noun/pronoun)+ main verb/additional parts

When	+ do	+ you	+ want to leave?
What	+ would	+ you	+ like to eat?

Formula 2—Word order when using 'which' and 'what' (question words):

Question word + subject noun + verb + additional parts

Which	+ computer	+ are	+ you buying?
What	+ mobile phone	+ works	+ the best?

Formula 3—Word order when using verbs:		
Verb + subject (noun/pronoun) + main verb/additional parts		
Do	+ you	+ want anything?
Would	+ you	+ like to eat?

Don't get nervous because of all these rules. To make things easier, write these rules on small pieces of paper and go through them over time to help you learn.

Tips

1. Avoid starting a question with a noun or a pronoun.
   ✗ **I** should go study?
   ✓ Should **I** go study?
   ✗ **Jatin** should go study?
   ✓ Should **Jatin** go study?
2. Always place a question mark at the end of questions.
   ✗ When will the movie start.
   ✓ When will the movie start**?**
3. While speaking, avoid saying 'no' or 'yes' at the end of a sentence to make it a question. This is slang.
   ✗ It is nice, **no**?
   ✓ Isn't it nice?

Once you have gone through this chapter, try watching news shows in English on TV, and pay attention to how questions are asked. This will help you understand how to form questions.

Exercise 12.7

Correct the following sentences. Check your answers before moving on.

1. You'd like to come for shopping with me?
2. Why you looking for a change?
3. You've been to other interviews?

4. For what reason you are in America?
5. How can I improve my English skills.
6. What else you want?
7. Will it be hard to qualify for the job.
8. What you did?
9. In which standard he is?
10. How he will come on his own?
11. How to get rid of this panic at interviews and at group discussions.
12. You are suggesting something to me?
13. Where you are going?
14. How you like your bread?
15. What movie you are watching?

Exercise 12.8

Read the questions below. Identify and rewrite the incorrect questions. Check your answers before moving on.

1. Whether there would be any improvements in my English?
2. How can I improve my communication skills in English?
3. Can I get a job in a telecom company?
4. Is it possible to work part-time shifts during the summer?
5. You can give me some advice about my problem?
6. What you did do?
7. What skills do I need to get a BPO job?
8. How I can learn to work more effectively?
9. Why do you want to work for this company?

Exercise 12.9

Given below is part of an interview between Kartik (interviewee) and Big Boss (interviewer). Correct Big Boss's questions where they have not been properly framed. Also, correct Kartik's sentence construction errors. (We went over this in chapter 1.)

Big Boss:	Why you want this job?
Kartik:	Getting this job I believe is good for me.

Big Boss:	What you want to get out of it?
Kartik:	To learn more.
Big Boss:	You been to other interviews?
Kartik:	Many interviews I have gone to.
Big Boss:	So why you not take up other jobs?
Kartik:	Not interesting.
Big Boss:	Where you live?
Kartik:	Living in Borivali.
Big Boss:	So what you are doing now?
Kartik:	Now just with my dad working.
Big Boss:	You can start next week?

! Make sure you have done the exercises and checked your answers before moving on.

12.7 HOW TO AVOID RUN-ON QUESTIONS

As with sentences, questions need to express one complete thought. Sometimes, we tend to create run-on question sentences that other people find hard to understand. Take a look at this:

```
I am interested in becoming a soft skills trainer
and I would like to know what are the basic
requirements needed to be a soft skills trainer in
a BPO and how to go about looking for higher posts.
```

This question is not concise. The first part of the sentence is not even a question—it is a statement. Be sure to separate the parts of the sentence that are statements from the parts that are questions. The statements usually come first. The first part of this sentence should have been written as:

✓ I am interested in becoming a soft skills trainer.

The rest of the sentence is actually a combination of two questions. It is also not really necessary to add phrases such as 'I would like to know' to the beginning of questions. Since you are asking, it is obvious that you want to know. Also, questions should always end with a question mark. The two questions should have been written as:

✓ What are the basic requirements needed to be a soft skills trainer in a BPO? How do I go about looking for job positions?

Thus, that one long sentence really should have been written as three short sentences: one statement and two questions.

✓ I am interested in becoming a soft skills trainer. What are the basic requirements needed to be a soft skills trainer in a BPO? How do I go about looking for job positions?

Keep these tips in mind while attempting exercise 12.10. As you go through them and try to shorten the long sentences, you will get better at professional writing and speaking.

Exercise 12.10

The following are run-on questions. Separate the statements from the questions and rewrite them. Also, correct any mistakes in the structure of the sentence. While there is no one correct answer, make sure your answer is similar to the one in the answer key. Check your answers before moving on.

1. My problem is I am confident when I speak one on one, but if I have to speak in front of a crowd I get nervous and stammer, what can I do to solve this problem?
2. When in an interview I am asked about my strengths and weaknesses how do I reply my weaknesses to the satisfaction of the interviewer.
3. I am a commerce student and I have just completed my second year of college, do I stand any chance of getting a job in banking industry.
4. Is it advisable for me to look for a career in counselling as I am only moderately fluent in English.
5. So I would like to know if the interviewer asks me why you shift from BPO industry to software services industry what I can answer him.
6. I would like to be a flight steward and I have one year of experience in the hospitality industry if you could suggest any courses.
7. I have been working in a medical transcription company for the

last six years and would like to switch to a sales job because I have reached the top level and I find no growth forward, so will I be able to get a job in sales and what are my growth chances.

8. And your articles are in Marathi Language, so did you write in Marathi language or did the newspaper translate the articles into Marathi?
9. Hi I am completing B.Com. final year and I want to be an MBA please can you give me some information about MBA entrance I am preparing for CE.

APPLYING WHAT YOU HAVE LEARNED

1. When asking questions in English, you must use certain types of words and follow a specific word order.
2. When starting a question, you should only use one of the following words:
   - Question words—Who, What, When, Where, Why, How and Which
   - Forms of 'to be', 'to do' and 'to have'
   - Can, Could, Would, Should, May
3. Most question words cannot be followed by a noun or pronoun. (They must be followed by a verb.):
   ✗ Why **she is** going there?
   ✓ Why **is she** going there?
4. Only the question words 'which' and 'what' are followed by a noun:
   ✓ Which **company** do you work for?
   ✓ What **factory** does he own?
5. Verbs are followed by a noun or pronoun:
   ✓ Are **you** coming?
   ✓ Did **Manjeet** write the article?
6. Depending on the question word or verb you use to start your question, you will get a different answer. You should generally use 'can', 'could', 'would', 'should' or 'may' when you want to be more formal or polite.
7. Questions should not end with a 'yes' or 'no'. They should also always have a question mark.

✗ You liked the food, no?
✓ Did you like the food?

8. Just like run-on sentences, run-on questions are confusing and should be avoided.

RECAP OF VERBS AND MATCHING PRONOUNS

Many of you may have forgotten the various forms of these verbs and what their compatible pronouns are (these topics are covered in the chapters on verbs and pronouns). Let's do a little recap:

Verbs used for forming questions

Past	Present	Future	Compatible Subject Pronoun
TO BE			
Was	Am	Will be	I
Were	Are	Will be	You
Was	Is	Will be	She/He/It
Were	Are	Will be	They/We
TO DO			
Did	Do	—	I/You
Did	Does	—	She/He/It
Did	Do	—	They/We
TO HAVE			
Had	Have	—	I/You
Had	Has	—	She/He/It
Had	Have	—	They/We

As you can see, when asking questions, only the verb 'to be' is used in the future tense.

CHAPTER 13

What is your good name? What is your bad name?

'Indianisms' (Part 1): Grammatical errors and slang

> Dear **Miss Nasha**,
>
> I am **very much** interested in working for you. I **came to know** of your company two days **back**. Can you **say** me the **concerned person** whom I can send my CV to? Please write back to me and I will **reply you** right away. **That's it I would like to talk about** in this email.
>
> **Yours faithfully**,
>
> Arjun

This is an example of a typical email I receive from people who want to work in my company. Apart from grammatical errors, this email has slang, as well as 'Indianisms' (all the words are marked in bold).

Indianisms are words and phrases that are commonly used in India, but are not accepted as correct English elsewhere in the world. Multinationals do not like the use of Indianisms. Also, in most business environments around the world, slang is considered unacceptable. If you speak and write using Indianisms, you will sound unprofessional. See if you use any of the following Indianisms:

Common Error 1:

✗ What is your good name?

- Can you have a 'bad' name? Of course not! Then you can't have a 'good' name either!

- The 'good' in the above sentence comes from a direct translation of the Hindi equivalent: '*Aapka shubh naam kya hai?*'

The correct way to ask someone their name is to simply say:

✓ What is your name?

Common Error 2:

✗ I want to tell to the concerned person my problem.

- This sentence contains two Indianisms. First, you can't use 'tell' in this situation, you must use 'speak'.
- Next, 'concerned person' is not grammatically acceptable in this context.

This sentence could have been better phrased as follows:

✓ I want to **speak** to **the person in charge** about my problem. Or, I want to **speak** to **someone who can help me** with my problem.

These are just a couple of examples. In this chapter and the next we will go over some of the most common Indianisms and slang that prevent young people from getting the jobs they want. It is extremely important that you learn to recognize Indianisms and stop yourself from using them.

What will I learn in this chapter?

13.1 Different types of Indianisms.
13.2 Putting it all together.

13.1 DIFFERENT TYPES OF INDIANISMS

Many Indianisms are formed due to errors in grammar. Others are because of slang words and phrases that have become common. Quite a few of these phrases are old expressions left behind by the British that we are still using in India. Sometimes, there is no clear reason *why* an Indianism is wrong—it just isn't a word or phrase that is globally accepted or understood.

Here are some examples of common Indianisms. Next to each one is an explanation (where possible) of why it should not be used, and examples of how you could get the same meaning across more clearly by using alternative words. Read one set at a time. Then, make flashcards to help you remember them. Don't get intimidated if you think there are too many to learn. After you read them a few times and do the exercises, you will get the hang of it!

Indianism	Explanation	What sounds better
✗ It happened several years **back.**	Never use 'back' to express time; use 'ago' instead.	✓ It happened several years **ago**.
✗ I went on a holiday two weeks **back.**	Never use 'back' to express time; use 'ago' instead.	✓ I went on a holiday two weeks **ago**.
✗ I am **very much** happy. ✗ I am **much** happy.	You can't use 'very much' or 'much' after 'I am.'	✓ I am very happy.
✗ It is **very much** expensive. ✗ She is **very much** beautiful.	Only use 'very much' to express emotion or desire.	✓ It is very expensive. ✓ She is really very beautiful. ✓ I would like it very much. ✓ I love you very much. These last two sentences express emotion/desire
✗ How **much dogs** do you have?	'Many' is used for countable nouns (like 'dogs').	✓ How **many dogs** do you have?

Indianism	Explanation	What sounds better
✗ How **many water** do you drink?	'Much' is used for non-countable nouns (like 'water').	✓ How **much water** do you drink?
✗ I am **staying** in Bandra. ✗ I am **put up** in Andheri.	You use the word 'stay' for a temporary situation and 'live' for a permanent one. You should never use 'put up'.	✓ I **live** in Bandra. When I travel to Delhi, I **stay** in south Delhi.
✗ The **female** from Wipro is coming tomorrow. ✗ She is the prettiest **female**. I know	Never use the word *'female'* to refer to a woman. (Just as you never use the word 'male' to refer to a man.)	✓ The **lady** from Wipro is coming tomorrow. ✓ She is the prettiest **woman** I know.
✗ I can **tell this** to you because you are smart. ✗ She **told to** my mother that I was wrong. ✗ She **said to me** about her boyfriend cheating on her. ✗ Did you **say to her** hi?	If using 'told' or 'tell', place *who* is being told right after. If using 'say' or 'said', state what is being said right after.	✓ I can **tell you** this because you are smart. ✓ She **told my mother** that I was wrong. ('You' and 'my mother'.) ✓ She **said that** her boyfriend was cheating on her. ✓ Did you **say** hi to her?
✗ I don't **think so** I am going. ✗ I don't **think so** he is right.	Rarely do we have nouns and verbs after the word 'so'.	✓ I don't think I am going. ✓ I don't think he is right.

Indianism	Explanation	What sounds better
		✓ I don't think so. ✓ I think so.
✗ Can you please **explain me**? ✗ Please **repeat me.** ✗ She **explained us** about the process. ✗ I **will explain** you.	You need to use 'to' in a sentence when the action of the verb originates from one subject and is directed to another.	✓ Can you please explain it **to** me? ✓ Please repeat it **to** me. ✓ She explained the process **to** us. ✓ I will explain it **to** you.
✗ She **committed a mistake** when she crashed her car into a tree. ✗ He **committed** another **mistake**—he forgot to get his timesheet signed.	For something done wrong out of carelessness (not a crime), we don't use the word 'committed'.	✓ She **made** a mistake when she crashed her car into a tree. ✓ He **made** another mistake—he forgot to get his timesheet signed.

Exercise 13.1

The following sentences contain some of the Indianisms that have been explained above. Correct them. There may be more than one way to rewrite some of the sentences. Make sure your answers are similar to the ones in the answer key.

1. I think so he will be here.
2. She came to meet me eight days back.
3. She is very much looking forward to it.
4. She always commits mistakes in class.
5. How much people will come to the party?
6. I stay in Belapur and commute to work every day by train.
7. She can tell these things to me because we are best friends.

8. The female will call you in two hours.
9. There is very much food on my plate.
10. She always explains me when I don't understand.

! Make sure you have done the exercises and checked your answers before moving on.

SOME MORE INDIANISMS

Indianism	Explanation	What sounds better
✗ What is your **good name**?	You can't have a 'bad' name, and thus, you can't have a 'good' name!	✓ What is your **name?**/What is your **first name?**/ What is your **last name?**
✗ I **feel** you are right. ✗ I **feel** the economy will improve. ✗ I **feel** he is an amazing person.	Only use 'feel' for feelings, not thoughts or opinions.	✓ I **think** you are right. ✓ I **believe** the economy will improve. ✓ In my **opinion** he is an amazing person.
✗ How **would I come to know** about her address?	'Come to know' is too wordy and not direct enough.	✓ Will you give me her address? ✓ Where can I get her address? ✓ What is her address?
✗ I **came to know** today that they ran away.	'Came to know' is too wordy and not direct enough.	✓ I found out today that they ran away. ✓ I realized today that they ran away.

Indianism	Explanation	What sounds better
✗ I am not **able to get** you.	'Able to get' sounds harsh and rude.	✓ I didn't **understand** what you said. ✓ Could you please **repeat** what you said?
✗ Why **not** you try this idea?	After the question word 'why', you generally need a verb *('not' is not a verb')*	✓ Why **don't** you try this idea?
✗ You can **communicate** to the person to whom you want.	'Communicate' is usually followed by 'with' and not 'to'.	✓ You can **speak to** whoever you want. ✓ You can **speak to** anyone here. ✓ You can **communicate with** anyone here.
✗ I will transfer you to the **concerned person**.	Just don't use it!	✓ I will transfer you to **someone who can assist you**.
✗ **Mention not**.	Just don't use it!	✓ Don't mention it. ✓ You're welcome.

Exercise 13.2

The executive in the following sentences has used many of the Indianisms mentioned in this chapter, as well as grammatical mistakes explained in previous chapters. Correct the mistakes. There may be more than one way to rewrite some the sentences. Make sure your answers are similar to the ones in the answer key:

Executive:	Thank you for calling Bank of Baroda, please can I help you?
Client:	Yes, I am calling to find out why my mutual fund account is doing so poorly.
Executive:	Let me pull up your account, sir. What is your good name?
Client:	My name is Tarun Khan.
Executive:	I am sorry, I was not able to get you.
Client:	I said my name is Tarun Khan.
Executive:	Thank you. There are a few stocks in your mutual fund whose prices have dropped a few days back.
Client:	Well, will you guys do anything about this?
Executive:	I can put you on hold for one moment to check this?
Client:	Sure.
Executive:	Thank you for staying on the line. I came to know that these particular auto stocks have dropped because of the budget that just came out. But we feel that they will bounce back in a few days.
Client:	I have not been happy with this mutual fund for some time now.
Executive:	Why not see if there are other mutual funds you would rather invest in?
Client:	Can I speak to someone about this matter?
Executive:	You can communicate to our investment manager.
Client:	Fine.
Executive:	Okay, I will transfer your call to the concerned person.
Client:	Thank you.
Executive:	Mention not.

! Make sure you have done the exercises and checked your answers before moving on.

MORE INDIANISMS

Indianism	Explanation	What sounds better
✗ I was here **only**.	Don't place 'only' at the end of sentences.	✓ I have been here.
✗ They speak very **friendly.**	Just don't use it!	✓ They speak **nicely**. ✓ They speak **in a friendly way**.
✗ They should **take care.** ✗ They should **be taken care.**	Do not use this phrase without sufficient explanation.	✓ They should be careful when crossing the road. ✓ They should take care of themselves. ✓ You should be careful not to hit the delete button.
✗ I am going to **gift** you a pen./I **gifted** her a pen.	Just don't use 'to gift' as a verb.	✓ I will **buy** you a pen **as a gift**./I **gave** her a pen **as a gift**.
✗ I'll **just go and come.**	Not direct—using too many words.	✓ I'll be back. ✓ I'll be right back.
✗ That's **it** I would like to talk about.	'It' does not mean the same thing as 'all'.	✓ That's **all** I would like to talk about.

Exercise 13.3

In the following dialogue, Natasha makes mistakes with Indianisms, as well as grammatical mistakes from previous chapters. Correct Natasha's dialogue. There may be more than one way to rewrite some of the sentences. Make sure your answers are similar to the ones in the answer key.

Natasha:	Rohan, I am very much upset with you.
Rohan:	Why?
Natasha:	I don't want to be your girlfriend any more.
Rohan:	But what have I done?
Natasha:	Weren't you supposed to meet me today itself at the store in Bandra?
Rohan:	I did go to the store, but I couldn't find you. Your cellphone wasn't working so I couldn't even call you. I should be the one who is upset!
Natasha:	I was there only. You should have taken care.
Rohan:	Well, I am sorry. But it is no reason for you to be so upset.
Natasha:	I feel you are being very rude. You are not speaking very friendly.
Rohan:	Natasha, I am sorry.
Natasha:	I was even going to gift you a shirt when I saw you.
Rohan:	Can I come and meet you right now?
Natasha:	No, that's it I wanted to talk about with you. I have to go out now.
Rohan:	Natasha, I am really sorry and I want to meet you today.
Natasha:	Okay, fine. I will just go and come. I will call you then.

! Make sure you have done the exercises and checked your answers before moving on.

SOME MORE INDIANISMS

Indianism	Explanation	What sounds better
✗ How long you'll be **accommodating** at my place?	'Accommodating' is too formal for normal speech.	✓ How long will you be **staying** at my place?
✗ **Today evening** ✗ **Today morning** ✗ **Today afternoon**	Just don't use it!	✓ This evening ✓ Tonight ✓ This morning ✓ This afternoon
✗ Please do the **needful.**	Just don't use it! Be precise about what you want the person to do.	✓ Please get back to me by tomorrow afternoon. ✓ Please notify me when the bug is fixed.
✗ I will **give** my exam next week. ✗ I have been studying English and practicing **the same.**	You can't 'give' an exam. Use 'take' instead. Using 'the same' is repetitive and unnecessary.	✓ I will **take** my exam next week. ✓ I have been studying and practising English.

Indianism	Explanation	What sounds better
✗ I would like to **make friendship** with you.	Just don't use it!	✓ I would like to **be friends** with you. ✓ I would like to **become friends** with you.

Exercise 13.4

Read the following email and correct any Indianisms and grammatical errors that you may find. There may be more than one way to rewrite some of the sentences, but make sure your answers are similar to the ones in the answer key.

```
Hi, myself Arjun, will be accommodating at your guest house today evening. My sister stayed at your guest house a few months back. She told me a lot about your place. But she forgot to say me your address. How would I come to know about your address?

Also, I hope that your guest house is quiet as I have to study for an exam that I am giving in a few weeks. If it will be noisy, please let me know about the same. That's it I wanted to know. Please do the needful.

I look forward to meeting you and making friendship with you.
```

! Make sure you have done the exercises and checked your answers before moving on.

MORE INDIANISMS

Indianism	Explanation	What sounds better
✗ I will **SMS** you from my **mobile phone**.	Words like 'SMS' and 'mobile' are not commonly used in the USA.	✓ I will **text** you from my **cellphone.**
✗ The number is **double zero**, three, **triple five**, one.	Words like 'double' and 'triple' are not commonly used in the USA. Americans Americans tend to say each number separately.	✓ The number is zero, zero, three, five, five, five, one.
✗ I am sorry **for that**.	Just don't use it!	✓ I am sorry **about** that. ✓ I am sorry **to hear** that.
✗ **What all things** are listed on your computer screen? ✗ I see **your all things** listed on my computer screen.	Just don't use it!	✓ What do you see on your computer screen? ✓ I see your information on my computer screen.
✗ Do you have **any other** shirt?	'Another' is a much better way to say 'any other'.	✓ Do you have **another** shirt?

Indianism	Explanation	What sounds better
✗ Can I meet the HR manager **out there**? ✗ Can I meet the HR manager **over here**?	Either leave these terms out or be more specific—instead of saying 'over here', say the name of the location.	✓ Can I meet the HR manager? ✓ Can I meet the HR manager for this office?
✗ I have **lot many** questions to ask you.	'Lot' is not a word. Either use '**a** lot **of**' or 'lot**s of**'. Also, you cannot use both 'a lot' and 'many' at the same time—choose one.	✓ I have **a lot** of questions to ask you. ✓ I have **many** questions to ask you.
✗ I will **intimate** you with the details. ✗ I will **intimate** you on the agenda.	'Intimate' is not a commonly used word for business purposes.	✓ I will let you know the details. ✓ I will talk to you about the agenda. ✓ I will go over the agenda with you.

Exercise 13.5

In the following conversation a company agent is talking to a customer in America. The company agent's has used many of the Indianisms you have learned about so far in this chapter. Correct his mistakes. There may be more than one way to rewrite some of the sentences. Make sure your answers are similar to the ones in the answer key.

Customer:	I am having a lot of trouble with the cellphone I just bought from your company. I am unable to send text messages.
Company agent:	I am sorry you are having lot many problems with your phone. What is your mobile number so I can look your account up?
Customer:	My number is 98-777-43341.
Company agent:	I am sorry but we don't have that number listed. Do you have any other number?
Customer:	No! This is my only number!
Company agent:	Okay, let me repeat the number. Nine, eight, triple seven, double four, three, four, one.
Customer:	That is wrong! I said 43341 not 44341.
Company agent:	I am sorry for that. Yes, I see your all things listed on my computer screen. It seems that you have no balance on your phone. That is why you are unable to send any SMSs.
Customer:	I just paid for more credit on my phone. I should have a positive balance on this phone!
Company agent:	Would you like to speak to our accounts department over here? You can intimate them on the details. They will be able to help you.
Customer:	Fine. Please transfer the call.

! Make sure you have done the exercises and checked your answers before moving on.

13.2 PUTTING IT ALL TOGETHER

This chapter needs to be read a few times for you to recognize all the different Indianisms. Flip through it from time to time, and you will find yourself getting comfortable with the rules.

Also, when you receive emails or talk to other people, start watching out for Indianisms. This will help you identify Indianisms more naturally, and help you eliminate them from your own speech.

The following exercises include a mix of the Indianisms we have read about in this chapter. The sentences in the following exercises have all been taken from actual emails and dialogues. As you go through them, keep referring to the tables in this chapter to help yourself along.

Exercise 13.6

The following sentences contain Indianisms as well as grammatical mistakes. Correct them. There may be more than one way to rewrite some of the sentences. Make sure your answers are similar to the ones in the answer key.

1. Those guards are telling that I cannot come into the building.
2. I have a group of people out here who are working along with me.
3. I went to meet the concerned person over there.
4. What you feel about Delhi?
5. I am accommodating at the hotel for one night.
6. I'll try to reply you.
7. I am going to give my exam on the 11 April.
8. I was capturing data for the project today morning.
9. I am in college only.
10. I like to make friendship with different types of people.
11. Is there any other manager I can talk to over here?
12. What is your good name?
13. I don't like this sari! Do you have any other sari I can wear?
14. My sister is smart, she will learn to drive herself only.
15. She said me that she will come at 10 p.m.
16. Did she intimate you on what was happening?

Exercise 13.7

The following sentences contain Indianisms as well as grammatical mistakes. Correct them. There may be more than one way to rewrite some of the sentences. Make sure your answers are similar to the ones in the answer key.

1. Please confirm receipt of the same.
2. I don't think so it is a good idea.
3. He told to me that the class was on Sunday.
4. When will I come to know about the plans for Saturday?
5. That female from the bank called for you in the afternoon.
6. Wait for me, I'll just go and come.
7. Q: Do you have anything else to say?
   A: No, that's it I wanted to talk about.
8. I am staying in Mumbai for the last ten years.
9. You can communicate your thoughts to the HR manager.
10. She is the very much best at work.
11. We were not able to get what he said.
12. Can you please explain me the math problem?
13. Will you say to her hello?
14. I need help bringing my things from the car. Can you do the needful?
15. I used to live in Mumbai five years back.
16. When we see them, they always have lot many advice for us.

Exercise 13.8

The following sentences contain Indianisms as well as grammatical mistakes. Correct them. There may be more than one way to rewrite some of the sentences. Make sure your answers are similar to the ones in the answer key.

1. What all things you need for your trip?
2. How much glasses of water are there on the table?
3. Q: Why didn't you call me last night?
   A: I'm sorry for that but I was very busy.
4. She is very much pretty.
5. I came to know about the problem after my senior told me about it.

6. Sameer came to my house some time back.
7. She gifted Ranvir a book for Diwali.
8. I can tell this to you because I trust you.
9. Can I know your good name, ma'am?
10. I am put up in Borivali.
11. I will explain you the Pythagorean Theory.
12. What is your mobile number?
13. Please call me. I will intimate you about the plan.
14. Why not you take a look at my CV?
15. I am very much happy with the food.
16. I feel the interview will be very hard.
17. She speaks very friendly to me.

! Make sure you have done the exercises and checked your answers before moving on.

CHAPTER 14

Is it 'Dear Miss Nasha', 'Dear Ms Nasha' or 'Dear Ms Fitter'?

Indianisms (Part 2): SMS slang, punctuation and writing professional emails

```
Dear Miss Nasha,

This is with regard to u r posting. I want to work for u. I am very good at training n HR and lot many other things . . . So I am applying to your company bcoz I think it is very good . . . Please go through my CV_

Tks.
Sheetal
```

This is another email I received from someone interested in working with me. When you send your CV to someone for the first time, you are hoping to make a good impression. But, if you send an email like this, it is likely the person will not even look at your CV because you have already made a terrible impression.

What is wrong with the above email?

- The email is filled with 'SMS slang'.
- Punctuation is either not used, or used incorrectly.
- The greeting and the signature are not professional.
- The structure of the email is not logical.

If you send a similar email to someone, you will immediately be thought of as unprofessional. In the last chapter we went over the Indianisms to avoid. In this chapter, we will go over a few more Indianisms and other errors people make when sending professional emails. Ultimately, you are presenting yourself to an employer who has never even met you, and it is crucial to come across as professional. This chapter will help you find a job, as well as become more professional at your current job. See if you can relate to any of the following mistakes:

Common Error 1:

✗ Dear Miss Nasha,

- It is incorrect to place someone's first name after a 'Miss', 'Ms', 'Mrs'or 'Mr'.

An email greeting should look like this:

✓ Dear **Nasha**, or Dear **Ms Fitter**,

Common Error 2:

✗ *I m writing to u bcoz of my wrk.*

- It is unacceptable to use SMS slang—words like 'bcoz' and 'u'—when writing *any kind* of email or letter.

This sentence should have been written as:

✓ I **am** writing to **you because** of my **work**.

Common Error 3:

✗ Please look at my CV . . . it contains my past work experiences. Please let me know if you have any openings.

- You must never use '. . .'—an ellipsis—in a professional email.
- You must capitalize the first letter of the next sentence after a full stop.
- You must always place a full stop, a question mark, or an exclamation mark at the end of a sentence.

With better punctuation, this sentence would read:

✓ Please look at my CV**. I**t contains my past work experience. **P**lease let me know if you have any openings.

What will I learn in this chapter?

14.1 How to avoid SMS slang emails and letters.
14.2 Poor punctuation can kill your chances of getting an interview.
14.3 How to write professional greetings and closings in business emails.
14.4 Writing professional emails to find a job.

14.1 HOW TO AVOID SMS SLANG IN EMAILS AND LETTERS

Sometimes we use spelling and grammar short cuts when writing emails to friends and family. Especially when sending SMSs, using short cuts helps save time. While it is okay to use SMS slang in informal messages, you should never use it when writing to anyone who is not a close friend or family member. Read the list of SMS slang words in the chart below. Make sure you avoid using any SMS slang in your emails.

Common SMS slang	Correct word
abt	about
bcoz	because
cudnt	could not/couldn't
gonna	going to
hai	Hi
hav or hv	have
i m	I am or I'm
m	I am
mam	ma'am
n	and
nxt	next

pls or plz	please
rgds	regards
tks or thanx	thanks
thru	through
trning	training
u	you
ur	your or you are
v	we
wanna	want to
wk	week
wrkin	working

Exercise 14.1

The following sentences have been taken from real business emails and contain SMS slang and other grammatical mistakes. Correct them. Check your answers before moving on.

1. Pls tell me why u want to join this company.
2. If an interviewer asks why u change ur job what do i tell him?
3. I m kousik. Pls tell me r u interviewing in town nxt wk?
4. I was looking at ur website today.
5. I m ready to interview for a job?
6. It's bcoz of her that I m here today.
7. I m a graduate in computer science.
8. I was asked, 'Why do u wanna work in an IT services company?'
9. Pl advise me how to get a job in a BPO.
10. I m wrkin in a multinational company and I would like to improve my communication skills.

! Make sure you have done the exercises and checked your answers before moving on.

14.2 POOR PUNCTUATION CAN KILL YOUR CHANCES OF GETTING AN INTERVIEW

Before you worry that this is going to be a long, boring lesson on punctuation, take a look at the five basic rules outlined below. These are simple rules that will not take you long to understand. Most of us already know them, but forget to use them in daily life.

1. If a sentence is a question, always place a question mark at the end.
   ✗ What kind of questions will they ask**.**
   ✓ What kind of questions will they ask**?**
2. For all other types of sentences, you must place either a full stop or an exclamation mark at the end. Ellipses (. . .) should not be used.
   ✗ I am going to take the exam tomorrow
   ✗ I am going to take the exam tomorrow . . .
   ✓ I am going to take the exam tomorrow**.**
3. After a full stop, question mark or exclamation mark, leave one space before starting the next sentence.
   ✗ I am looking for a new **job.Do** you think you can help me?
   ✓ I am looking for a new **job. Do** you think you can help me?
4. After a full stop, question mark or exclamation mark, the next sentence should start with a capital letter.
   ✗ She is always complaining**! d**o you know what her problem is?
   ✓ She is always complaining**! D**o you know what her problem is?
5. If you are joining two independent clauses (an independent clause contains a subject, verb and object and could be its own sentence) with an 'and' or a 'but', you should include a comma before the 'and' or 'but'. Try not to start your sentences with 'and' or 'but'.
   ✗ I am looking for a job in a multinational**. B**ut I am not confident of getting the job.
   ✓ I am looking for a job in a multinational**, b**ut I am not confident of getting the job.

Many of us already know these rules, but don't bother to follow them when writing emails. We either think these rules don't matter, or we are too lazy to follow them. Either way, please remember that there is no excuse for writing an email to *anyone* without following these basic punctuation rules.

Exercise 14.2

The following sentences are from real business emails and contain errors in punctuation and SMS slang. Correct them. Check your answers before moving on.

1. Could you please tell me the basic job profile of a team leader.
2. I want to grow in my profession.i know that is only possible if you have good communication skills. Am I right
3. Do u have any idea what I should do.
4. My name is Vibha and I hv recently joined a manufacturing company. i m really happy with this company
5. What are they looking for in a telephonic interview.
6. can u tell me what offshore outsourcing is all abt. I m interested in learning more abt this field.tks for your help.
7. I hav a couple questions. after my BCA I think I m proficient in English but I sometimes get confused. im confident in writing but hav some doubts in speaking.
8. Does the speed at which you talk matter.
9. Im Prakash from Chennai. I worked as a software professional. But i cudnt cope with the java technology and coding.
10. How are you,
11. If an interviewer asks me why I changed from the software field to the BPO field, what answer should I give him.
12. I have completed my SSC in Marathi medium. and I have just joined a new job
13. I am planning to join a training class to improve my English ... And can I come meet you. Also, how do i rate my vocabulary skills. Do you have any online test.

! Make sure you have done the exercises and checked your answers before moving on.

14.3 HOW TO WRITE PROFESSIONAL GREETINGS AND CLOSINGS IN BUSINESS EMAILS

So far, we have covered the slang and punctuation errors that are to be avoided when writing emails or letters. Now, let's learn how to write a proper email greeting (where you put the name of the person you are writing to) and closing (where you sign your name). For example, read the greeting and closing that Rohini chose for her email to Minal Patel, an HR manager:

> **Dear Miss Minal,**
>
> I am applying for a vacant position in your organization in research. I am herewith submitting my CV. I am looking to hear from you.
>
> **Yours Respectfully.**
> **Rohini**

In this email, both greeting and closing are wrong! To be taken seriously by an employer, a client or a colleague, every part of your email needs to come across as being professional. Let's learn the correct way to start and end emails.

THE GREETING

Rohini started her email with:

✗ **Dear Miss Minal,**

This greeting is unprofessional. The rules for greetings are:

1. Never use the prefix 'Miss' when sending an email to a woman, unless you know she prefers to be addressed in this way. You should only use the following:
   - Ms
   - Mrs (If you know the woman is married.)
2. Never place someone's first name after a 'Ms' 'Mrs' or 'Mr' If using these prefixes, only use the person's last name:
   ✗ Dear Ms **Minal**
   ✗ Dear Ms **Minal** Patel
   ✓ Dear Ms Patel

3. You should only use a person's first name if you know them well. Remember, when using first names, do not add a prefix:
   ✗ Dear **Ms** Minal,
   ✓ Dear,
   ✓ Minal,
4. If you don't know the person's name, use the following examples:
   - Dear HR Manager/Dear HR Representative, (if you know you are writing to the HR manager).
   - To whom it may concern, (always safe).
   - Dear Sir or Madam,

   If you don't know if the person is a man or a woman, do not just use 'Dear Sir'. You must then use 'Dear Sir or Madam'.
5. Never use the following greetings in professional emails:
   ✗ Hello
   ✗ Hi
   ✗ Dear Ma'am, (this is unprofessional)
   ✗ Dear Madum, (this is an incorrect spelling of 'Madam')

So, Rohini's email should have begun with:

✓ Dear Ms Patel,

THE CLOSING

Just like the greeting at the beginning of the email, the closing is extremely important. Rohini's closing in the email was:

✗ Yours Respectfully.
Rohini

There are several things wrong with this. Let's learn the rules for closing emails.

1. Closings like 'yours respectfully' are old, outdated British phrases that are not that common. Try to avoid closing your emails or letters using the following:
   ✗ Yours respectfully,
   ✗ Yours faithfully,
   ✗ Yours obediently,
   ✗ Yours kindly,/Kindly yours,
   ✗ Thanking you,

2. Stick to the following closings for business emails:
   ✓ Regards, (The best and most accepted salutation. You are always safe with this one.)
   ✓ Best regards,/Best wishes,
   ✓ Warm regards, (Use only when you know the person you are emailing as it could seem too forward otherwise.)
   ✓ Thanks, (This is more informal.)
   ✓ Sincerely, (This is more formal.)
   ✓ Yours sincerely,/Yours truly, (formal and not really necessary unless for a fancy letter).
3. Always place a comma ',' after the closing. Never place a full stop.
   ✗ Regards.
   ✓ Regards,
4. When signing your name at the end of an email, look at the greeting you chose. If you used the person's last name (Ms Patel) or if you didn't use a name at all (To whom it may concern/Sir or Madam), you must state both your first and last name in the closing:
   ✓ Regards,
   Rohini Gupta
5. If you used the person's first name in the greeting (Dear Minal or Minal), you must state only your first name in the closing:
   ✓ Regards,
   Rohini
6. Add your phone number below your name. Do this even if the person already has your phone number.

Thus, for this email, Rohini's greeting and closing would look like:

Dear Ms Patel,

[TEXT OF THE EMAIL]

Regards,
Rohini Gupta (Both first and last name used because she used 'Ms Patel' in the greeting.)

981-122-3456

Exercise 14.3

Correct the following emails so that they sound more professional. Look for incomplete sentences as well as misspelled words and incorrect punctuation. Make sure you add the proper greeting and closing phrases. There may be more than one correct answer. Check your answers before moving on.

1.

```
Dear Respected Madam,

I've looked at ur website. I would like 2 know if ur offering trning in Delhi. I m wrkin in a accounting firm and would like to improve my communication skills. If possible send details abt the trning course.

Yours faithfully.
Sanjay
```

2.

```
Hi,

I am working in a telecom company as a team leader and want to advance in my job. Could you send me the schedule of new course that are starting in September or November so I can start early and also let me know the fees for the programmes offered.

Kindly yours.
Mr Vikram
```

3.

```
Dear Ms Vipasha Khiantani,

i want to improve my communication skills pls help me with this. Are u offering any communication
```

```
courses?. Do you have courses in Mumbai. Pls send
me course details.

Thanking you,
Mr Lalit Joshi
```

! Make sure you have done the exercises and checked your answers before moving on.

14.4 WRITING PROFESSIONAL EMAILS TO FIND A JOB

We just learned how to begin and end emails professionally. Let's now learn how to write the actual contents of an email. One of the most important emails you will ever send to a company is the one with which you are applying for a job. Your goal is to make a good impression, so that you get invited for an interview. Therefore, the entire email needs to be professional, clear and logical.

Let's take another look at Rohini's email. She now knows how to start and end the email, but the content of her email is still not good enough for her to get called for an interview.

```
Dear Ms Patel,

I am applying for a vacant position in your
organization in research. I am herewith submitting
my CV. I am looking to hear from you.

Regards,
Rohini Gupta
```

This email has several things wrong with it. Let's go through each area together.

STEP 1: THE INTRODUCTION

Every email must have an introduction where you state clearly and briefly:

- Who you are—using both your first and last name
- Where you obtained the person's contact information from

For example, Rohini's introductory sentence was:

✗ I am applying for a vacant position in your organization in research.

This email goes straight into *why* Rohini is writing an email without stating *who* Rohini is, or *where* she found this person's email address. This is an unprofessional way to start an email. A better alternative is:

✓ My name is Rohini Gupta, and I found your contact information on your company's website.

Notice how Rohini introduces herself with both her first and last name. She also mentions where she found this person's contact details.

STEP 2: WHY YOU ARE WRITING

After the introduction, we should state *why* we are writing to the person. This part of the email should include:

- What position you want—include the position or type of position you are interested in
- Why you would be the ideal person for the position—a quick one-sentence background saying who you are and what it is that makes you a great fit for the position

Rohini did include some of this information in her email:

✗ I am applying for a vacant position in your organization in research.

This sentence is okay, in that it states why she is writing and the position she is interested in, but she could have done a better job explaining why she would be suitable for the position. Also, she could have been more polite. Take a look at the following sentence:

✓ I am interested in applying for a position in your research department. Currently, I have over two years of experience in this area.

Here, Rohini has said the same thing, but in a more polite way. Saying 'I am interested in applying' is just more polite than saying 'I am applying.' These are small variations, but if you can remember them, they will be helpful to you.

Also, Rohini added a quick line stating that she already has two years of experience in research. Information like this can create interest, encouraging the person to open and read your CV. Remember, just because you have emailed someone your CV does not mean they will actually take the time to open the attachment and read it. Your email must stir interest in them to do so, and that is up to you.

STEP 3: REFERENCE TO ATTACHED CV

Adding a line that refers to the CV you have attached is necessary. Let's read how Rohini did this:

✗ I am herewith submitting my CV.

There are a couple things wrong with how Rohini refers to her CV. For one, words like 'herewith' are old-fashioned and should be avoided in modern, professional situations. Also, Rohini did not actually say that the CV is attached to the email. The sentence could have been written as:

✓ Please find attached to this email a copy of my CV which details my past work experience.

STEP 4: CONCLUSION—REFERENCE FOR THE FUTURE

The last sentence of your email should be a conclusion, and should in some way refer to the future. It is a good idea to let the person know that you will call them later to follow up. This shows that you are truly interested in the position. Let's take a look at Rohini's conclusion:

✗ I am looking to hear from you.

First, this closing is a bit rude. It sounds like an order rather than a request. Also, Rohini did not indicate that she would follow up. Take a look at how she could have better concluded the email:

✓ I will call you up during the week to confirm you have received this email. I look forward to speaking with you.

Good work, you are done! That's all it takes to put together a professional email. Take a look at the new, improved email from Rohini to Ms Patel:

```
Dear Ms Patel,

My name is Rohini Gupta, and I obtained your contact information from your company's website. I am interested in applying for a position in your research department. Currently, I have over two years of experience in this area. Please find attached to this email a copy of my CV that details my past work experience.

I will call you up during the week to confirm you have received this email. I look forward to speaking with you.

Regards,
Rohini Gupta
981-122-3456
```

Competition for jobs is so strong these days that you can't afford to make mistakes in your emails. You've only got one chance to make a good impression on recruiters—so make sure it's perfect.

Exercise 14.4

Your friend Ramesh is looking for a new job and has been sending his CV to lots of different companies. He hasn't been having much luck getting a job, and asks you for help. When you see his email, you realize why he has not been called for interviews.

First, correct only the SMS slang, punctuation and sentence structure mistakes in Ramesh's email. Check this with the answer key. Then rewrite Ramesh's email using the professional structure you learned above. There may be more than one way to rewrite the email, but make sure your answer is similar to the example in the answer key.

```
Dear Sir/Ma'am,

I m Ramesh Desai from Bangalore, I m a Commerce Graduate from Pune University,
```

```
Last five years working in a software Company in
Bangalore as an Accountant. I saw ur ad for an
accountant. I wld like to wrk for ur company.

I hv attached my CV.

Expecting a call or a line from you.

Thanks,
With Regards.
Ramesh
```

APPLYING WHAT YOU HAVE LEARNED

1. It is extremely important when sending an email to come across as professional and clear.
2. Including any type of SMS slang (examples: 'bcoz', 'pls', 'u r') in business emails is unprofessional and inappropriate.
3. It is important to follow the rules of punctuation throughout the email.
4. When beginning emails, you must follow certain rules. For example, you should not include the person's first name after 'Ms', 'Mrs' or 'Mr' Only include the person's last name.
   ✗ Ms Kavita,
   ✗ Ms Kavita Singh,
   ✓ Ms Singh,
5. Likewise, when signing off emails, it is important to avoid phrases like 'Yours faithfully', 'Bye' and 'Thanking you' as closings. Instead it's safest to stick to the following:
   ✓ Regards,
   ✓ Thanks,
   ✓ Sincerely,
6. Additionally, when ending emails, the way you sign your name is extremely important. For example, if your greeting is to 'Ms Singh', then you must include both your first and last name in the signature. Remember to add your phone number after your name.
   ✓ Regards,
   Amit Joshi
   983-453-4578

7. When writing to a recruiter for the first time your email should include the following:
   - Introduction—who you are; where you obtained the person's information from.
   - Why you are writing—the position you are applying for; why you are a good candidate for that position.
   - A mention of your CV—a polite statement that your CV is attached in the email.
   - Conclusion—indication that you will follow up; a polite line saying you are looking forward to speaking with the person.

SECTION II

Pronunciation, speech and accent

Rashmi wants to work in a respected multinational company where she can earn a good salary. She is a smart girl with a degree in commerce, and believes she will be a valuable asset to the organization she works for. Her English is quite good, so she can't understand why she keeps getting rejected. After ten interviews an HR manager finally tells her, 'Rashmi, your accent is too hard to follow. You need to work on neutralizing your accent and improving your pronunciation.' Rashmi feels like crying when she hears this. She has no idea what the HR manager is talking about. No one has ever told her she should 'neutralize her accent' before.

Has this ever happened to you or to someone you know? Did you feel as confused as Rashmi?

In the previous section, we worked on perfecting your English grammar. Consider that to be your foundation, the framework essential for becoming an effective communicator. Now, let's add to those grammar skills by improving the way you *sound* when you speak. In this section, you will learn what it means to 'neutralize' your accent. Through various pronunciation techniques, you will learn how to manipulate your vocal cords, mouth, tongue and teeth in order to speak more clearly.

Speaking with the correct pronunciation is useful for everyone—not just those interested in jobs in a particular field. As India becomes more global and the domestic economy strengthens, any successful business person will need to be able to communicate effectively with a global audience.

This section includes the following chapters:

CHAPTER 15

I keep getting rejected because of my accent!

An overview of sounds

> Dear Nasha,
>
> My name is Karthik. I am currently working in a S/W company in Bangalore. I'm basically from Kerala with a typical Malayalam accent. I'm doing exceptionally well in my current position but people have started to complain about my accent. Yesterday I had a party and one of my colleagues suddenly said, 'I don't know how you get so much appreciation from your clients with a typical Malayalam accent, and how you are communicating with your clients.' So my question is what shall I do to neutralize my accent?

This is an email I received from a rediff.com reader. It is one that you will perhaps be able to empathize with. Many of us are now being told that we need to 'neutralize' our accents or improve our pronunciation. This can seem both insulting and annoying at times. Why should anyone have to change his or her accent? Is it really necessary? In this chapter, we will tackle these questions and begin the process of helping you learn how to 'neutralize' your accent.

What will I learn in this chapter?

15.1 It is not necessary to 'put on' a foreign accent.
15.2 Why pronunciation is important.
15.3 The difference between sounds and letters.
15.4 How to pronounce three types of consonant sounds.

15.1 IT IS NOT NECESSARY TO 'PUT ON' AN ACCENT

Many of you are probably wondering if accent neutralization means 'putting on' a foreign accent. The answer is no. Accent neutralization is about speaking clearly and being understood globally. You should not at any time try to *copy* a foreign accent, as you will end up sounding funny and unnatural. Instead, this section will teach you to fine-tune and make your own accent clearer and easier to understand.

15.2 WHY PRONUNCIATION IS IMPORTANT

If you speak perfect English but no one can understand you because your voice is muffled or unclear, then what is the point? Now, you may be thinking, 'I was born with my accent and it will always be difficult for people in other countries to understand me. There is nothing wrong with that.'

I disagree. Yes, everyone should keep their unique accent; however, in today's global world, it is crucial to be able to speak to, and be understood by, people in different countries. I also disagree that people in different countries always find it difficult to understand one another.

You might have noticed that English spoken in England sounds different from English spoken in America. Similarly, English as it is spoken in America sounds different from the English spoken in Hong Kong or Singapore or Australia.

But interestingly, for the most part, people from these different countries do not have great difficulty understanding one another. Why is this?

The answer is actually quite simple: people around the world pronounce their *consonant sounds* in pretty much the same way. That's right—Australians and Americans pronounce almost all their consonant sounds alike!

Accents in these countries are varied mostly because people pronounce their *vowel sounds* differently.

! In case you have forgotten—the vowels are: a, e, i, o, u. The remaining twenty-one letters in the alphabet are called consonants.

In India, many of us actually pronounce our consonant sounds differently from the rest of the world. This makes it difficult for us to be understood at times. Also, this is a major reason why many of us are told that we have 'mother tongue influences' or thick regional accents.

In truth, we are not focusing on our consonant sounds enough. By doing so, anyone can become an effective global communicator. This chapter, as well as the following chapters, will help you improve your consonant sounds.

Before you proceed, take a deep breath. Don't get frustrated if you can't understand a particular sound, or if you find some sounds hard to create. This is normal. To succeed in improving your accent, you have to learn to really *listen* to yourself. Don't just *think* about the way you speak; instead, learn to *feel* the way you speak—pay attention to how your lungs, mouth, teeth and tongue work together to create different sounds. Let's start the lesson by trying to understand what a sound actually is.

15.3 SOUNDS VERSUS LETTERS

It is very important to understand the difference between *letters* and *sounds*. Two words containing the *same letter* may produce *different sounds* when spoken. Likewise, one letter may produce several different sounds.

The Alphabet

- In the English language, we have one alphabet.
- This alphabet contains twenty-six letters (a-z).
- These twenty-six letters produce forty-four sounds.

For example, try saying the two words below, and pay close attention to how they sound:

- Giraffe
- Goat

Notice that the 'g' in 'giraffe' and the 'g' in 'goat' do not sound the same. Even though these two words start with the same *letter* 'g', they produce *different sounds*.

Now, see how the following words start with either the letters k, c or q, but produce the *same* 'kah' sound:

- **C**at
- **K**ing
- **Q**uick

This does not mean, though, that all words that begin with the letters c, k or q will produce the 'kah' sound. For example:

- **C**ease—Here, the letter 'c' takes on a 'sah' sound.
- **K**nack—Here, the 'k' is silent so the word is pronounced 'nack'.

For Hindi speakers, this may be confusing because in Hindi, letters and sounds match each other. As we can see from the above examples, English sounds are more complicated. But they are not completely random. In the English language, just as we have a dictionary of words, we also have a dictionary of sounds called the phonetic dictionary. Here, each word is defined by the way it sounds.

! How can I possibly learn how each and every word sounds?

Well, you can't exactly memorize the entire phonetic dictionary! But what you *can* do is pay attention to the rest of this section while also increasing your exposure to spoken English. Watch English TV programmes, news shows and movies, and practise speaking English as much as possible, and you will find yourself making progress surprisingly fast.

15.4 DIFFERENT TYPES OF CONSONANT SOUNDS

Let's start with the ways in which we make different consonant sounds.

Most consonant sounds have one or more of the following three qualities:

1. Strong, aspirated, 'air' sounds, like 'kah!', which is technically called the 'plosive'.
2. Weak, throat sounds like 'ba', which are technically called the 'voiced'.
3. Friction sounds like 'sah'.

Before we get into learning about individual consonant sounds, let's learn what these three qualities mean.

1. Strong, aspirated 'air' sounds like 'kah'

Definition of the sound:

- For 'air' or aspirated sounds, air from our lungs is held back either by our lips or our tongue, and then released to cause a small explosion. For this kind of sound, you need to 'let the air come out'.
- This is a strong sound because the air needed is forceful.
- We do not use the vocal chords in our throat to produce this type of sound. Whispering, for example, is always aspirated (try whispering and notice the amount of air that comes out of your mouth).

! While practising this sound, place one hand in front of your mouth so you feel the gush of air.

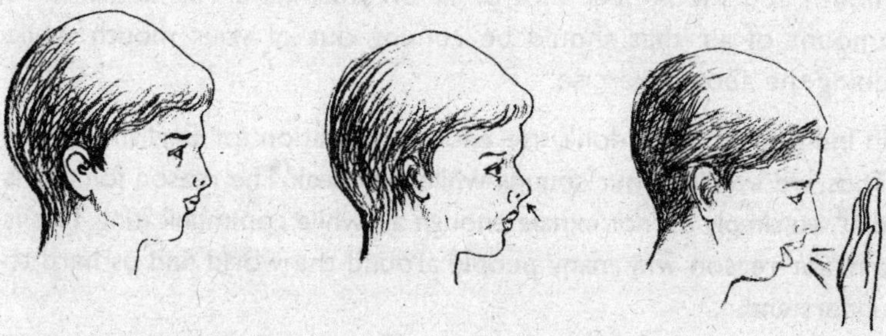

How to do it

- Put your hand in front of your mouth.
- Close your lips together so that no air can escape.
- Take a deep breath through your nose.
- Open your lips, but keep the air in your mouth.
- Let out a loud gasp of air from your mouth in a 'kah!' sound.
- The 'ah' signifies the large gasp of air you should have felt on your hand. This is what we mean by 'letting the air come out'.
- Do this a few times until you are completely comfortable with this concept.

Use Hindi sounds to understand aspiration

If the above instructions sounded confusing and you still can't understand the concept of aspiration, take a look at the exercise below.

1. Try saying the Hindi sound क (ka)—This sound has no aspiration (air).
2. Now try saying the Hindi sound ख (kha)—This is an aspirated (air) sound.

Now go back and forth between क (ka) and ख (kha). Place one hand in front of your mouth to feel the difference. You should feel more air on your hand for the ख (kha) sound.

- The Hindi sound ख (kha) is closest to the English sound 'Kah'.
- Any time you are confused about how to aspirate, remember the difference between the Hindi क (ka) and ख (kha) sounds.

If you are still not quite sure if enough air is coming out of your mouth, try whispering while keeping one hand in front of your mouth. You should feel a lot of air on your hand. This is the same amount of air that should be coming out of your mouth while doing the above exercise.

In India, most of us don't use enough aspiration for English sounds. Thus, we 'swallow' our sounds while we speak. The reason for this is that we simply do not exhale enough air while communicating. This is a major reason why many people around the world find us hard to understand.

Now, let's compare this with a throat, non-air sound (the opposite of what we just did).

2. Weak, throat ('non-air') sounds like 'ba'

Definition of the sound:

- Produced using the vocal chords in our throat.
- This is a weak sound because we don't aspirate, or use air.

! While making this sound, place one hand in front of your mouth and place your other hand on your throat. You should *not* have felt a gush of air on your hand. You should instead have felt a vibration in your throat.

How to Do It
- Close your lips together so that no air can escape.
- Sharply open your mouth and get out a 'ba' sound.

! There is no aspiration required for throat sounds. The Hindi sound क (ka) that we covered above is an example of a throat sound.

Now compare 'kah' to 'ba':

Make the 'kah' sound again and then alternate to the 'ba' sound with one hand in front of your mouth and other the on your throat. You will notice two things:

- The 'kah' sound results in *more* air (which you should feel on your hand in front of your mouth), and *less* movement in the throat (which you should feel on the hand placed on your throat). This is called an aspirated (air) sound simply because it is caused by air.
- The 'ba' sound results in less air on the hand and a lot of movement in the throat. This is called a throat sound because its strength comes from your throat.

Why is it so important to bring out air for certain sounds like 'kah'?

- It will make your words more easily understood.
- It makes what you're saying more audible, helping your words sound clearer.
- It slows down the rate of your speech, which also helps you to sound clearer.

Next, let's move on to tongue and teeth placements.

3. Friction sounds—like 'sah'

Definition:

- Can be both a throat or an aspirated sound.
- To produce this type of sound, push air out from your lungs through a narrow opening in our mouth. As the opening is narrow, friction will result in a hissing noise.
- The opening in your mouth is narrowed or widened by the way you place your teeth.

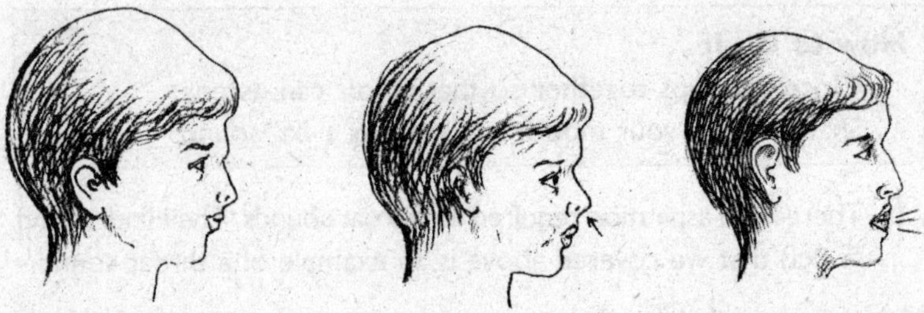

How to do it

- Place your upper teeth on top of your lower teeth so they just touch.
- Take a deep breath and blow a strong amount of air out so that it sounds like 'ssss'.
- Air will escape through an opening between your teeth.
- This 'ssss' hissing noise is referred to as 'friction'.

These are the three main qualities that consonant sounds have. The individual sounds that we will learn about in the following chapters will have one or more of these qualities.

Exercise 15.1

Answer the following questions.

1. What differentiates the way English is spoken around the world?
2. Why do so many Indians find it hard to communicate globally?
3. Does each letter of the alphabet have one particular sound?
4. What is an aspirated sound? What is another name for it?
5. What is the opposite of an aspirated sound? Give an example.
6. What is a friction sound?

APPLYING WHAT YOU HAVE LEARNED

1. Around the world, people tend to pronounce their consonant sounds the same way. However, in India, we tend to 'swallow' our consonant sounds, therefore sometimes making our accent hard to be understood globally.

2. Improving your consonant sounds will help you sound clearer, more articulate, more professional and be easily understood globally.
3. The twenty-six letters in the English alphabet produce forty-four sounds. Don't make the mistake of thinking the same letter will always create the same sound.
4. There are three main qualities that sounds have:
   - Aspirated, 'air' sounds are caused when lots of air comes out of the mouth.
   - Throat sounds are caused by a strong vibration in the throat. Very little air should escape from the mouth.
   - Friction sounds are formed by the placement of the teeth. These sounds can be aspirated or throat based.

CHAPTER 16

Neutralizing your accent through 'air' sounds

The 'pah', 'kah' and 'tah' sounds

In the previous chapter, we learnt how to use air, our vocal chords and teeth to create different types of sounds. In this chapter, we will focus specifically on aspirated sounds (like 'kah'). Refer to the previous chapter if you need to refresh your memory on how to produce an aspirated sound.

What will I learn in this chapter?

16.1	How to make the 'pah' sound.
16.2	How to make the 'kah' sound.
16.3	How to make the 'tah' sound.
16.4	Mastering the 'pah', 'kah', 'tah' sounds.

Don't worry if you are uneasy or feel out of breath while practising these sounds. It is normal to feel uneasy when using so much air at once.

16.1 HOW TO MAKE THE 'PAH' SOUND

Basic sound rules:

1. Strong sound.
2. Aspirated, 'air' (lots of air through the mouth).

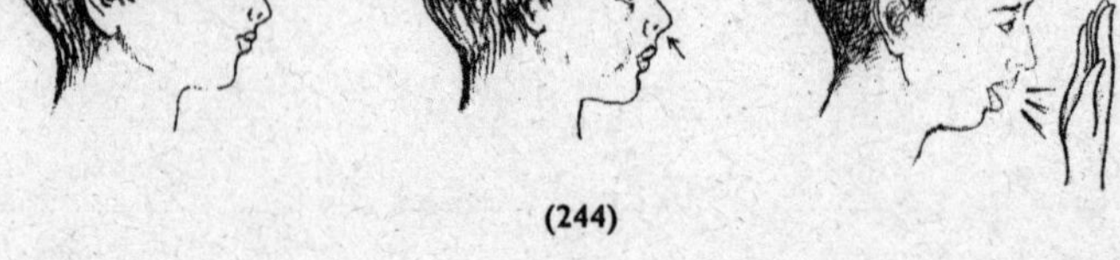

How to make the 'pah' sound:

1. Close your lips.
2. Take a deep breath from your nose and hold the air in your mouth.
3. Open your lips and say 'pah!' while letting out a gasp of air.
4. Hold the palm of your hand in front of your mouth and repeat the exercise—you should feel a lot of air on your palm.

! Any time you see the letter 'p' in an English word, pretend there is an aspirated 'ah' sound after every 'p' sound and let out a gasp of air so it sounds like a 'pah'.

Compare it to Hindi: Don't use the Hindi प (pa) sound!

1. Try saying the Hindi प (pa) sound while placing your hand in front of your mouth. You will notice there is little or no aspiration (air) coming out of your mouth.
2. The English 'pah' sound is different—it needs lots of air.
3. To create the English 'pah' sound, start with the Hindi प (pa) sound, and add lots of aspiration.

Practice exercise

Practise saying the following words with 'pah' sounds while keeping your hand in front of your mouth. It is very important that air comes out of your mouth when saying the 'pah' sound, regardless of whether the letter 'p' falls in the *beginning, middle* or *end* of the word.

For example, the word 'paper' should sound like 'payh-pehr'.

Paper	Up	Pepsi	Support
Page	Party	Apply	Please
Expect	Passionate	Position	Tape
Apologize	Pause	Apparel	People
Possible	Coop	Possessive	Pay
Put	Pen	Purpose	Leap
Help	Per	Japan	Type
Keep	Per cent	Nap	Open

16.2 HOW TO MAKE THE 'KAH' SOUND

Basic sound rules:

1. Strong sound.
2. Aspirated, 'air' (lots of air through the mouth).

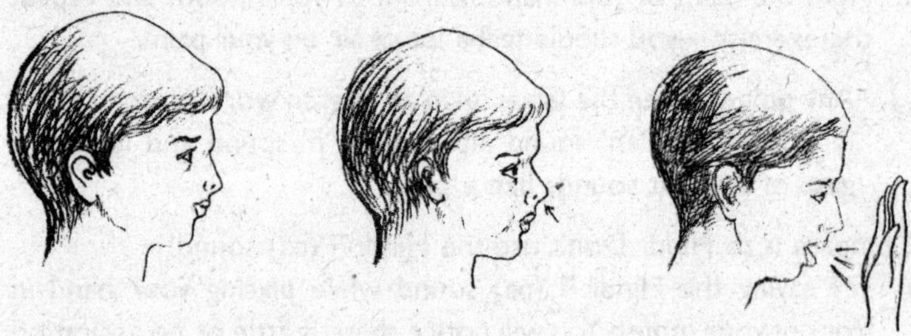

How to make the 'kah' sound:

1. With your mouth open, take a deep breath through your nose and hold the air in your mouth.
2. Let out a gasp of air and say 'kah!'
3. Repeat the exercise while holding the palm of your hand in front of your mouth—you should feel a lot of air on your palm.

Common error: don't use the Hindi क (ka) sound!

1. Try saying the Hindi क (ka) sound while holding your hand in front of your mouth. You will notice there is very little aspiration (air) from your mouth.
2. Do not use the Hindi क (ka) sound.
3. Now, try saying the Hindi ख (kha) sound while placing your hand in front of your mouth. You will feel much more air on your hand.
4. The English 'kah' sound is similar to the Hindi ख (kha) sound. You just need to add more air.

Practice exercise

Practise saying the following words with 'kah' sounds while holding your hand in front of your mouth. When the letters 'k', 'c' or 'q' fall in the middle of the word, the 'kah' sound will be slightly less forceful than if the letters 'k', 'c' or 'q' fall in the *beginning* or *end* of the word.

Can	Second	Calcutta	Music
Can't	Quick	Campaign	Black
Account	Take	Cash	Courage
Call	Customer	Pack	Courier
Tackle	Count	Compliment	Perfect
Cat	Cake	Comprehend	Tick
Case	Morocco	Kosher	Lacking
Become	Mistake	King	Kiss

16.3 HOW TO MAKE THE 'TAH' SOUND

The 'tah' sound is another 'air' sound. However, it is more complex than the 'pah' and 'kah' sounds—it requires careful concentration on tongue placement. Pay close attention to the directions below and keep the 'air' in mind while you focus on your tongue.

Basic sound rules:

1. Strong sound.
2. Aspirated, 'air' (lots of air comes out of the mouth).

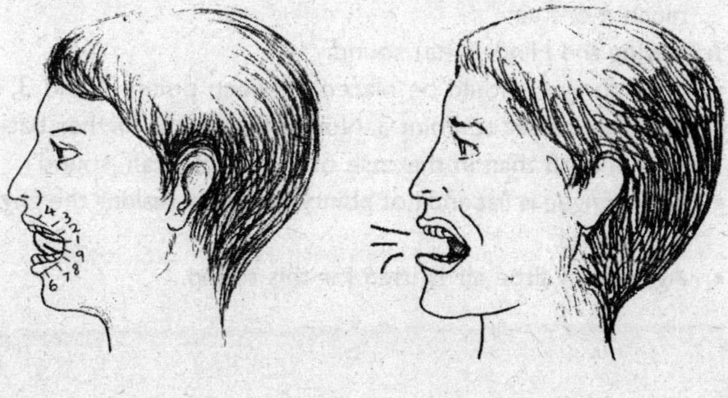

Explanation:

1. Place *only the tip* of your tongue on Point 4—this is the area on the roof of your mouth where the skin touches the teeth.
2. Lower your tongue sharply and let out a gasp of air (as when you were producing the 'pah' and 'kah' sounds) out of your mouth.
3. Do the exercise again while holding the palm of your hand in front of your mouth—you should feel a large amount of air on your palm.
4. Be careful that your tongue does not go further back than Point 4—even Point 3 is too far back.

! As with the 'pah' and 'kah' sounds, pretend there is an aspirated 'ah' sound after every 't' sound and let out a gasp of air—so it sounds like 'tah'.

Common error: don't use the Hindi त (ta) and ट (ta) sounds:

1. Try saying the Hindi त (ta) sound.
   - The tip of your tongue should be placed below Point 4. Notice that this is just a bit lower than where you placed your tongue for the English 'tah' sound.
   - Your tongue is flat and the sides touch the area below Point 4. This is quite different from the English 'tah' sound where your tongue needs to be pointy and only the tip is used (not the sides).
   - Hold your hand in front of your mouth. You will *not* feel much air for the Hindi त (ta) sound. The English 'tah' sound requires much more air.
2. Try saying the Hindi ट (ta) sound.
   - Your tongue should be placed between points 2 and 3, but probably closer to Point 3. Notice that this is further back in your mouth than in the case of the English 'tah' sound.
   - Your tongue is flat and not pointy like when making the English 'tah' sound.
   - Again, very little air is used for this sound.

	English 'Tah' Sound **T**atter	Hindi त (ta) Sound कुर्ता (kurta)	Hindi ट (ta) Sound बेटी (beti)
Tongue Placement	Point 4	Just Below Point 4	Between Point 2–3 (closer to 3)
Tongue Width	Use tip of the tongue	Flat (use tip and sides)	Flat (use tip and sides)
Aspiration	Lots of air	No air	No air

! As you can see from the above chart, tongue placement for the English 'tah' sound is similar to the Hindi त (ta) sound. Remember to keep the tip of your tongue pointed and add air.

Practice exercise

Practise saying the following words with 'tah' sounds while holding your hand in front of your mouth. It is very important that air comes out of your mouth when saying the 'tah' sound, regardless of whether the letter 't' falls in the *beginning*, *middle* or *end* of the word.

For example, the word 'tatter' should sound like 'tah-tehr'.

Take	Telephone	Eight	It
Tall	Temporary	Today	Sitting
Table	Tide	About	Positive
What	Let	Ten	Outing
Tax	Time	Interview	Tunnel
Teacher	Tiger	Activities	Suggest
Tell	Attack	Not	Might
At	Tomorrow	Tube	Complete

As a rule, when the letter 'h' follows the letter 't' in any word, a 'THah' sound is produced. The 'THah' sound is different from the 'tah' sound we just learned. We will cover the 'THah' sound in the next chapter.

Exercise 16.1

Answer the following questions:

1. How would you describe the 'pah', 'kah' and 'tah' sounds?
2. Where should you place your tongue for the 'tah' sound?

16.4 FLUENCY WHILE PRACTISING AIR SOUNDS

Let's try a practice exercise. Try saying these sounds in the order given. First say them slowly, then more quickly. Hold one hand in front of your mouth at all times to ensure that the flow of air is forceful.

Pah – Kah – Tah
Pah – Kah – Tah
Pah – Pah – Kah – Kah – Tah – Tah
Pah – Pah – Pah – Kah – Kah – Kah – Tah – Tah – Tah
Pah – Kah – Pah – Kah – Tah – Pah
Pah – Tah – Kah – Tah – Pah – Kah – Pah – Kah – Tah
Pah – Kah – Tah – Pah – Kah – Tah – Pah – Kah – Kah – Tah – Tah – Pah – Pah – Kah

Exercise 16.2

Read the following sentences. Underline all the 'pah', 'kah', 'tah' sounds you see. Remember that letters and the sounds they create can be different. For example, the letter 'd' in 'wished' actually produces a 'tah' sound, so the word should sound like 'wisht'. We are only concerned with sounds in this exercise. Check your answers in the answer key. Then read these sentences out loud while focusing on the sounds you have learned. Repeat if necessary.

1. Pinky is a polite person with polished English, nice purses and lots of lipsticks.

2. It is customary to carry a container when coasting through customs.
3. Take a cookie from the cabinet and pack the cake from the table.
4. Tell me tonight what to take on the hunting trip.

Exercise 16.3

Read the passage. Underline all the 'pah', 'kah', 'tah' sounds that you see. Remember that letters and the sounds they create can be different. In this exercise we are concerned only with sounds. Check your answers against the answer key. Then read this passage out loud while focusing on the sounds you have learned. Repeat if necessary.

Kartik wanted to join Capita, a call centre for the position of agent. But, during his interview, his speech was unclear and he made many mistakes. His interviewer, Tanvi, told him to go home and practise speaking English clearly. At first Kartik was disappointed. After a few days, though, he decided to take Tanvi's advice and started practising. He bought a grammar book. He also started watching TV shows in English. Kartik spent night after night working to improve his English. After two months, he went back to Capita. Tanvi was impressed with him and his determination to improve his skill-set. Kartik got the job and also learned a very important lesson—hard work is the secret to success!

APPLYING WHAT YOU HAVE LEARNED

1. 'Pah', 'kah' and 'tah' are all aspirated, 'air' sounds. They require lots and lots of air from the mouth. The most common mistake people make is to not use enough air while making these sounds.
2. It doesn't really matter where in a word—the beginning, middle or end—these sounds fall. They tend to require lots of air regardless.

3. The 'tah' sound also requires you to be careful where you place your tongue. The tip of your tongue should be placed right where your skin touches your teeth on the roof of your mouth. If you place the tip of your tongue too far back in your mouth, you won't get the correct sound.
4. The 'tah' sound also requires your tongue to be pointy, so that only the tip is used. This is different from the other Hindi 'ta' sounds.

CHAPTER 17

Stick out your tongue!

The 'THah' sound

In the last chapter we focussed on aspirated sounds, or sounds requiring lots of air. In this chapter, we will look at the 'THah' sound—a sound that, believe it or not, requires you to stick out your tongue!

The idea of sticking out your tongue may sound weird or awkward to you, but don't worry. Once you get the hang of it you'll see that this pronunciation technique will start occurring naturally.

What will I learn in this chapter?

17.1 How to make the 'THah' sound.
17.2 An exception to the 'THah' sound.
17.3 Compare and master the 'tah' and 'THah' sounds.

17.1 HOW TO MAKE THE 'THAH' SOUND

The 'THah' sound is different from the 'tah' sound we covered earlier in this section. When the letter 'h' follows the letter 't' in any word, it creates a sound of its own—'THah'. Many people find this sound slightly difficult to learn, as it requires you to focus on where you place your tongue as well as to use lots of air. Be careful not to confuse the 'THah' sound with the 'da' or 'tah' sounds. Follow the instructions given below carefully, and you should be able to learn this sound easily.

Basic sound rules:

1. Strong sound.
2. Friction sound.
3. Aspirated, 'air' (lots of air through the mouth).

Common errors:

1. You don't stick your tongue out, instead you tend to keep your tongue placed behind your teeth.
2. You don't release enough air.

How to make the 'THah' sound:

1. Put the tip of your tongue (and even a little more for clarity) between your upper and lower teeth (touching your upper teeth)—so your tongue should be 'sticking out'.
2. Blow hard and feel the air coming out on the sides of your tongue—this 'friction' sound is what you want to feel when pronouncing words with this sound.
3. To make this sound, blow out air while your tongue is sticking out, and then bring your tongue back into your mouth to form a 'THah!'
4. Hold your hand in front of your mouth and repeat this exercise—you should feel a sharp gush of air on your palm.

! It is crucial that your tongue is 'sticking out' a bit (even if you feel funny doing so). Hold a mirror in front of you while practising to make sure you are doing this correctly.

Compare the English 'THah' sound to the Hindi थ (tha) sound:

1. Try making the Hindi थ (tha) sound while holding your hand in front of your mouth. You will notice there is a good amount of air coming out of your mouth.
2. Make the Hindi थ (tha) sound again, but this time pay attention to where you place your tongue. You will notice the tip of your tongue is behind your top teeth, almost sticking out.
3. The English 'THah' sound is similar to the Hindi थ (tha) sound. You just need to add more air and stick your tongue out even further.

! Make sure that your tongue is in the position described above. Also, it is very important that air comes out of your mouth when making the 'THah' sound, regardless of whether the letters 'th' fall in the *beginning, middle* or *end* of the word.

Practice exercise

Practise saying the following words while keeping your tongue in the position described. Hold your hand in front of your mouth. In these examples the 'THah' sound is at the beginning of the word.

Thank	Thirsty	Thought
Thaw	Thirty	Thorough
Theory	Thing	Thorny
Thermal	Throw	Thumb
Thistle	Therapy	Thunder
Three	Thug	Thigh

Practice exercise

Practise saying the following words while keeping your tongue in the position described. Hold your hand in front of your mouth. In these examples the 'THah' sound is in the middle of the word.

Healthy	Mathematics	Something
Wealthy	Catholic	Anything
Cathy	Earthy	

Practice exercise

Practise saying the following words while keeping your tongue in the position described. Hold your hand in front of your mouth. In these examples the 'THah' sound is at the end of the word.

Bath	Death	Mouth
Both	Earth	Myth
Breath	Fourth	South
Cloth	Month	Path

17.2 AN EXCEPTION TO THE 'THAH' SOUND—THE WEAK 'TH'

There is one exception to the 'THah' sound. Sometimes we don't need to stick our tongue out and release that much air. We call this type of exception the weak 'th' sound. For the weak 'th', keep your tongue behind your teeth and lessen the amount of air you use. The weak 'th' sound occurs for the following types of words:

The	Those	Them
Then	Thus	Their

Also, when the letter 'e' follows the letters 'th' (to form a 'the') in any word, the same weak 'TH' sound exception applies. This tends to occur when 'the' falls in the *middle* or *end* of a word. Examples include:

Brea**the**	Fa**the**r	Ga**the**r	Ba**the**

For the most part though, stick to practising the 'THah' sound. Chances are you will automatically know when to use the weak 'th' sound.

Practice exercise

Let's practise going back and forth between the 'THah' and the weak 'th' sounds. Remember to stick your tongue out and exhale air for the 'THah' sounds. For the weak 'th' sounds, keep your tongue behind your teeth and lessen the amount of air you expel.

Normal: Therapy	Normal: Thunder	Normal: Thank
Weak: Then	Weak: Thus	Weak: Than

Normal: Author	Normal: Anything	Normal: Something
Weak: Brother	Weak: Clothes	Weak: Neither

Normal: Bath	Normal: Cloth	Normal: Teeth
Weak: Bathe	Weak: Clothe	Weak: Teethe

Exercise 17.1

Read the following sentences. Underline all the 'THah' sounds. Check your answers against the answer key. Then read these sentences out loud while focusing on the 'THah' sounds. Repeat if necessary.

1. Think about the theory of thermal thunder.
2. The growth of thorns is anything but earthy.
3. 'Have faith,' said the father to the thief.
4. Death is nothing but a path to take.

Exercise 17.2

Read the passage given below. Underline all the 'THah' sounds and circle all the weak 'th' sounds. Then read these sentences out loud while focusing on these sounds. Repeat if necessary.

```
The theory that Theodore thought of was nothing
but wrong math. Thus, Theodore's father paid a
wealthy sum to Cathy to further think through the
theory.
```

17.3 COMPARE AND MASTER THE 'TAH' AND 'THAH' SOUNDS

In the previous chapter we went over the 'tah' sound. Just so that you don't get confused, let's compare the 'tah' sound with the 'THah' sound:

- What the 'tah' and 'THah' sounds have in common: both sounds require lots of air so hold one hand in front of your mouth when practising to ensure you are using enough air.

- How the 'tah' and 'THah' sounds are different: for the 'tah' sound your tongue should remain behind your teeth whereas for the 'THah' sound your tongue should touch the teeth but also slightly stick out beyond them.

Let's practise the 'tah' and 'THah' sounds. Try making the sounds given below in the correct order. First say them slowly, then more quickly. Make sure you are focusing on your tongue placement.

THah – Tah – Tah
Tah – THah – THah
THah – Tah – THah – Tah – THah – Tah
Tah – Tah – THah – THah – Tah – THah – Tah – THah – Tah
THah – Tah – THah – Tah – Tah – THah – Tah – THah – THah – Tah
THah – THah – THah – THah

Exercise 17.3

Read the passage given below. Underline all the 'THah' sounds and circle all the 'tah' sounds. Then read these sentences out loud while focusing on the 'THah' and 'tah' sounds. Hold one hand in front of your mouth to make sure you are aspirating properly. Repeat if necessary.

> Tonight is Martha's birthday party. I have not got her anything yet. I think I will take her a tennis racket as she has a thing for sports. On Thursday I am taking her, Thelma, and my three brothers to a tennis tournament.

Exercise 17.4

Answer the following questions:

1. Where should your tongue be placed for the 'THah' sound?
2. What are some of the characteristics of the 'THah' sound?
3. What is the difference between the 'THah' sound and the weak 'th' sound?
4. How are the 'tah' and 'THah' sounds different? In what way are they similar?

APPLYING WHAT YOU HAVE LEARNED

1. The 'THah' sound requires the tip of your tongue to come out of your mouth.
2. For the 'THah' sound you need to aspirate, so you also need air to come out of your mouth. As your tongue is sticking out, the air will cause a 'friction' sound as it makes its way through the gap between your tongue and teeth.
3. The 'THah' sound has one exception—the weak 'th'. For certain words like 'the', 'thus', 'then' and other words containing 'the' within them (ba**the**, bro**the**r), you don't stick your tongue out between your teeth. Also, you don't aspirate.
4. It's good to practise the 'THah' sound with the 'tah' sound as they both are strong, require air, and need concentration on tongue placement.

CHAPTER 18

Common consonant sound errors—tongue related

'Da', 'tah', 'na' and 'ra' sounds

Dear Nasha,

I have a peculiar problem with my voice. I often have to repeat the same thing three to four times in order to communicate with others. This problem gets intensified when I am in a noisy room, or if I have to speak to a person standing far away from me. Most of the time, the people I am speaking to can hardly follow what I am saying. I am a competitive professional and I have never had a big setback in my educational and professional career. However, I really worry that I am losing many opportunities, as I often fail to communicate properly. Could you please suggest a remedy for this?

I received this email from one of my students. This person is clearly frustrated at being misunderstood while speaking. It may make him feel better to know that many of us have the same problem—of confusing certain sounds with others, resulting in people not being able to understand what we are saying. This happens because many consonant sounds are actually very similar. If you place your tongue even slightly in the wrong place or aspirate improperly, you create the wrong sound.

From the previous chapter, you should have understood the importance of tongue placement. This chapter will continue to focus on sounds that require careful attention to tongue placement.

What will I learn in this chapter?

18.1 MAKING THE 'DA' SOUND

Basic sound rules:
1. Weak sound.
2. Throat (no air).

How to make the 'da' sound:
1. Place only the tip of your tongue on Point 4—this is the area on the roof of your mouth where the skin touches the teeth. (See diagram on page 262)
2. Lower your tongue sharply, but do not let out a gasp of air.
3. Repeat the exercise while holding one hand in front of your mouth, and placing the other hand on your throat—you should feel little or no air on your palm and lots of vibration in your throat.
4. Be careful that your tongue does not go further up than point 4—even Point 3 is too high.

Common mistake: don't use the Hindi ड (da) sound!
1. Try making the Hindi ड (da) sound. You will notice that your tongue placement is between Points 2–3 in the diagram on page 262, and your tongue is flat.
2. For the English 'da' sound, you need to bring your tongue forward to Point 4.
3. Also, you need to use only the tip of your tongue for the English 'da' sound.

18.2 COMPARE THE 'DA' AND 'TAH' SOUNDS

The 'tah' sound we covered previously is often confused with the 'da' sound. This happens because the two sounds share similar traits. Let's see what these sounds have in common, and how they are different. Pay close attention while you practise these sounds to make sure you are differentiating between them correctly.

How the 'tah' and 'da' sounds are similar

1. Both sounds have *identical* tongue placements. For those of you who have forgotten where the tongue should be placed for the 'tah' sound, let's do a quick recap:
   - Place *only* the tip of your tongue on Point 4—this is the area on the roof of your mouth where the skin touches the teeth.
   - Be careful not to place your tongue too far back in your mouth (at Points 3, 2 or 1).
2. Both sounds require the tongue to be pointed and not flat.

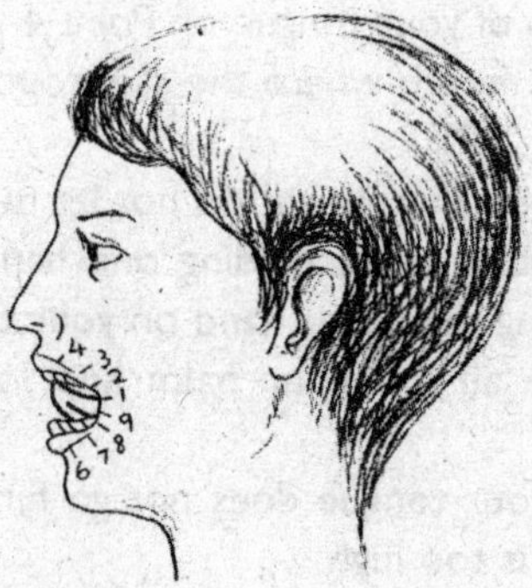

How the 'tah' and 'da' sounds are different

1. The 'tah' sound is an aspirated sound, created by using lots of air.
2. The 'da' sound is a throat sound, created by vibration in your throat and with very little or no air coming out of the mouth.

18.3 PRACTISING THE 'TAH' AND 'DA' SOUNDS FLUENTLY

- For both the 'tah' and 'da' sounds, make sure the tip of your tongue stays at Point 4.
- As the 'tah' and 'da' sounds have identical tongue placements, don't forget to use lots of air for the 'tah' sound. This is very important in order to distinguish it from the 'da' sound.

Remember the above rules while doing the following exercises.

Practice exercise

Try making the sounds given below in order. First say them slowly, then more quickly.

Tah – Da – Da
Da – Tah – Tah
Tah – Da – Tah – Da – Tah – Da
Da – Da – Tah – Tah – Da – Tah – Da – Tah – Da
Tah – Da – Tah – Da – Da – Tah – Da – Tah – Tah – Da – Tah – Tah – Tah – Da

Practice exercise

Practise saying the following words containing the 'tah' and 'da' sounds while holding your hand in front of your mouth. You should feel a gush of air on your hand *only for the 'tah' sound*. For both the 'tah' and 'da' sounds, make sure your tongue is pointed and touches the roof of your mouth where the skin touches your teeth.

Ten	Tan	Bed
Den	Dan	About
Time	At	Should
Dine	Had	Eight
Tummy	Let	Bade
Dummy	Dog	Tag

Exercise 18.1

Read the following sentences. Underline all the 'tah' sounds and circle all the 'da' sounds. Check your answers against the answer key. Then read these sentences out loud while focusing on your tongue placement and aspiration. Pay attention to the difference between the 'tah' and 'da' sounds. Repeat if necessary.

1. I want to eat dinner downstairs tonight.
2. Madonna is a music star with lots of beauty, diamonds and dollars.
3. I had tears tonight when I dreamt of dancing with Dev Anand.
4. Dwarnik submitted the tax deposit ten days after it was due.

Exercise 18.2

Read the passage given below. Underline all the 'tah' sounds and circle all the 'da' sounds. Check your answers against the answer key. Then read the passage out loud while focusing on your tongue placement for both sounds. Also, pay attention to the difference between the 'tah' and 'da' sounds. Repeat if necessary.

> Tarun took too much time to study and turn in his presentation. It was due on Tuesday but Tarun finished it on Wednesday. His teacher, Mrs Jadhav, was impatient and upset. Tarun felt terrible and thought, 'What's the matter with me?' Tarun promised to do a better job next time around and during the week was extra polite to Mrs Jadhav.

18.4 HOW TO MAKE THE 'NA' SOUND

The 'na' sound is fairly easy to learn. It has the exact same tongue placement as the 'tah' and 'da' sounds.

Basic sound rules:

1. Weak sound.
2. Throat (no 'air').
3. Nasal sound.

How to make the 'na' sound:

1. Just like for the 'tah' and 'da' sounds learned earlier in this section, place only the tip of your tongue on Point 4—this is the area on the roof of your mouth where the skin touches the teeth.
2. Lower your tongue sharply, but do not let out a gasp of air.
3. Repeat the exercise while holding one hand in front of your mouth and keeping the other hand on your throat—you should feel little or no air on your palm and lots of vibration in your throat.
4. Take care that your tongue does not go further up than Point 4—even Point 3 is too high.

Common error: don't use the Hindi न (na) sound!

1. Try making the Hindi न (na) sound. You will notice that your tongue is placed between Points 2–3 (see diagram on page 262) and your tongue is flat.
2. For the English 'na' sound, you need to bring your tongue forward to Point 4.
3. Also, you need to use only the tip of your tongue for the English 'na' sound.

- The 'tah', 'da' and 'na' sounds all share the same tongue placements.
- Only the 'tah' sound requires the use of lots of air.
- The 'da' and 'na' sounds should both result in lots of vibration in your throat.

Practice exercise

Practise the following words containing the 'tah', 'da' and 'na' sounds while holding your hand in front of your mouth. You should feel a gush of air on your hand *only for the 'tah' sound*. For all three sounds, make sure your tongue is pointed and touches the roof of your mouth where the skin touches the teeth.

Table	Dampen	Nagpur
Data	Neglect	Temporary
Neat	Tangible	Duplicate
Talking	Disappoint	Afternoon

Exercise 18.3

Read the passage given below. Underline all the 'tah' sounds and circle all the 'da' and 'na' sounds. Check your answers against the answer key. Then read the passage out loud while focusing on your tongue placement for all three sounds. Also pay attention to the difference between them. Repeat multiple times if necessary.

```
The house that Anand and Tinaz lived in was divided into nine sections. Anand never felt the need to hang out in the top two sections. He instead spent time during the day in the drawing room and time at night in the master bedroom. Teresa on the other hand, did something different. She spent her time in the typing room, nursery room and dining area.
```

From the explanations given above, you should have noticed that English sounds differ from Hindi sounds in the following ways:

- The tongue is more forward and is placed closer to the teeth.
- Most sounds require you to use only the tip of the tongue.

! Many of us use Hindi sounds while speaking in English and thus either don't bring our tongues close enough to our teeth, or don't use enough air. We should be mindful of this so that we do not 'swallow' our English sounds.

18.5 HOW TO MAKE THE 'RA' SOUND

Try making the Hindi र (ra) sound. Now say the Hindi word मेरा (mera). You will notice that your tongue curls back in your mouth and the tip of your tongue rubs the roof of your mouth.

This should not occur while making the English 'ra' sound—your tongue should not, at any time, touch the roof of your mouth.

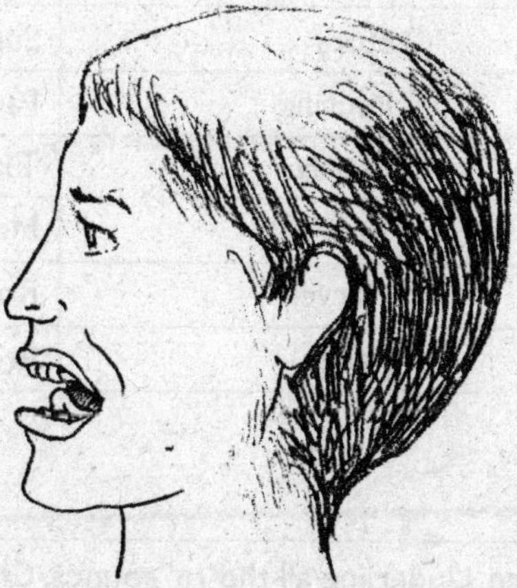

Basic sound rules:
1. Weak sound.
2. Throat (no 'air').

How to make the 'ra' sound:
1. Open your mouth like you are about to make the Hindi र (ra) sound.
2. However, unlike the Hindi र (ra) sound, make sure your tongue *does not* touch the roof of your mouth.
3. To do this, try dropping your jaw so that your tongue is further away from the roof of your mouth.

Practice exercise

Practise saying the following words containing the 'ra' sound. Make sure your tongue does not touch the roof of your mouth. Pay attention to the position of your jaw.

Ran	Righteous	Borrow
River	Are	Sorry
Ronald	Already	Caring
Rose	Arrange	Star

Very	Story	Super
Real	Pouring	Parent
Morning	Clarify	Turkey
Purge	Tariff	Murky
Rearrange	Marvel	Roar
Rectify	Range	Row

Exercise 18.4

Read the passage. Underline all the 'ra' sounds. Check your answers against the answer key. Then read the passage out loud while focusing on your tongue placement. Repeat if necessary.

> The arrow broke in three parts. Ruki ridiculously rotated it and then ripped her dress. She then rode her horse to Rajasthan while making her poor dog run with her. What a terrible person she is!

Exercise 18.5

Answer the following questions.

1. What does it mean to 'swallow your sounds'?
2. What do the 'tah' and 'da' sounds have in common?
3. How are the 'tah' and 'da' sounds different?
4. How is the 'na' sound similar to the 'tah' and 'da' sounds?
5. What should you always avoid when making the 'ra' sound?

APPLYING WHAT YOU HAVE LEARNED

1. When making the 'da' and 'na' sounds, your tongue should be at Point 4 in the diagram provided in this chapter (where the skin on the roof of your mouth touches your teeth). If your tongue is placed further back in your mouth, these sounds will come out wrong.

2. For the 'da' and 'na' sounds, your tongue should always be pointed and not flat (only the tip should touch the roof of your mouth).
3. The 'da' and 'na' sounds are similar to the 'tah' sound in that they all share the same tongue placement. The 'tah' sound is the only one out of the three that requires aspiration, or 'air'. The other two—'da' and 'na'—are throat sounds and thus require little or no air. The 'da' and 'na' sounds will both cause a vibration in your throat.
4. You should not let your tongue touch the roof of your mouth when making the 'ra' sound. To do this, make sure you drop your jaw.

CHAPTER 19

Common consonant sound errors—teeth related

The 'fah', 'va' and 'wa' sounds

In the previous chapter we learnt various sounds, which if made incorrectly can easily be mistaken for other, similar sounds. We learned that where you place your tongue and how much air you use changes the way people understand you. In this chapter, we will continue those lessons and learn about sounds that require focus on your teeth and lips.

What will I learn in this chapter?

19.1 How to make the 'fah' sound.
19.2 The difference between the 'fah' and 'pah' sounds.
19.3 Practising the 'fah' and 'pah' sounds fluently.
19.4 The 'va' sound.
19.5 Practising the 'fah' and 'va' sounds fluently.
19.6 The 'va' sound versus the 'wa' sound.
19.7 The difference between the 'va' and 'wa' sounds.
19.8 'Bite your Vs and kiss your Ws'

19.1 HOW TO MAKE THE 'FAH' SOUND

The English 'fah' sound is similar to the Hindi फ (fa) sound. You can start with this sound and then add lots of additional air to make the English 'fah' sound.

Basic sound rules:

1. Strong sound.
2. Aspirated, 'air' sound.

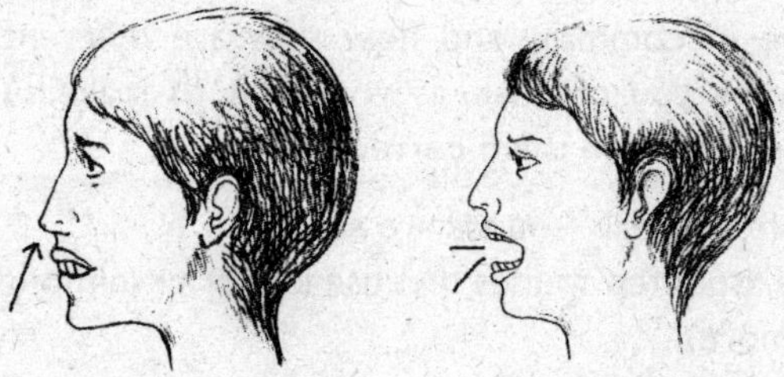

How to make the 'fah' sound:

1. Take a deep breath through your nose and hold the air in your mouth.
2. Bite your upper teeth down on your lower lip like you are about to make the Hindi फ (fa) sound.
3. Drop your lower lip and let out a gasp of air and say 'fah!'.
4. Repeat the exercise while holding the palm of your hand in front of your mouth—you should feel a lot of air on your palm.

! Whenever you see the letter 'f' in an English word, try to make an aspirated 'ah' sound after every 'f' sound and let out a gasp of air so it sounds like a 'fah'. It is very important that air is expelled from your mouth when making the 'fah' sound, regardless of whether the letter 'f' falls in the *beginning*, *middle* or *end* of the word.

Practice exercise

Practise saying the following words while holding your hand in front of your mouth. Remember to bite down for the 'fah' sound!

Face	Fill	Calf
Fall	Laugh	Full
Feel	Fun	Future
Afford	Fool	Offer
Feather	Forty	Loafer

19.2 THE DIFFERENCE BETWEEN THE 'FAH' AND 'PAH' SOUNDS

The 'pah' sound is often confused with the 'fah' sound. This happens because the two sounds share similar traits. Let us learn what these sounds have in common, and how they are different. Pay close attention while you practise, as you want to make sure you are differentiating between them correctly.

How the 'fah' and 'pah' sounds are similar:

1. Both are aspirated sounds that use lots of air (although 'pah' uses slightly more).
2. Both are strong sounds.

That's right—if you hold your hand in front of your mouth while making both the 'fah' and 'pah' sounds, you should feel a similar gush of air. Now let's see how they are *different*.

How the 'fah' and 'pah' sounds are different:

1. The 'pah' sound is formed when you join your upper lip with your lower lip.
2. The 'fah' sound is formed when you join your upper *teeth* with your lower lip ('biting down').

As you can see, the key difference between these two sounds is the use of teeth for the 'fah' sound.

19.3 PRACTISING THE 'FAH' AND 'PAH' SOUNDS FLUENTLY

Let's attempt a practice exercise. Try making the following sounds in the given order. First make them slowly, then more quickly. Remember the rules you just learnt. You may want to look in a mirror while doing this exercise to make sure you are biting down for the 'fah' sound and joining your lips together for the 'pah' sound.

Fah – Pah – Pah
Pah – Fah – Fah
Fah – Pah – Fah – Pah – Fah – Pah
Pah – Pah – Fah – Fah – Pah – Fah – Pah – Fah – Pah
Fah – Pah – Fah – Pah – Pah – Fah – Pah – Fah – Fah – Pah – Fah – Fah – Fah – Pah

Practice exercise

Practise saying the following words containing 'fah' and 'pah' sounds while holding your hand in front of your mouth. You may want to look in a mirror while doing this exercise to make sure you are biting down for the 'fah' sound and joining your lips together for the 'pah' sound.

Father	Fickle	Foot	Furnace
Patter	Pickle	Put	Purpose

Exercise 19.1

Read the sentences given below. Underlinc all the 'fah' sounds and circle all the 'pah' sounds. Check your answers against the answer key. Then read these sentences out loud while focusing on the difference between the 'fah' and 'pah' sounds. Repeat if necessary.

1. Praful put on his flip-flops and flew to Paris.
2. Puffing away, Piyush appeared in front of the fort.
3. The party for Farukh was fun and was filled with family, friends and people from the office.
4. I support profit and will fight those who oppose self-made people.

Exercise 19.2

Read the passage given below. Underline all the 'fah' sounds and circle all the 'pah' sounds. Check your answers against the answer key. Then read the passage out loud while focusing on the difference between the 'fah' and 'pah' sounds. Repeat if necessary.

Payal and Firoze were pondering over their problem. They found that filling out forms was purposeless and felt they should focus on finer things. Firoze loved opera and painting pictures of flapping fireflies. Payal instead loved parties filled with food and fun people.

19.4 THE 'VA' SOUND

You should now be comfortable with the concept of biting down to produce the 'fah' sound. There is another sound that requires this same technique—the 'va' sound.

Most of us already know how to form the 'va' sound because it exists in Hindi—व (va). This sound is made pretty much the same way in English.

Basic sound rules:

1. Weak sound.
2. Throat (no 'air').

The 'fah' sound versus the 'va' sound

1. Similarities—they are both formed using the teeth-to-lower-lip placement.
2. Differences—the 'fah' sound requires lots of air and the 'va' sound requires none.

Hold the palm of one hand in front of your mouth, and place your other hand on your throat. Now, interchange between the 'fah' and 'va' sounds.

1. For the 'fah' sound, you should feel a large amount of air on your palm. You should feel very little vibration in your throat
2. For the 'va' sound, you should feel *no* air on your palm and *lots* of vibration in your throat.

! Remember to bite down for both sounds—teeth to lip interaction should be the same, regardless of whether the 'fah' or 'va' sound falls in the *beginning*, *middle* or *end* of the word.

Remember these rules while doing the following exercise.

19.5 PRACTISING THE 'FAH' AND 'VA' SOUNDS FLUENTLY

Let's try a practice exercise. Try making the following sounds in the order given. First make them slowly, then more quickly. Remember the above rules while doing this exercise, and the ones that follow.

Fah – Va – Va
Va – Fah – Fah
Fah – Va – Fah – Va – Fah – Va
Va – Va – Fah – Fah – Va – Fah – Va – Fah – Va
Fah – Va – Fah – Va – Va – Fah – Va – Fah – Fah – Va – Fah – Fah – Fah – Va

Practice exercise

Practise saying the following words while holding your hand in front of your mouth. Notice the difference in the air exhaled between the 'fah' and 'va' sounds. Remember to bite down for both.

Fast	Feel	Ferry	Focal
Vast	Veal	Very	Vocal

You should now understand that the 'va' sound is formed by biting your upper teeth down on your lower lip and that no air is needed.

19.6 THE 'VA' SOUND VERSUS THE 'WA' SOUND

The real issue with the 'va' sound comes when we compare it to the 'wa' sound. In Hindi, there is no sound that is similar to the English 'wa' sound. For this reason, many of us are in the habit of confusing the 'va' and 'wa' sounds.

Let's learn how to make the 'wa' sound.

Basic sound rules:

1. Weak sound.
2. Throat, no 'air' (except when followed by 'tah' and 'kah' sounds).

How to make the 'wa' sound:

1. Round up your lips as if you are about to say the vowel 'U'.
2. Your tongue should be drawn back.
3. Create a humming sound in your throat and say 'wwww'.
4. Now try saying the word 'wow'.
5. Repeat the above exercise while keeping one hand on your throat—you should feel a vibration in your throat.

Let's now take a look at how these two sounds are similar, and the ways in which they are different.

The 'va' sound versus the 'wa' sound

1. Similarities—they are both throat sounds that need lots of vibration in the throat, and no air is expelled.

2. Differences—the formation of your mouth is different for these two sounds. For the 'va' sound, you bite your upper teeth down on your lower lip. For the 'wa' sound, you scrunch your lips together in a 'u' form.

19.7 'BITE YOUR V'S AND KISS YOUR W'S'

The above phrase says it all. For the 'va' sound, remember to bite down. For the 'wa' sound, remember to make a kissing face.

The problem is not that we don't know how to make these two sounds. Instead, the issue is that we mix them up. So, for example, the word 'vowel' will end up sounding like 'wowel', or the word 'water' will end up sounding like 'vater'.

It is very important to pay attention when making these sounds. For the next exercise, stand in front of a mirror. Try making the following sounds in the given order while looking at your mouth in the mirror. Make sure that you are 'biting your v's and kissing your w's' correctly. First make the sounds slowly, then more quickly.

Wa – Va – Va
Va – Wa – Wa
Wa – Va – Wa – Va – Wa – Va
Va – Va – Wa – Wa – Va – Wa – Va – Wa – Va
Wa – Va – Wa – Va – Va – Wa – Va – Wa – Wa – Va – Wa – Wa – Wa – Va

! Remember to bite your upper teeth down on your lower lip for the 'va' sound. Remember to scrunch your mouth in a 'u' shape for the 'wa' sound.

Practice exercise
Underline all the 'va' sounds and circle all the 'wa' sounds. There could be multiple sounds in the same word. Then practise saying the following words while looking in the mirror. Pay attention to your mouth.

Wary	Wail	Wave
Very	Veil	Weave
Wine	Volkswagen	Woven
Vine	Vowel	Well-versed

Exercise 19.3

Read the sentences given below. Underline all the 'va' sounds and circle all the 'wa' sounds. Check your answers against the answer key. Then read these sentences out loud while focusing on the difference between the 'va' and 'wa' sounds. Look at yourself in the mirror for better results. Repeat multiple times if necessary.

1. Why wonder about very useless events?
2. Vertigo makes you wavy and uneven.
3. Wednesday is a wonderful day to visit active women.
4. Wacky, wild visitors are always welcome in my winter tavern.

Exercise 19.4

Read the passage given below. Underline all the 'va' sounds and circle all the 'wa' sounds. Check your answers against the answer key. Then read the passage out loud while focusing on the difference between the 'va' and 'wa' sounds. Look in the mirror for better results. Repeat multiple times if necessary.

> One day Vinaya was walking towards her valuable Volkswagen when she saw a woman she knew waiting near a veranda. Vinaya wondered what her name was. She questioned the woman who revealed she had met Vinaya several weeks ago. Her name was Wanda; she was twenty-two years old and had a lovely wristwatch on.

Exercise 19.5

Answer the following questions:

1. How are the 'fah' and 'pah' sounds similar? How are they different?
2. How are the 'fah' and 'va' sounds similar? How are they different?
3. What is the saying to remember about your vs and ws?

APPLYING WHAT YOU HAVE LEARNED

1. If you do not bite down your upper teeth to your lower lip while producing the 'fah' sound, you will end up with a 'pah' sound. They are both very similar as they require lots of air. Thus, it is important to pay close attention to ensure that that you are biting down for the 'fah' sound.
2. The 'va' sound requires the same teeth-to-lower-lip placement as the 'fah' sound. The only difference is the use of air for the 'fah' sound and the use of the throat for the 'va' sound.
3. It is very common to confuse the 'va' sound for the 'wa' sound while speaking. Remember to 'bite your Vs and kiss your Ws', and pay attention while you speak.

CHAPTER 20

I talk too fast and tonelessly!

Vowel sounds

> Dear Nasha,
>
> Does the speed at which you talk matter? I speak at a normal pace, but the listener always comments that I speak too fast. I don't know why. For quite a few years, I am watching Star World, BBC, Star Movies—all English channels. Do you think I can get used to the speed in which they speak? Please advise.

I received this email from one of my students. Speaking too quickly is a problem many of us face. For one, we tend to think faster than we speak, so we are always in a hurry to finish our sentences. Unfortunately, listeners cannot absorb information at the same rate. This is why we must try to slow down our pace and take deep breaths while we speak.

It may come as a surprise that the pace of your speech is linked to vowel sounds. We can decrease the speed at which we speak by stretching vowel sounds while speaking. In India, many of us *shorten* our vowel sounds to such an extent that not only do we speak too fast, but the actual words start sounding like other, similar words.

Vowel sounds also add flavour and excitement to our voices. By stretching them and adding emotion to them, we can become more persuasive and effective speakers.

In the previous sections, we learnt various consonant sounds. In this chapter we will focus on techniques that will help to improve our vowel sounds.

What will I learn in this chapter?

20.1 How consonant sounds affect the length of vowel sounds.

20.2 Why stretching certain words is very important for good communication.

20.3 Using vowel sounds to improve intonation.

20.1 HOW CONSONANT SOUNDS AFFECT THE LENGTH OF VOWEL SOUNDS

In the previous chapters, we learnt the differences between aspirated and throat sounds.

- Aspirated (air) sounds are caused by expelling air from the mouth—examples are the 'pah', 'kah', 'tah', 'fah' sounds.
- Throat sounds are caused by vocal chords in the throat—examples are the 'da', 'na', 'va', 'ra', 'wa' sounds.

As we have already learned, aspirated sounds are stronger than throat sounds because they are caused by the force of air coming out of the mouth.

- Air sounds—strong, forceful.
- Throat sounds—weak.

When a vowel sound falls *before* a consonant sound that is an air sound (strong sound), it is cut short. For example, let's take the word 'm**a**t'. Just as you begin getting the 'a' sound out, the strong consonant 'tah' sound follows and cuts the 'a' in half.

Now, let's look at the word 'm**a**d'. Here, the 'a' sound is followed by a consonant sound that is a weak, throat sound. Since 'da' is a weak sound, it cannot cut the 'a' sound in half. In fact it joins hands with the 'a' sound as they complete the word together.

So, what we see is that in the word 'mat', the 'tah' sound does not need the 'a' sound to finish the word. It is strong and can complete the word on its own.

The 'da' sound on the other hand, needs the 'a' sound's help to finish the word 'mad'. So, the 'a' sound becomes even longer.

Because of this, the word 'm**a**t' will always be shorter in length than the word 'm**a**d'.

Rules to remember:

! When vowel sounds come before strong consonant sounds, they are shorter. When vowel sounds come before weak consonant sounds, they are longer.

Exercise 20.1

Using the rules you just learned, identify which of these consonant sounds are strong or weak. We have covered some of these sounds in previous chapters. For others, make the sound while holding one hand in front of your mouth and placing the other on your throat. Remember, any sound that requires the use of air is a strong sound. Any sound resulting in vibration in your throat is a weak one.

Ba	Ga	La	Pah	Tah	Ya
Da	Ja	Ma	Ra	Va	Za
Fah	Kah	Na	Sah	Wa	

It is important to concentrate and make sure that you extend vowel sounds if they come before weak consonant sounds.

20.2 WHY STRETCHING WORDS IS IMPORTANT FOR GOOD COMMUNICATION

It is very important that you stretch your vowel sounds when required and make sure the words you say are of a proper length. For instance, let's take the two words we used earlier—'mat' versus 'mad'.

As it is, the 'tah' and 'da' sounds are very similar—they have identical tongue placements. If you are speaking to someone over the phone, it is possible that they may not be able to differentiate between your 'tah' and 'da' sounds. But they will be able to tell what you are saying by the *length* of the vowel sounds in the words.

That's right! Human beings actually programme themselves to recognize words *based on the length of the word.*

If we fail to stretch our vowel sounds when required, we end up being misunderstood, especially when talking to a larger global audience.

Practice exercise

Practise saying the following words out loud row by row. First say the short word, and then say the long one. For the long word, make sure that you stretch the vowel sound so that the word sounds longer than the corresponding short word.

Short word	Long word
Bit	Bid
Beat	Bead
Let	Led
Calf	Halve
Life	Strive
Safe	Cave
Tack	Tag
Luck	Mug
Back	Bag
Lock	Log
Prop	Snob
Trap	Slab
Cap	Cab
Mace	Maze
Case	Craze
Lease	Freeze

Exercise 20.2

1. What happens to vowel sounds which fall before a strong consonant sound?
2. What happens to vowel sounds which fall before a weak consonant sound?

20.3 USING VOWEL SOUNDS FOR BETTER INTONATION

What is intonation?

Intonation is the tone and pitch of your voice.

- Tone—the 'music' in your voice. The manner in which you speak.
- Pitch—the degree of highness and lowness of your voice (the volume).

Changing your pitch is not a very effective way to communicate. Changing the *tone* is what will make your speech more interesting.

Why intonate?

- It breaks communication barriers.
- It allows people to trust you more easily.
- It allows others to feel comfortable when you speak.
- It helps you to hold the attention of the person you are speaking to.

! No matter whom you are speaking to—your employer, a business associate, your wife, husband, girlfriend or boyfriend, even your children—you will be far more effective if you modulate the tone of your voice.

How do I intonate?

Vowel sounds add to the emotion, or intonation in our voices. Good communicators know how and when to stretch or emphasize certain vowel sounds to get their meaning across.

Practice exercise

Let us pretend someone has asked you to do something, which you just cannot do.

- First, say 'I can't do it' out loud in a nice, friendly tone.
- Then, say 'I can't do it' out loud in an angry, frustrated tone.

Many of you will have emphasized on the word 'can't' while changing your tone. Do the exercise again, and this time pay attention to the fact that when you changed your tone, the consonant sounds in the word 'can't'—the 'kah', 'na' and 'tah' sounds—pretty much stay the same.

The reason the word 'can't' sounded friendly the first time and angry the second was really due to the way in which you altered the *vowel* sound 'a'.

Practice exercise

Say the phrases given below out loud while emphasizing on the vowel sounds.

• I d**o**? (As a question.)	• I l**o**ve you (Emotionally.)
• I d**o**! (Excitedly.)	• I l**o**ve you (Excitedly.)
• I d**o**n't! (Angrily.)	• I h**a**te you! (Angrily.)
• I d**o**n't (Unhappily.)	• I h**a**te you? (As a question.)

Practice exercise

Say the following statements out loud, and emphasize the vowel sounds in bold.

- M**Y** brother got admission in a GR**EA**T university; Y**OU**RS couldn't even P**A**SS his exams!
- My BR**O**THER got admission in a great UNIV**E**RSITY; yours couldn't **E**VEN pass his EX**A**MS!

Tips for intonating your vowel sounds:

- Feel when you speak—speak from your heart.
- Move your hands around when you speak—even if you are on the phone.
- Smile when you speak.
- Focus on giving a personality to your voice.

A good way to improve intonation is to read fairy tales out loud. That's right! Fairy tales are filled with great adjectives and verbs.

Also, because they are made for children, it is easy to make them sound exciting.

Practice exercise

Buy a fairy tale or download one from the internet. *Little Red Riding Hood*, for instance. Now, follow these steps to improve your intonation:

1. Read the fairy tale and record your own voice.
2. Play it back and listen to yourself speaking.
3. Go back to the fairy tale and underline the verbs and adjectives that you think you could say in a more interesting way.
4. Read the fairy tale again and record yourself again. Work on stretching or adding excitement and emotion to some of the words you underlined. (Remember, excitement and emotion need to come from *within* you.)
5. Listen to the recording again and compare it with the first one.
6. Analyse the differences. Repeat this process on an ongoing basis with different books and articles.

APPLYING WHAT YOU HAVE LEARNED

1. If you want to reduce the speed at which you speak or improve your intonation, focus on your vowel sounds.
2. When vowel sounds come before an aspirated (strong) consonant sound, they are cut short.
   - P**a**t is shorter in length than P**a**n.
3. When vowel sounds come before a throat (weak) consonant sound, they become longer.
   - S**a**d is longer in length than S**a**t.
4. Emphasizing certain vowel sounds will help you sound more interesting and full of life. Try and make sure that in each sentence you say, a few of the words have a different tone.

SECTION III

Interpersonal Communication

In the last two sections we covered language fluency and pronunciation. These are the basic tools you need for effective speaking. In this section, you will learn how to use communication as a powerful tool to build relationships with co-workers, superiors, clients and customers. In business, your ability to make people like and trust you is as important as being smart and hardworking. This section will help you improve your personality and become more successful at the workplace and in your personal life.

Chapters in this section:

21. People like people who can talk well, right? Wrong!
    Extraordinary listening for building business relationships
22. Talking to new people is scary!
    Building conversations by asking good questions
23. I am an average conversationalist. Can I become an extraordinary one?
    Probing, assuring and reading between the lines
24. Get to the point—I don't have time to listen!
    Speaking concisely

CHAPTER 21

People like people who can talk well, right? Wrong!

Extraordinary listening for building business relationships

Gaurav just couldn't understand it. He was a funny guy. He was smart and good at his work. Yet, most of his company's clients seemed to like Nandan better. 'Nandan is no better than me!' thought Gaurav. 'Why is he always invited to more parties than I am? Why does he seem to have better relationships with our clients than I do? Why do all our colleagues consider Nandan such a good friend? I am a good friend too. Why don't people trust me with their problems?'

Have you ever met someone like Nandan? Someone who is popular with everyone? Do you wish you could be like them? In this chapter you will learn how to become well liked and build extraordinary relationships.

What will I learn in this chapter?

21.1 The difference between an average and an extraordinary listener.
21.2 Building business relationships through extraordinary listening.
21.3 Why people find it so hard to listen.
21.4 How to become an extraordinary listener.

21.1 THE DIFFERENCE BETWEEN AN AVERAGE AND AN EXTRAORDINARY LISTENER

Everyone tells us that effective listening is important. We have heard this a million times over. But what is the big deal—how important is listening, really?

Let's analyse the dialogue given below. Sameer is at the office speaking to a few of his colleagues:

Mohan:	Sameer, what did you do over the weekend?
Sameer:	Well, I actually had a really fun weekend. I went to a new theatre in Andheri to watch a movie. The theatre has these amazing reclining seats . . .
Mohan:	Did you hear about Sunil's engagement? He told me about it yesterday!

- What went wrong?

Sameer was in the middle of a sentence when Mohan cut him off rather rudely.

- What could the repercussions be?

It's possible that Mohan suddenly remembered Sunil's engagement and wanted to share the news immediately. But Sameer now probably thinks that Mohan wasn't listening to him in the first place. And this probably made Sameer feel that what he had to say was not interesting enough. Now, for no fault of his own, Sameer's self-esteem may suffer.

- Can you think back to a time where you were speaking and someone cut you off in the middle of what you were saying?

Try and remember who cut you off (you will most probably be able to), and how it made you feel. Take a look at the following dialogue. Sonia is speaking to her friend Anu.

Sonia:	I have a problem with my boss at work. He always takes out his anger on me and yells at me for every little thing.
Anu:	Oh, really?
Sonia:	Yes, just the other day I was sitting at my desk and he came out, and for no reason at all told me I need to start doing better work!

Anu:	[Glances quickly at her watch] Oh really? That's too bad.
Sonia:	Umm . . . yeah that is all.
Anu:	Okay, so do you want to see a movie later on?

- What went wrong? Why did Sonia stop talking about her problem all of a sudden?

Well, for one, she saw Anu glance at her watch and sensed her disinterest. Also, Anu didn't ask her any follow-up questions; she just kept saying 'oh really'. Sonia suspected that Anu was getting bored, so she quickly ended the conversation. This fear was confirmed when Anu abruptly asked if Sonia wanted to go to a movie.

- Think back to times when you were speaking to someone and it seemed like they were not paying attention. How did it make you feel?

In the following dialogue, two close friends are talking about a private issue. Sometimes we discuss personal things about ourselves and our lives with people who are close to us, but regret doing so later because of their reactions. We feel sad when they don't respond in ways we expected them to. See if you can identify with this dialogue.

Ruby:	Tasha, I feel so awful. I just had a horrible fight with my brother.
Tasha:	What happened?
Ruby:	He told me I wasn't doing enough to help out our family, and that I was only concerned with myself.
Tasha:	What did you say?
Ruby:	I yelled at him and we fought for almost an hour. I feel terrible about it and have been crying ever since.
Tasha:	Ruby, you just have to get over it! You can't let your family problems get you down! Come on, let's go have a coffee and talk about something else.

- What went wrong?

The problem was not that Tasha was not listening. In fact, she kept asking Ruby questions—'What happened? What did you say?' However, something changed in the end. After Ruby shared how terrible she was feeling, that she had been crying, Tasha told her to 'get over it'. While Tasha may have thought this was great advice, to Ruby it signaled that her friend really did not want to sit down and listen to her problem. Instead, she just told her to 'get over it'.

- Has something similar ever happened to you? Do you remember how you felt?

The truth is that when people don't listen to us we tend to feel rejected, unimportant and sad. We usually avoid building relationships with people like this.

21.2 BUILDING BUSINESS RELATIONSHIPS THROUGH EXTRAORDINARY LISTENING

Today, business is more about relationships than products. With intense competition, there will always be companies carrying similar products and people possessing similar skill sets. Each one of us needs to find ways to differentiate ourselves from the competition. One easy way is to listen and build unique relationships with others. Extraordinary listening is a powerful tool to win in a competitive environment. Take a look at the example below:

One morning, Nitin decided to buy coffee and a piece of cake before going to work. There were two stores right next to each other near Nitin's house, both selling coffee and cake. Nitin went into the first store and bought his coffee and cake. The woman behind the counter was nice—she took his money and thanked him before he left. The coffee and cake were good.

The next day, Nitin decided to try the second store—perhaps the coffee would be even better! The

```
woman behind the counter smiled, asked Nitin how he was doing, seemed genuinely interested when Nitin answered, and took his money and thanked him. The coffee and cake were just as tasty as in the first store—there was no difference in the product.

The next day, without hesitation, Nitin chose the second store. Both served the same coffee and cake, but in the second store there was a nice lady who had asked Nitin how he was doing, and had genuinely listened to his answer.
```

The woman in the first store did nothing wrong. She may even have been a good listener. But the woman in the second store was an *extraordinary* listener. Extraordinary listeners make us feel they are more concerned about us than themselves. They make us feel important and appreciated. Extraordinary listeners tend to have have more friends and are more popular.

The easiest way to get people to like you, to get more business, and to build better relationships, is to become an extraordinary listener.

21.3 WHY PEOPLE FIND IT SO HARD TO LISTEN

It seems so easy—just listen to others while they are talking! Why aren't we all extraordinary listeners? Well, here are a few reasons:

- It is much more fun to talk than to listen.
- We often assume we already know what the other person is going to say.
- We often assume that we already know the right answer and we have little to learn from others.
- It is boring to listen to someone complain about their problems.
- We like to give advice rather than just listen.
- We are self-conscious while we speak, so we keep on talking to make a good impression.

21.4 HOW TO BECOME AN EXTRAORDINARY LISTENER

First, you must understand the difference between *hearing* and *listening*. Listening involves using your eyes, mind and heart.

USE YOUR EYES

Have you ever been in a conversation in which the person you are speaking to is not looking at you or meeting your eye? Perhaps they are looking at their watch, or the floor, or the sky, or even someone else. That is the first sign of a terrible listener.

Or how about the opposite? Instead of looking away, the person you are talking to just stares at you blankly! Even while they look into your eyes, it seems as if they are looking right through you and that that their thoughts are a million miles away.

There is a saying that 'the eyes are the windows to the soul.' This is true—your eyes convey your emotions, your enthusiasm, and your interest in the other person.

How to use your eyes for extraordinary listening:

- Look into the eyes of the person who is talking—show him/her that you *are* listening.
- Don't just stare blankly.
- Refrain from thinking about how you can break away to speak to someone else or do something else—your eyes can't conceal this.
- Use your eyes to show emotion.
- Raise your eyebrows when necessary.

USE YOUR MIND

Think back to conversations with people in which it seemed that the other person was responding without actually *listening* to what you said.

For example, read the following dialogue between Raman and Sonali. They are talking about working in a call centre.

Raman:	Sonali, I can't believe that you are going to work in a call centre. Your shift will be late at night and it will completely ruin your sleeping habits.

Sonali:	Raman, I will be earning twice as much as before. And I get free training!
Raman:	But what about what you will be doing to your body? You will have to sleep all day and work all night! Also, what about your family? You won't be able to spend any time with them.
Sonali:	Raman, it is very important to save money. With this job I will be able to save almost 10,000 rupees every month! How can you say it is not worth it?

In this conversation, both Raman and Sonali are making valid points. However, neither is responding to what the other is saying. Especially Sonali—she completely ignored all of Raman's comments. It is almost as if she was talking to herself. She doesn't even think about his questions about her health and her family. Raman, too, doesn't really think about what Sonali is saying about earning more money. He has his fixed views and he is just reaffirming what he already knows.

This was a wasted conversation. Raman and Sonali did not *think* about what the other was saying before they spoke. Neither person listened with their minds, and consequently, did not learn anything new from this conversation.

Everyone does this. Have you ever been in a situation in which you already know what your response will be to what the other person is saying? Even before they are done speaking you already know what *you* will say? It's like you are bursting to speak and just waiting for them to quickly stop talking! If you are familiar with this feeling, you are certainly not listening with your mind.

! Smart people talk less and listen more. You already know what you think. It's much smarter to learn what other people know.

How to use your mind for extraordinary listening:

- Do not begin formulating your next sentence while the person is still is speaking.
- Follow the other person's train of thought.

- Take in the meaning and the intent of the words.
- Comprehend the message before responding to it.
- Give non-verbal and verbal responses that show you are listening.
- Use reassurances such as yes, okay, correct in the course of the conversation.

USE YOUR HEART

This is the most crucial step in extraordinary listening. Most of us are average listeners—we use our eyes and our minds. *Extraordinary* listeners know how to use their hearts.

Let's take the following example:

You finally get a break from work and decide to go to Goa for a holiday. You are very excited and run to share the good news with one of your friends.

You:	Hey, guess what? My boss finally gave me leave! I'm going to Goa! I'm so excited!
Friend:	Ugh. I haven't been on a vacation in months. I really need a break as well.

Try and imagine how would you feel. You wanted to share something positive that happened to you but your friend immediately began talking about himself. Moreover, he was so negative that it killed your excitement.

Let's take another scenario:

You:	Hey, guess what? My boss finally gave me leave! I'm going to Goa! I'm so excited!
Friend:	Oh my god! I love Goa. It's such a great place. You know what, I will tell you exactly where you should eat and stay. Last time I went there I had the most amazing time. I spent every morning swimming and then had a long lunch, a nap and then went out partying all night. I love Goa!

Does your friend come across as a better listener in this situation? Well, he was certainly better than in the first scenario! At least he wasn't negative. But what did he do when you went to share your news with him? Was he happy for you? No, he was much happier for himself—notice how he immediately began sharing his own experience about going to Goa. He also started giving you advice on where to stay, what to do, etc.

This is an example of an average listener. Most of us fall into this category.

Now, let's look at one last scenario.

You:	Hey guess what? My boss finally gave me leave! I'm going to Goa! I'm so excited!
Friend:	That is so fantastic! I am so happy for you! You have deserved a vacation for a long time now. I have noticed how hard you have been working. What do you plan to do while you are there?

This is an example of an extraordinary listener. He was genuinely happy and excited for you. He congratulated you. From his empathetic response you know that he *truly listened* when you told him that your boss *finally* gave you a vacation.

And last, he did not push his advice on you, as then he would have been doing all the talking. He asked instead if you knew what you were planning to do in Goa thus allowing you to talk and him to listen.

We tend to think that people always want our advice. That is not usually true. People sometimes just want someone who they can share their joy and their pain with. They just want someone who will listen to them talk.

! We are not listening if we only respond with advice, criticism or narrations of our own experiences.

How to use your heart for extraordinary listening:

- Share enthusiasm—show you are happy for others.

- Empathize with others' pain—let people unload their emotions.
- Try not to always make a connection with one of your own experiences.
- Try not to offer advice on how it could have been done better or criticize.

The difference between these three situations was that the last example showed a friend who actually *cared* that you finally got a chance to take a vacation. He was genuinely interested in finding out what you would be doing in Goa—his questions had more depth than the others.

We can all be extraordinary listeners. It's just a matter of putting other people before us.

Exercise 21.1

A woman decides to start a stock portfolio with her multinational bank. She picks up the phone and calls the local Mumbai help desk number. She explains her query to the customer service agent. This is the dialogue that follows. Underline and explain where in this dialogue the agent did not listen to the customer.

Agent:	'Okay, someone will call you back in two days.'
Customer:	'No, I won't have time in two days; I'd like to speak to someone now.'
Agent:	'Ma'am, someone will surely call you in two days.'
Customer:	'Did you not hear me? I won't have time in two days! I'd like to speak to someone now.'
Agent:	'Sorry ma'am, but someone will call you in two days surely.'
Customer:	'Are you telling me no one is available in the entire bank to speak with me? And why does it take two days to return customers' calls?'

Agent:	'Yes, sorry ma'am it takes two days. But don't worry, someone will surely call you.'
Customer:	'This is so frustrating. You aren't even answering my questions. Fine, have someone call me in two days.'
Agent:	'Thank you ma'am, goodbye.'
Customer:	'Wait! You haven't taken down my contact information . . .'

Exercise 21.2

You tell a friend that you just had a great weekend. Which response corresponds to a bad, average and extraordinary listener?

1. 'That's fantastic. You have deserved a good weekend for some time. What did you do?'
2. 'You're lucky, I had an awful weekend!'
3. 'What did you do over the weekend?' or 'Maybe I should hang out with you over the weekends!'

CHAPTER 22

Talking to new people is scary!

Building conversations by asking questions

Anahita was nervous. She had to go to a function at work. 'I hate networking,' thought Anahita. 'It's so hard to make conversation with new people.'

Do you sometimes feel like this? Do you sometimes run out of things to say when talking to new people? Do you get nervous having to start conversations with people?

In the last chapter, we talked about the importance of extraordinary listening. In this chapter we will focus on another powerful communication tool—effective questioning. When speaking to people, asking relevant and interesting questions will not only help the conversation stay alive, but also let the other person know that you are interested in them.

What will I learn in this chapter?

22.1 How to ask thoughtful questions.
22.2 Linking questions to responses.
22.3 How to seem interested in people.
22.4 Tips for effective questioning.

22.1 HOW TO ASK THOUGHTFUL QUESTIONS

Take a look at the dialogue between Vikram and his colleague Bhavani at an office function. Observe Bhavani's responses.

Vikram:	Hi Bhavani. How are you doing?
Bhavani:	I'm good. How is your work coming along? I hear you are working late regularly?
Vikram:	Yes, things are getting very hectic. I stay back every day until almost 10 p.m.!
Bhavani:	Oh, that is too bad! How is your wife?
Vikram:	Oh, she is fine.
Bhavani:	Good to hear. How are your children?
Vikram:	They are also fine.
Bhavani:	That's good. I see Anu, let me go say hello to her. It was nice talking to you!
Vikram:	Okay. Nice talking to you too.

Have you ever had a conversation of this sort? Do you find these encounters extremely boring? Well, you are right—they are! If the conversation between Vikram and Bhavani did not happen *nothing would be lost* because *nothing was gained*. Bhavani learned nothing new about Vikram. This happened because she only asked shallow, disconnected questions instead of thoughtful ones.

Let's analyse the conversation between Vikram and Bhavani to understand this difference. The first question Bhavani asked Vikram was:

Bhavani:	How is your work coming along? I hear you are working late.
Vikram:	Yes, things are getting very hectic. I stay back everyday until almost 10 p.m., working!

Wow! Every day until 10 p.m.! Poor Vikram must be so tired! Also, what could he be working on until so late? A new project? Or perhaps he has done something wrong at work so he has to stay late. There are so many questions that Bhavani could have asked Vikram.

Let's take a look at how Bhavani responded to Vikram:

Bhavani:	`Oh, that is too bad! How is your wife?`

What does Vikram's wife have to do with his working late? Nothing. Instead of asking Vikram a follow-up question about his work, Bhavani decided to ask Vikram a broad, unrelated and therefore shallow question about his wife. This is where the conversation broke down. From this point onward, the dialogue is boring and static.

How could this have been avoided?

Bhavani could have asked more thoughtful, interesting follow-up questions. Take a look at the dialogue below and see if you notice any difference.

Vikram:	`Hi, Bhavani. How are you doing?`
Bhavani:	`I'm good. How is your work coming along? I hear you are working late these days?`
Vikram:	`Yes, things are getting very hectic. I stay back every day until almost 10 p.m.!`
Bhavani:	`Oh, that is too bad! Why are you working so late?`
Vikram:	`Well, we just landed a big client so everyone in our group is working late.`
Bhavani:	`Really? Well, that's good news! Who is the client?`
Vikram:	`Oh, a large airline company. Yes, it is very exciting for us! Especially for me because I have all these new responsibilities and I am learning so much.`
Bhavani:	`That is so nice. How are you involved in the project? Are you still doing marketing work?`
Vikram:	`Yes, I handle the billboard marketing. It is very exciting because . . .`

- What is the difference between the two dialogues?

In the first dialogue, Bhavani asked Vikram three broad, unrelated questions:

1. How is work?
2. How is your wife?
3. How are your children?

In the second conversation, Bhavani asked Vikram questions *only* about work.

1. Why are you working late?
2. Who is the client?
3. How are you involved in the project?
4. Are you still doing marketing work?

Bhavani stuck to one topic, and therefore had one, good, meaningful conversation. And look how much more Bhavani has learned in this conversation compared to the first one: Vikram is working on a project with a large airline company, he is excited about the project, and he is handling billboard marketing. All in all, the second conversation was more interesting and more thoughtful than the first.

Thoughtful questions allow us to probe the other person for reasons, their way of thinking, and help us to understand their real motives and feelings. Usually 'how' and 'why' are question words that allow for more open-ended, thoughtful responses.

Exercise 22.1

The person you are talking to says: 'I want to run in the Bombay marathon.' Try to come up with five interesting, thoughtful questions to ask this person. Then think of five shallow questions and compare the difference.

22.2 LINKING QUESTIONS TO RESPONSES

By now you should have understood how to ask thoughtful, meaningful questions. It is equally important to know how to link questions with answers in order to build good conversations.

Take a look at the dialogue between Vipasha and Neil. Pay attention to Vipasha's responses.

Vipasha:	Hi Neil, how are you?
Neil:	Okay, I just decided to go to Matheran for the weekend.
Vipasha:	Well, that is great! When are you leaving?
Neil:	Friday evening. I'm so tired of work. I can't wait for the break.
Vipasha:	I can understand. Where are you staying?
Neil:	Oh, at this little bungalow my family owns.
Vipasha:	Lucky! How are you getting there?
Neil:	By car—we are driving there.

There is nothing glaringly wrong with this conversation. Vipasha was a good listener and was excited that her friend Neil was going to Matheran. But this conversation lacked depth and was not particularly interesting. Can you think why?

Let's take a look at one of Neil's responses to a question Vipasha asked:

Vipasha:	Well, that is great! When are you leaving?
Neil:	Friday evening. I'm so tired of work. I can't wait for the break.

Up until this point, the conversation has been about going to Matheran. But now, Neil has just spoken about something else: he told Vipasha that he is tired of work. In a way, Neil has given a small opening into his personal life and troubles. Vipasha responded to this by saying:

Vipasha:	I can understand. Where are you staying?

Instead of picking up Neil's clue that something was not right at work, Vipasha went back to the original topic of conversation: going to Matheran.

When building conversations, it is important that we not only ask meaningful questions, but we listen to the *last thing the other person said* and respond to that. Take a look at how Vipasha could have asked better questions:

Vipasha:	Well, that is great! When are you leaving?
Neil:	Friday evening. I'm so tired of work. I can't wait for the break.
Vipasha:	I can understand. Why are you tired of work? Is everything okay?
Neil:	Well, not really. I just got a new boss and he is really tough on me for no reason. I am just not enjoying my work anymore.
Vipasha:	I'm sorry to hear that. Are you looking for a new job?
Neil:	Yes, I have been for some time. I'm looking in the field of finance.
Vipasha:	Really? I didn't know you were interested in finance.
Neil:	I wasn't earlier, but now . . .

- How is this dialogue better?

In this dialogue, Vipasha responded to the *last thing* that Neil mentioned. Because of this, she built a meaningful conversation in which she began to understand a problem that Neil was facing. When he said, 'I'm so tired of work. I can't wait for the break,' he was giving Vipasha a window of opportunity to talk about his personal life. People do not tend to come straight out and tell other people their personal issues. However, everyone gives small hints and clues, and it is up to good listeners and questioners to make the best of these rare openings.

Also, notice how the conversation started with Neil going Matheran, then went on to Neil's work issues and then finally became about Neil's interest in finance. This is a sign of a good conversation—one that moves and grows.

Remember, if you want to build strong, special business relationships, you have to become an extraordinary listener and an effective questioner.

Exercise 22.2

Read the following conversation between Nitin and Anand. Identify where Nitin makes the mistake of not responding to the last thing Anand says.

Nitin:	Hi Anand, did you hear about Anu's party?
Anand:	Yes, I did, but I won't be able to make it.
Nitin:	Oh really? Well that is too bad. How is your girlfriend doing?
Anand:	She's doing okay. She's really busy on a new project right now.
Nitin:	Well that is exciting! Hey, are you guys attending Rohan's wedding later this month?
Anand:	Yes, both of us are going to his wedding.

22.3 HOW TO SEEM INTERESTED IN PEOPLE

Learning to have a thoughtful, meaningful conversation is not just about building an interesting conversation. It is also about showing the other person that you are truly interested in their life. We do this by not just responding to the last thing someone said, but by showing empathy.

Take a look at the conversation between James and Nishita. James is trying to get Nishita to go on a date with him to watch a movie. Let's see if he is successful:

James:	Hi Nishita, do you want to go see a movie this Saturday night?
Nishita:	No, I can't. I'm going to my grandmother's house.

James:	Okay . . . umm . . . what time are you coming back?
Nishita:	Not until very late.
James:	Well, can you come back earlier? The movie starts at 8.
Nishita:	No, I can't. It's quite an important visit.
James:	Oh come on Nishita! Try to do something! I'm sure you can try and come back by 7.30 or so.
Nishita:	No, I really can't, and now you are starting to annoy me.

Well, James clearly failed in his goal to get Nishita to go on a date with him! Can you think why? Let's analyse the dialogue. When James asked Nishita to go to the movies, her response was:

Nishita:	No, I can't. I'm going to my grandmother's house.

Now, do we know *why* Nishita is going to her grandmother's house? It could be her grandmother's birthday. It could be that her grandmother is very sick. So far we have no idea. Let's look at what James's response was.

James:	Okay . . . umm . . . what time are you coming back?

James certainly did not listen and respond appropriately. By not asking Nishita why she was going to her grandmother's house, he made it clear that he was thinking only of himself. Finally, Nishita did give James a more straightforward clue that something important was happening at her grandmother's house.

James:	Well, can you come back earlier? The movie starts at 8.

Nishita:	No I can't, it's quite an important visit.

At this point, James should have realized that perhaps something out of the ordinary was happening at Nishita's grandmother's house, and he should have asked her if everything was all right. But instead look at what James's response was:

James:	Oh, come on Nishita! Try to do something! I'm sure you can try and come back by 7.30 or so.

James has not thought about Nishita's needs and her feelings even once. He has come across as being selfish and only interested in his *end goal*—watching the movie. The truth is that because he was only focussed on his end goal, he was unable to achieve it.

Take a look at how the dialogue could have gone better if James had been more concerned and empathetic towards Nishita.

James:	Hi Nishita, do you want to go see a movie this Saturday night?
Nishita:	No, I can't. I'm going to my grandmother's house.
James:	Oh, okay. Any special reason?
Nishita:	Actually, she is not feeling too well.
James:	Why, what happened?
Nishita:	Saturday is my late grandfather's birthday and she always becomes quite sad. So we all try to visit and cheer her up.
James:	That is really wonderful of your family. I am sure she will feel better when she sees you!
Nishita:	Thanks, James. Perhaps we can see the movie another time?

James:	No problem, Nishita. I'll give you a call on Sunday and maybe if you're free we can see it then.
Nishita:	That sounds good. I'll talk to you later.

- How was this dialogue better?

In this dialogue James did not force Nishita to agree to see the movie on Saturday. Because he was listening to her, responding to the *last thing* she said and being empathetic, his questions came across as thoughful and caring. His chances of seeing the movie with her on Sunday are much higher now.

Make being a good listener and questioner a habit, and you will automatically achieve what you set out to.

22.4 TIPS FOR EFFECTIVE QUESTIONING

- Ask thoughtful questions instead of shallow ones.
- Ask follow-up questions instead of broad, unrelated ones.
- Ask questions based on the last thing a person says.
- Be genuinely interested in and empathetic towards other people.

CHAPTER 23

I am an average conversationalist. Can I become an extraordinary one?

Probing, assuring and reading between the lines

So far we have learned how to listen effectively to what others are saying and how to take conversations forward in an interesting way. We have also learned how to build powerful relationships through empathetic and caring responses.

In many situations, though, people will not give you all the information you need to empathize properly or to build interesting conversations. In this chapter, you will learn how to listen to what people *don't* say. Silence teaches you a lot—understanding people's insecurities always helps in dealing with them better. And finally, learn how to make people feel comfortable enough to talk to you more freely.

What will I learn in this chapter?

23.1 How to read between the lines.
23.2 How to reassure people.
23.3 How to gain additional insight into people's personalities.
23.4 Tips for extraordinary conversations.

23.1 HOW TO READ BETWEEN THE LINES

Yes, sometimes people just do not tell us enough! At other times, people simply don't say what they really mean. Keep in mind that we all have our own insecurities and tend to be careful about sharing too much information with others. In order to create a strong bond with another person, you need to be sensitive about their insecurities and look for clues in unsaid statements. Take a look at the dialogue between Parul and her husband Samir, which illustrates this point.

Parul:	Samir, I think I look fat in this skirt. Should I change it?
Samir:	No, you look fine. Hurry up and finish getting ready.
Parul:	But ... are you sure ...?
Samir:	Yes, Parul you look fine, just hurry up or we will be late!

- What is special about this dialogue?

This dialogue may seem unimportant, but within Samir's responses lay an opportunity to build a stronger bond. In this situation, Parul was questioning whether a certain skirt made her look fat. Her husband promptly responded by saying no. However, did he really read between the lines and try to understand what his wife could have been asking? If he had looked a bit deeper, he would have realized that Parul was feeling insecure about her weight. She was not only concerned with what she did openly say—looking fat in the skirt—but also with what she *did not say*—looking fat in general.

You are probably saying to yourself, 'But I am no mind reader! How can I figure out what people are *not* saying?' You are right, this is a difficult task. It requires attentiveness and the ability to read other people's tone of voice and body language. Also, you need to be able to put other people's feelings first.

If you can learn to do this, the benefits are enormous. Once you understand what people want to say but can't, you have the opportunity to respond in a way that will win their affection. It is a wonderful thing to be able to address someone's insecurities without them having to ask you to.

23.2 HOW TO REASSURE PEOPLE

Let's take another look at the dialogue between Parul and her husband. This time, we will have Samir *read between the lines*. Pay close attention to his responses.

Parul:	Samir, I think I look fat in this skirt. Should I change it?
Samir:	Absolutely not. You look fantastic.
Parul:	But ... are you sure ...?
Samir:	How could you look fat in that skirt when you are not fat at all? Trust me—I think you look just perfect. Please wear the skirt.

- How was this dialogue different from the first?

Well, for one thing, Samir listened to what his wife *did not say*. He inferred that she must be feeling insecure about her weight. Next, he assured his wife that she was not fat at all.

Samir:	How could you look fat in that skirt when you are not fat at all?

He also convinced Parul that she looked great in the skirt. He did this by choosing reassuring words that made her feel good about herself:

Samir:	Trust me, I think you look just perfect. Please wear the skirt.

To reassure someone, don't avoid the situation—deal with it and take responsibility for making the other person feel more secure. Also, don't forget to intonate and show emotion when you speak.

So far, we have learned a simple two-step method. First, read between the lines. Second, assure people. Let's look at the following dialogue between Ajay and one of his clients. This dialogue represents a work situation that many of us have to deal with—keeping our clients and customers satisfied.

Ajay:	Mr Joshi, have you had a chance to read the report I sent you?

Mr Joshi: Yes, I noticed that it is only thirty pages long?
Ajay: Yes, that is correct.
Mr Joshi: Umm...okay. It was a good report. I will get back to you tomorrow with our feedback.

- Did Ajay read between the lines?

No, he did not. Look back to when Mr Joshi commented that the report was only thirty pages long. He was probably implying that the report was shorter than he had expected. From that we can infer that he thinks the quality of the report may be in doubt because of its size. If Ajay had read between the lines, he could have replied to Mr Joshi in a more reassuring manner. Read the following dialogue and notice the difference.

Ajay: Mr Joshi, have you had a chance to read the report I sent you?
Mr Joshi: Yes, I noticed it is only thirty pages long?
Ajay: Yes, but don't worry Mr Joshi, that is not because we have left anything out. In fact, the report is extremely detailed, but we have taken time to make sure the writing is as concise as possible.
Mr Joshi: Oh, well that is good to hear. Yes, it did read very nicely. I will get back to you tomorrow with our feedback.

- How was this dialogue different from the previous one?

Ajay read between the lines and gave Mr Joshi a response that left him feeling reassured.

Exercise 23.1

Rohan is being interviewed for a job in the advertising department of a marketing company. Identify where in the following conversation Rohan fails to read between the lines. Think of what he could have done to reassure his interviewer.

Interviewer:	Your CV looks okay.
Rohan:	Thank you.
Interviewer:	You do seem though to have a lot of experience in the finance field.
Rohan:	Yes, I definitely have a lot of experience in the finance field.
Interviewer:	Okay, we will consider your application and call you if we are interested.

23.3 HOW TO GAIN ADDITIONAL INSIGHT INTO PEOPLE'S PERSONALITIES

So far we have covered techniques in reading between the lines and reassuring other people. But sometimes there are situations in which we just don't have enough information to understand someone's true feelings. We may want to be there for the person and reassure them, but we just don't have enough information to know how. Take a look at the following dialogue.

Yasmin:	Hi Shabana, how are you doing?
Shabana:	Umm...okay.
Yasmin:	What is wrong? Are you feeling all right?
Shabana:	Umm...yes, everything is fine.
Yasmin:	No, you are not fine. What is wrong?
Shabana:	Everything is just fine! Let's talk about something else!
Yasmin:	No, Shabana, I know something is bothering you. What happened?

Have you ever found yourself in a situation like this? You know that something is wrong with your friend but they just won't tell you what. Later, they may even get upset with you for not trying to help! In situations like this, effective probing is very important.

Probing means asking for more information in a sensitive way. Don't get discouraged if all the questions you ask are not answered. It is important not to make the other person think you are interrogating them or putting them on the defensive. Keep your tone kind, and gently ask for more details. It is useful to try and ask detailed questions when probing. For example, instead of asking, 'Is something wrong?' try asking, 'Is something wrong with work?'

Let's see how Yasmin could have probed more effectively.

Yasmin:	Hi Shabana, how are you doing?
Shabana:	Umm...okay.
Yasmin:	What is wrong? Are you feeling okay?

So far, Yasmin has been a brilliant listener. She read between the lines and immediately realized something was wrong with Shabana. The conversation then went on to:

Shabana:	Umm...yes, everything is fine.
Yasmin:	No, you are not fine. What is wrong?

- What did Yasmin do wrong?

Yasmin has the very best intentions. She is concerned about Shabana and wants to understand her problem. However, the way she is probing comes across as sounding aggressive and confrontational. Also, the questions are not specific and thus it is easy for Shabana to brush them off.

- How could have Yasmin have conducted this conversation better?

Yasmin could have responded by saying:

Shabana:	Umm...yes, everything is fine.
Yasmin:	Are you sure? It looks as though you are a bit upset. Is everything okay at work?

Notice how the essential meaning is the same, but there is a subtle difference in the way Yasmin has carried out her probing. She states her *observation* that Shabana *seems* upset and not her *opinion* that Shabana *is* upset. (For example, when Yasmin previously said, 'No, you are not fine.') Also, Yasmin asked an extremely specific question about Shabana's work. By asking more specific questions, Yasmin might be able to come closer to the truth.

Take a look at how the entire dialogue could have turned out if Yasmin had probed more effectively.

Yasmin:	Hi Shabana, how are you doing?
Shabana:	Umm...okay.
Yasmin:	What is wrong? Are you feeling okay?
Shabana:	Umm...yes, everything is fine.
Yasmin:	Are you sure? It looks as though you are a bit upset. Is everything okay at work?
Shabana:	No, work is just fine.
Yasmin:	Is it something to do with with your family? Why don't you try talking about what happened—it might make you feel better.

Shabana will be more inclined now to share her problem. Of course, it is up to Yasmin to keep probing effectively and continue to read between the lines. And finally, once Yasmin comes close to understanding Shabana's problem, it is up to her to properly reassure Shabana. If Yasmin gets it wrong, the chances of Shabana opening up to her again will be slim.

This basic example can be applied to many personal or business situations. To find out the truth we must probe and read between the lines. To build relationships we must then use this knowledge to reassure others and gain their confidence.

Exercise 23.2

Take a look at a dialogue between Gurjot and his client, Ms Chandra. Identify where Gurjot does not do a good enough job probing for details and write how you think it could have been done better.

Gurjot:	Ms Chandra, did you have a chance to look at our work?
Ms Chandra:	Yes I did. I'm just not happy with the work your team has done.
Gurjot:	But why?
Ms Chandra:	Why? Isn't it obvious? This is terrible work!
Gurjot:	Okay, I apologize on behalf of my team, but what are you unhappy with?
Ms Chandra:	Why don't you try going through the report yourself and figure it out!

23.4 TIPS FOR BECOMING AN EXTRAORDINARY CONVERSATIONALIST

- Read between the lines—listen to what people *don't* say.
- Empathize with the insecurities of others and learn to reassure people.
- Probe to find out more information by asking detailed, sensitive, non-confrontational questions.

CHAPTER 24

Getting to the point

Speaking concisely

So far we have covered various forms of interpersonal communication—listening, questioning, probing and reassuring. Focusing on these areas will help you conduct conversations easily and strengthen your business and personal relationships. In this chapter we will address another important aspect of effective communication—speaking and presenting information concisely, i.e., getting to the point quickly! This skill is an especially crucial one in today's hectic world, where everyone is constantly running out of time. No one has the time or patience to listen to endless, unnecessary rambling. Particularly in business, we are increasingly expected to state our thoughts quickly and crisply—as the old saying goes, 'time is money'.

In your own experience, have you ever come across people who talk on and on? Doesn't it always seem like it takes them ten times longer than necessary to say what they mean? People like this are called *ramblers*—they are annoying and, quite frankly, can be a waste of time. When you are presenting an idea, a statement or answering a question, it is crucial that you are concise and to the point. Similarly, it is essential to focus on your voice quality and body language. Whether you are speaking to one person or giving a presentation to a group, learning these skills will set you apart from the crowd and help you in your professional life.

What will I learn in this chapter?

24.1 How to get to the point and speak logically.

24.2 Step 1—the introduction.

24.1 HOW TO GET TO THE POINT AND SPEAK LOGICALLY

The content of what you say is very important. Whether you are answering a simple question or presenting an idea to a crowd, the way you frame your thoughts should be logical and easy to follow. Logic and order are extremely important when it comes to speaking.

- Why does logic matter in conversation?

It is important to remember that no matter how interesting you may think you are, people will not listen to every word you say. Others will daydream while you are speaking. Thus, it is important to keep from wandering from the main point. For one, people are less likely to start daydreaming if you are concise and crisp. Second, when their mind does wander, it will be easy for them to jump back into the conversation and start following you again.

No matter how hard you try, there are times where your mind starts wandering when other people are speaking. Your boss could be speaking to you about a new project, but you might be thinking of what movie you are going to watch later in the evening. This is normal. We all daydream. Usually, we catch ourselves and quickly snap back into the conversation and start paying attention. However, for the few seconds that our mind was wandering, we lost out on what the other person was saying. Now, if the other person is a logical speaker, it will be easy for us to snap back into the conversation. However, if the other person is a rambler, we will be lost when we re-enter the conversation, and will most likely start daydreaming again.

No one wants to be known as a rambler. Sometimes, though, we hear ourselves and know that we are rambling, but just don't know how to stop. This easy-to-follow structure will help you become a more concise speaker. Remember, this is a format you can follow whether you are answering a simple question or putting together a presentation.

24.2 STEP 1: THE INTRODUCTION

The introduction should be self-sufficient. It should in itself tell the other person the core of what they need to know. The way to structure an introduction is as follows:

Part A: WHO, WHAT, WHEN, WHERE
+
Because
+
Part B: WHY – 1 or 2 reasons only

Let's use an easy example to illustrate the above. You are speaking to a friend and he asks you, 'What do you like to do for fun?' By using the above introduction structure, you could say:

```
'I love to paint pictures because painting allows me to release my frustrations and make presents for the people I love.'
```

Part A: I love to **paint pictures**

+

Because

+

Part B: Painting allows me to **release my frustrations** and **make presents for the people I love**.

When we break this down, we can see that:
- WHAT (Part A) = Painting
- WHY (Part B, reason 1) = Release frustrations
- WHY (Part B, reason 2) = Make presents for people who are loved

It is important that the introductory sentence be brief and you only state a few 'why' reasons. These 'why' reasons should *only* relate to the 'who', 'what', 'when', 'where'—in this example, painting.

24.3 STEP 2: THE CONTENT

Here, you provide the facts, opinions, examples and quotes that supporty the 'why' given in your introduction.

Support for 'why' (reason 1): release frustrations

```
'The other day I was extremely angry with my boss, and when I came home I started to paint a picture of the sea. Within twenty minutes, I was so absorbed in the painting I forgot I was angry. By the time I finished the painting I had completely forgiven my boss and was able to have a wonderful evening.'
```

Support for 'why' (reason 2): make presents for people who are loved

```
'It is also great to always be able to give people I love my own paintings as presents. The other day it was my best friend's birthday, and I gave her a picture of her that I had painted. She was so touched, and it felt so wonderful to be able to give her something no one else could give.'
```

Notice that these two things *only* support the 'why' reasons given in the introduction. These two things include actual reasons and examples. Thus, the listener will have something that makes them remember why you love painting. At this juncture, a common mistake is to start listing other 'what' or 'why' reasons. For example:

```
'I also love swimming and golfing and reading to my little sister'.
```

By listing too many other reasons, you are flooding the listener's mind with too much information and are rambling. Remember to support the introductory sentence with the reasons why you love painting rather than listing all the other things you like doing for fun. People do not have large enough attention spans to remember long lists of data. Thus, pick one thing to talk about and talk about it properly.

24.4 STEP 3: THE CONCLUDING SENTENCE

There is a famous saying that goes, 'Tell people what you are going to tell them, then tell them, at the end tell them what you have told them.' Remember how I mentioned earlier that people's minds tend to drift while other people are talking? It is crucial that you conclude by *re-stating* your original thought. This jolts people back into remembering what you began speaking about.

> 'Painting offers me a chance to give back to the people I love and become a calmer person, and so it is what I like to do most for fun.'

Notice that both the 'why' reasons from the introduction are stated again:

- 'Why' (reason 1): release frustrations—restated as 'to become a calmer person'.
- 'Why' (reason 2): make presents for people who are loved—restated as 'give back to people I love'.

So a conversation like this would read:

> 'I love to paint pictures because painting allows me to release my frustrations and make presents for the people I love. The other day I was extremely angry with my boss, and when I came home I started to paint a picture of the sea. Within twenty minutes, I was so absorbed in the painting I forgot I was angry. By the time I finished the painting I had completely forgiven my boss and was able to have a wonderful evening. It is also great to be able to give people I love my own paintings as presents. The other day it was my best friend's birthday,

```
and I gave her a picture of her that I had painted.
She was so touched, and it felt so wonderful to be
able to give her something no one else could.
Thus, because painting offers me a chance to give
back to the people I love and become a calmer
person, it is what I like to do most for fun.'
```

Exercise 24.1

Take a look at the response to the question, 'What is your favourite festival?' While reading the response, identify the following:

1. Step 1 (Introduction)—Who, What, When, Where.
2. Step 1 Why reasons.
3. Step 2 Backup for why reasons.
4. Step 3 Concluding sentence.

```
My favourite festival is Diwali, because I love
firecrackers and having my entire family together.
When we burst firecrackers the entire sky lights
up and it seems as if the whole world is happy.
Before my family goes out to burst firecrackers,
we have a large meal where we laugh together, talk
to one another and in general catch up with each
other's busy lives. All in all, Diwali, through
lights, laughter and fun, brings my family together.
```

Exercise 24.2

Ajit asks his friend Rajal, 'Why didn't you call me yesterday?' Rajal responds by saying:

```
'I forgot to call you because I was studying and
looking after my little brother. Also, I had to
pick up something for my mother and clean my room.
I just had so much to do!'
```

Identify the parts of the introduction in Rajal's response. Then write down the error with Rajal's response based on the structure we learned earlier. Give an example of a correct, concise response she could have given.

Exercise 24.3

Ami Badani is the marketing head at Sigma Communications. She is furious with one of her subordinates, a young new executive named Vipasha for a report she recently submitted. Ms Badani angrily asks Vipasha, 'Why was the marketing report you submitted incomplete?'

> Vipasha responds, 'Ms Badani, I was unable to find the necessary data because my computer was not working properly and I was unsure whether I was supposed to concentrate only on the client's marketing plan. While I was going through the client records, I found that their in-house information was not properly stated. Their product figures did not match their sales figures and thus I decided not to include any financials. It was a very confusing project.'

Identify the parts of the introduction in Vipasha's response. Then write down the error in Vipasha's response based on the structure we learned earlier. Give an example of a correct, concise response she could have given.

24.5 TIPS FOR SPEAKING CONCISELY

- Whether you are answering a simple question or giving a presentation, structure your thoughts logically and concisely.
- Anything you say should include an introduction, the main content and a concluding sentence.

Section IV

Professional Etiquette

We all want to get the job of our dreams—one that pays us more money and gives us more responsibility. But, to get a better job, we have to prove we are worthy of that job. To do so, our image really matters. How nicely we dress, how well we stand and look, how strongly we shake our interviewer's hand, how well we write our CV, and how professionally we talk to recruiters—all this adds up to give us our image. In this section, you will learn how to create a more professional image for yourself and how to get the job of your dreams!

Chapters in this section:

CHAPTER 25

Is etiquette important? Does image really matter?

Etiquette (Part 1): Dressing and grooming professionally

Amit joins a multinational bank as a junior associate. On his first day at work, he is asked to accompany a senior banker to a meeting with a client and take notes. The client is waiting for the two bankers, and as they walk in he frowns in disapproval. Amit's shirt is too thin, and it is obvious that he is wearing a sleeveless undershirt instead of a short-sleeved one. His watch is too loose and dangles distractingly off his wrist. It was hot outside and Amit, who rushed from the train to the office, is also releasing a tinge of body odour.

During the initial greetings, the client notices that Amit's handshake is not firm. The meeting continues and towards the end, the senior banker asks Amit to send a follow-up email to the client. A few hours later the email is received and the client's image of the company sinks further: the email is badly formatted and lacks professional etiquette.

What has gone wrong here?

- Amit has not dressed properly.
- Amit has not accessorized properly.
- Amit smells bad.
- Amit does not know how to shake hands in a meeting.
- Amit wrote an unprofessional email.

Overall, Amit has shown a lack of both grooming and professionalism.

When working in today's business world, grooming and etiquette are extremely important—image really does matter.

In this chapter we will go over some basic dressing and grooming tips that you can easily incorporate into your everyday life.

What will I learn in this chapter?

25.1 Men—how to dress to impress.
25.2 Women—how to dress to impress.
25.3 Ways to groom yourself.

25.1 MEN—HOW TO DRESS TO IMPRESS

Before we begin, an important point—you do not have to buy designer brands or spend a lot of money to look professional. All you need to do is avoid certain fabrics, choose certain colours and wear accessories correctly.

We will also go over some basic tips for dressing professionally at the workplace. Remember that every workplace will have its own rules. These are some general tips for looking sharp and appropriate in a business setting.

TROUSERS

- Colours:
  - ✓ Stick to black, grey or dark blue.
- Fabrics:
  - ✗ Do not wear 100 per cent cotton trousers to interviews as they wrinkle easily. Cotton khakis can be worn to work, but not to interviews or meetings.
  - ✗ Do not wear shiny polyester trousers (100 per cent polyester trousers).
  - ✗ Do not wear jeans to meetings and interviews.
  - ✓ Wear trousers that are a combination of polyester/rayon or cotton/synthetic. While trousers that are 100 per cent wool, 100 per cent micro-synthetic and wool/synthetic combinations are very nice, they are impractical in a hot country like India.
- Size:
  - ✓ Make sure your trousers fit well—do not wear baggy trousers.
  - ✗ Trousers should not be rolled at the end.

✗ Trousers should not be too long and not touch the floor when you walk.
✗ Trousers should also not be too short. Your socks should not be visible when you walk.
✓ Look at men's fashion magazines to get an idea of how good trousers should fit.

SHIRTS

- Style:
  ✓ Wear shirts with collars.
  ✗ Avoid wearing shirts that are too thin.
- Colours:
  ✓ Avoid wearing shirts with flashy designs or patterns—stick to one colour or simple stripes.
  ✓ Light blues, greys, whites and crèmes are the best.
  ✗ Avoid colours like red and purple.
- Fabrics:
  ✓ Wear shirts that are 100 per cent cotton or cotton/synthetic combinations.
  ✗ Do not wear silk, 100 per cent polyester and 100 per cent rayon.

- Size:
  - ✓ Make sure your shirt fits well. When you tuck it in, it should not look baggy.
  - ✓ Try to wear shirts with removable stays—this will keep your collar looking firm.
  - ✓ Iron your shirts properly before wearing them.
  - ✓ Tuck your shirts into your trousers, do not leave them hanging out loose.
  - ✓ Try to match your shirts with your trousers. Look at men's fashion magazines for tips.

UNDERSHIRTS

✓ Wear undershirts under collared shirts so that sweat does not seep through.

✗ Do not wear sleeveless undershirts.

SHOES

✓ Shoes should be black or brown. Avoid white and other light-coloured shoes.
✓ If possible, buy leather shoes—they are the best.
✗ No tennis shoes, sandals or slippers.

TIES

✓ Wear a tie to all interviews and meetings.
✓ Ties can be single coloured or multicoloured. If multicoloured, make sure that at least one of the colours on the tie is the same as your shirt or your trousers. Avoid ties with floral patterns, cartoon characters or anything too flashy.

✓ The tie should be knotted so that it is just long enough to touch the belt.

JACKETS

✓ It's best to take a suit jacket along with you for an interview. There is no harm in looking extra professional. Also, you can always take off your jacket if you are feeling hot, or if you feel you are overdressed. For an interview, make sure your jacket is the same fabric and colour as your trousers. If you are not going to an interview, your jacket and trousers can be different colours, like a black jacket and grey trousers. For meetings, ask your superior if you should take a jacket. For the most part, if you are wearing a tie, you don't really need to wear a jacket.

ACCESSORIES

✓ Trousers should always be worn with belts. Belts should not be wider than one inch and the colour should match your shoe colour (e.g. brown belt with brown shoes).

✗ Avoid large silver and gold buckles, as they are too flashy.

✓ A watch should be fitted, it should not dangle off your wrist like a bracelet.

✗ Don't wear sunglasses (on your face or on your head) for an interview or meeting.

25.2 DRESS TO IMPRESS—WOMEN

Here too, one thing is certain—you do not have to buy designer brands and spend a lot of money to look professional. All you need to do is avoid certain fabrics, choose certain colours, and wear accessories correctly.

Let's go over some basic tips for dressing professionally at the workplace. Remember, every workplace will have its own rules. These are general tips for looking sharp and appropriate in a business setting.

Women can wear both western clothes and Indian clothes to the workplace. Let's first look at some tips for western clothes.

TROUSERS AND SKIRTS

- Colours:
  - ✓ Almost any colour works. To be extra safe, stick to black, grey, blue, green and crèmes.
  - ✗ Avoid colours like bright pink, bright orange and red as they are too distracting.
  - ✓ For the most part, avoid flashy patterns—stick to single-coloured trousers and skirts.
- Fabrics:
  - ✗ Do not wear shiny, 100 per cent polyester skirts or trousers.
  - ✗ Do not wear jeans.
  - ✓ Wear skirts and trousers that are 100 per cent wool, 100 per cent linen, wool/synthetic combinations, cotton/synthetic combinations or silk/synthetic combinations.
  - ✓ If wearing a thin skirt or trousers, make sure your underwear does not show through. You must always check how you look in the back in a mirror before leaving the house.
- Size
  - ✓ Skirts should be knee-length or longer. (No mini-skirts please.) A-line skirts without slits are the best.
  - ✓ Trousers should be fitted, but not too tight. If you have big hips, make sure your trousers are straight-leg, or that they flare out lightly at the end. (Do not wear tapered trousers.)
  - ✗ Make sure your trousers are not too long and don't touch the floor after you put your shoes on.

SHIRTS

- Style:
  - ✓ Collared shirts, blouses or sweaters can be worn safely.
- Colour:
  - ✓ Almost any colour works for women. To be extra professional stick to whites, blues, greys and crèmes.
  - ✗ Try to avoid colours that are too distracting, like bright pink, bright orange and red.
  - ✓ Single colours or patterns are both acceptable. If wearing patterns, stick to stripes, checks and simple designs. Avoid floral patterns.

- Fabric:
  - ✓ When wearing collared shirts, wear 100 per cent cotton or cotton/synthetic combinations.
  - ✓ When wearing blouses, wear cotton, synthetic and silks (any combination).
  - ✓ When wearing sweaters, any material is fine.
  - ✗ Avoid wearing shirts that are too thin—your bra should not show through your shirt.
- Size:
  - ✓ For interviews, long-sleeved shirts are always safe.
  - ✓ For daily work, short sleeves are okay. Do not wear sleeveless shirts.
  - ✓ Iron your shirts (especially collared shirts) before wearing them.
  - ✓ Tuck in—tucking your shirt in looks sharper. However, if you are on the heavier side, it will look better if you leave your shirt untucked. If you do leave your shirt untucked, make sure your shirt is not too long or too short. It should fall halfway down your hip.
  - ✓ Try to match your shirts with your skirts and trousers. Look at women's fashion magazines for tips.

Let's now go over how you should dress if you are wearing Indian clothes.

SALWAR KAMEEZES

- Colour:
  - ✓ Stick to simple prints. Complicated and flashy designs are not good in the workplace.
  - ✓ Almost all colours are fine.
- Fabric:
  - ✓ Wear 100 per cent cotton, 100 per cent silk, cotton/synthetic combinations, cotton/silk combinations.
  - ✗ Do not wear 100 per cent synthetic material—these kinds of salwar kameezes look too shiny, too thin and too tacky. You want to make sure that the fabric is thick.

SARIS

- Only wear a sari if you are already used to wearing one. If you cannot walk or sit gracefully in a sari, then don't wear one to an interview or a meeting.
- Colours:
  - ✓ Stick to simple prints. Complicated and flashy designs are distracting at the workplace.
  - ✓ Almost all colours are fine—just avoid distracting colours like bright pink, bright orange and red.
- Fabric:
  - ✓ Wear 100 per cent cotton, 100 per cent silk, cotton/silk combinations or chiffon.
  - ✗ Do not wear synthetic saris. They look too shiny, too thin and too tacky. You want to make sure the fabric is thick.
- Blouse:
  - ✗ Your blouse should not be be low—minimum skin should be exposed.
  - ✗ Don't wear a sleeveless blouse. Wear a blouse with sleeves that fall before your elbows.

Now, lets go over shoes and the other accessories that go with both western and Indian clothes.

SHOES

✓ When wearing western clothes, you must wear close-toed shoes.
✓ When wearing Indian clothes, open-toed sandals are acceptable.
✓ Leather shoes are the best, but other materials will do.
✓ Stick to dark-coloured shoes. Avoid white and light coloured shoes.
✓ Heels are nice, but only wear them if you can walk in them properly.
✗ Do not wear tennis shoes or slippers.

ACCESSORIES

- Subtle jewellery should be worn.
  - ✓ One necklace, three rings or less (total, not per hand) and small earrings are acceptable.
  - ✗ Avoid wearing too much gold.
  - ✗ No bangles—one simple bracelet is more professional.

✓ Scarves are nice accessories and are fashionable. Only wear them if you can match them properly with your outfit.
✓ Belts are nice accessories when you are wearing trousers. Make sure the buckle is not too big. If you are wearing gold jewellery, make sure the buckle is gold. If you are wearing silver jewellery, make sure the buckle is silver.
✓ Make sure your purse looks professional. Do not go to an interview with a pink, synthetic purse you took to a party the night before.
✗ Don't wear sunglasses (on your face or on your head) for an interview or important meeting.

Now that we have covered how to dress, let's learn how to groom ourselves.

25.3 WAYS TO GROOM YOURSELF

India is a hot country, and you should keep this in mind when you dress. Especially during the summers, the temperature can be scorching. Many of us use public transport—buses, trains, auto rickshaws and taxis—in order to travel to and from work. Thus, smelling good and staying fresh are not always the easiest task.

Here are two sets of suggestions to help you present yourself better. The first set includes things you *must* do, no matter what. The second set includes things you *can* do, if you have a bit more money and time on your hands.

Things you *must* do:

CLOTHES

There is really no excuse for wearing dirty clothes. Make sure your clothes are always washed before you wear them. If you travel by train or bus and you know you will get dirty, don't wear white shirts—wear darker colours that can hide small amounts of grease or perspiration. You can also carry an extra shirt with you for emergencies.

HAIR

Shampoo your hair more than once a week—oily hair is not a pretty sight. If you use hair oil, always wash it out before going for an interview or professional appointment or meeting. For women, it may look more professional to keep your hair tied up and out of your face. For men, short hair is always more professional, as is a good, close shave. Don't overuse hair gels.

BODY ODOUR

You must have a bath every day and use soap to clean yourself properly. After you eat meals or go to the toilet, you must *always* wash your hands with soap.

You must apply anti-perspirant or deodorant. Please note that an anti-perspirant is different from a deodorant. A deodorant simply adds fragrance, but does not stop you from sweating. If you want to reduce sweating as well as smell good, you must buy products labelled 'anti-perspirant'. Also, make sure you keep a bottle of anti-perspirant with you at all times. This way, once you get off the train, you can quickly reapply your anti-perspirant before going into the office. You should periodically check if you smell bad and reapply when necessary. Wear a bit of cologne or perfume. Be careful not to wear too much.

BAD BREATH

When you know you are going for an interview or an important meeting, don't eat onions, garlic or other foods that you know will make your breath smell bad. Also, after lunch, go to the bathroom and rinse out your mouth. Keep chewing gum or breath mints with you so that if you have to meet someone suddenly, you can pop one in your mouth. Some people even keep a small tube of toothpaste and a toothbrush with them just in case.

It is also a very good habit to check that there is no food stuck in your teeth after you have finished eating.

NAILS—WOMEN

You do not *have* to wear nail polish. If you do, refrain from wearing red and bright pink (or any other bright colour) to an interview or an important meeting. Stick to light pinks, crèmes or clear nail polish. Also, make sure your nail polish is not chipped.

The length of your fingernails matters. Make sure your fingernails are not too long, and that there is no dirt stuck under them.

The appearance of your toenails is also extremely important. If you are wearing open-toed shoes you must make sure that your toenails look clean. They should be short, and if you have applied nail polish, make sure it is not chipped.

NAILS—MEN

Many men think that the appearance of their nails goes unnoticed. Nothing could be further from the truth. You must make sure your nails are always clipped short. Also, make sure there is no dirt stuck under your fingernails. You can remove the dirt in your fingernails by washing them, soaking them in water, or taking a nail file and removing the dirt.

FACIAL HAIR—WOMEN

As Indians, we naturally tend to have dark facial and body hair. It is very important that you wax or thread your upper lip, chin and cheeks if you have excessive hair growth (almost all women have to at least wax their upper lip). Additionally, shaping your eyebrows will make your eyes look cleaner.

If you have hair on your hands, fingers, feet and toes, make sure you remove it (especially fingers and toes). Also, do not wear a skirt without waxing or shaving your legs.

FACIAL HAIR—MEN

Keeping a moustache or beard is each man's personal preference. If you don't have a moustache or a beard, make sure you shave the day you have an interview or an important meeting. A stubble does not look sharp.

Also, make sure you check to see if you have nose hairs that show and if so, pluck or trim them.

THINGS YOU *CAN* DO

LOTION

When you wear short-sleeved shirts or short skirts, make sure you apply lotion on your elbows and knees. Dry, cracked skin is not a pretty sight.

FACIAL SKIN

Don't use the same soap you use on your body for your face. Use face soap or face wash, as it is less harsh and contains less oil. Face soaps that say 'hypo-allergenic' on the label are very good to use. If you tend to sweat a lot during the day, it may be a good idea to take a bar of soap to work and wash your face in the middle of the day.

MAKE-UP—WOMEN

Don't go overboard using make-up in the workplace. It should be worn within reason, or not at all. If you would like to wear a bit of make-up to help you look sharper, I recommend the following:

- Lips: Apply a little lip-gloss or natural-coloured lipstick on your lips.
- Eyes: Apply a touch of mascara on your eyelashes. Also, curling your eyelashes can make a world of difference to your eyes. You can buy an eyelash curler at a beauty supply store or chemist. A very small line of kajal on the top of your eyes also looks nice. Using dark brown eyeliner instead of black can be softer and better for the workplace.
- Skin:
  - ✓ If you have oily skin, use a face blotter. These are small sheets of paper also known as 'paper powders'. They can be found in department stores. Brands like Clean & Clear and Ponds sell them in India. Each slip of paper can be dabbed on your skin to remove excess oil. They are a bit expensive, but if you can afford them they are very useful right before an important meeting.
  - ✓ Face powders are great if you want your skin to look extra perfect. Refrain from using foundation, as it tends to look caked,

and in hot weather melts rather quickly. Also, foundation is not very good for your skin. If you do end up using foundation or face powder, make sure the colour is just a half shade lighter than your skin. Don't be fooled into thinking that lighter foundation makes your skin look lighter—you might just end up looking funny. Last, if you apply foundation or face powder on your face, apply it on your neck as well so that the colour matches.

✓ A small amount of blush on your cheeks can look nice as it can give you a healthy glow. But it is not really necessary, and if you don't know how to use blush properly, refrain from doing so. If you accidentally put on too much, you could end up looking like a clown.

Remember, make-up should enhance and highlight your features rather than draw negative attention to them.

You may feel that some of the above tips are trivial or cumbersome, but if followed, they can make a big difference to your overall appearance. And in the end, if you look good, you will also feel good.

CHAPTER 26

Is etiquette important? Does image really matter?

Etiquette (Part 2): Greetings and business cards

In the previous chapter we learned how Amit, a junior associate at a multinational bank, failed to make a good first impression with a client. We learned that many of his problems were to do with how he was dressed and groomed. In this chapter, we'll go over some of the other mistakes Amit made. There are also extra tips on business etiquette that will help you conduct yourself in interviews, meetings and other professional activities.

What will I learn in this chapter?

26.1 How to make a good first impression.
26.2 Business card etiquette.
26.3 Extra tips on professional etiquette.

26.1 HOW TO MAKE A GOOD FIRST IMPRESSION

Meeting someone for the first time can be nerve-racking. What if you extend your hand for a handshake and they don't shake your hand back? What if you ask them a question and they simply ignore you? What if they think you are stupid? What if they think you are unattractive? What if they just don't like you?

Take a deep breath. It might make you feel better to know that most people go through the same emotional turmoil before meeting someone new—especially if that someone is an interviewer or a client.

The trick to feeling confident is actually very simple—just act confident! And what's the easiest way to act confident? Give the perfect handshake of course!

Handshakes are very important. They reveal a great deal about your character and confidence. Follow these pointers for effective handshakes:

✓ Give a firm handshake. This shows you are confident in yourself and your abilities. If you are a woman, remember there is no reason why your handshake should be weak. If you are a man (especially a strong one), be careful that your handshake is not *too* firm. You don't want to hurt the other person.

✓ Who goes first? If you walk into a room for an interview or a meeting and the other person does not extend their hand, extend yours. Don't be shy. On the contrary, if you extend your hand first, it shows you are confident and not afraid to seize the initiative. Many women have problems extending their hand first. Women tend to wait for the other person (especially if the other person is a man) to extend their hand first. There is no need to do this.

✓ Look the person in the eye. When you shake someone's hand, make sure you are looking at them squarely in the eyes (not below or above).

✓ Stand up straight. Posture is important. When you walk into a room or when you get up to shake someone's hand, remember to stand up straight.

✗ Make sure your palms are not sweaty. In humid weather, you must always be careful about this before shaking someone's hand. If you are about to walk into a meeting, wipe your palms on a handkerchief or napkin first.

26.2 BUSINESS CARD ETIQUETTE

Giving and receiving business cards is another area where many of us unknowingly act in an unprofessional way. Read the tips given below:

✓ Always make sure you have your business card on you before going to a meeting, conference or other professional event.

✓ When handing your business card to someone, always make sure the print is facing the other person. Don't make them turn the card around to read it.

✗ Some people hand out their business cards using two hands. They also bow slightly when handing the card over. This is an extremely polite way to hand someone your business card. However, it can come across as being overly polite, overly formal and not modern. The more accepted way to hand out business cards is to use one hand.

✗ Don't pass your business cards around like flyers. Wait until you have had a conversation with someone, and then offer your business card before you go your separate ways. Especially if someone is senior to you, you must wait until you have had a dialogue before handing them your business card.

✓ When someone hands you their business card, take a second to read the card. It will make the person feel you are interested in them.

26.3 EXTRA TIPS ON PROFESSIONAL ETIQUETTE

✓ Standing up: If someone walks into a room and you are sitting down, it is polite to get up and then offer your hand for a handshake.

✗ Mobile phone: Turn the ringer of your mobile phone off during meetings. Also, don't keep looking at your phone during the meeting to check the time or to see if you've received a new text message.

✓ Posture: Keep your posture straight when you meet someone. When you are sitting behind a desk or table, make sure your back is straight. Don't slump.

CHAPTER 27

How can I come across as being professional over the phone?

Telephone etiquette (Part 1): General tips

So many potential jobs, networking opportunities, clients and customers are lost because of poor telephone etiquette. Much of today's verbal communication is done over the phone. This makes it absolutely necessary for everyone to know how to sound professional and polite over the phone. This chapter will cover basic, everyday telephone etiquette that will help you become more successful in the workplace.

What will I learn in this chapter?

27.1 Bad phone etiquette.
27.2 Good phone etiquette.
27.3 The rules of phone etiquette.

27.1 BAD PHONE ETIQUETTE

A young girl named Simran had an assignment from her university—she was to interview CEOs of Human Resource companies in order to learn more about their industry. After days of calling different companies, she finally found one CEO, Ms Mehta, who agreed to speak with her about the project. Ms Mehta told Simran to call her the next day and perhaps they could find a time to meet.

Simran was excited. Ms Mehta was well-known in the HR world, and Simran was sure she would be able to provide valuable insight into the industry. The next morning, Simran anxiously dialled Ms Mehta's cellphone. Let's see how the conversation went.

Ms Mehta answered the phone after several rings and in a rushed voiced said, 'Hello?' Simran immediately responded, 'Hi, this is Simran. What time can we meet today?'

Ms Mehta was confused. Who was Simran? A client? An employee? She didn't know what to say and answered, 'Uh, I'm sorry, who?' Simran quickly answered, 'This is Simran Shah!'

Ms Mehta suddenly recollected the young girl named Simran who had called her the day before. 'Oh yes, Simran from Delhi University.' Ms Mehta thought for a second, she had a very busy day lined up. She would have to take time out to see Simran. And judging from the way Simran had sounded on the phone, she was not really looking forward to helping her. 'You know Simran, today is not good for me. Why don't you try calling me later this week?'

'Uh, okay. Bye.' Simran hung up. She was sad; she had been looking forward to meeting Ms Mehta. Also, her project was due next week.

What went wrong here? Very simply, Simran did not show the correct phone etiquette—she did not sound professional or polite. Also, she did not make herself sound like an interesting, enthusiastic person. Why would Ms Mehta, a busy executive, want to make time for someone like that?

This example can teach us something about the different calls we have to make as business professionals. Whether we are calling a recruiter for a job, an HR representative to set up an interview, or a potential customer or client, we need to be courteous and friendly on the phone. Let's now take a look at how Simran's conversation with Ms Mehta could have gone better.

27.2 GOOD PHONE ETIQUETTE

We saw how Simran failed to make a good impression on Ms Mehta. Let's see what happens when Simran adds a little professional etiquette to her phone call.

Ms Mehta answered the phone after several rings. In a rushed voiced she said, 'Hello?' Simran immediately answered by saying, 'Hi, Ms Mehta, this is Simran Shah from Delhi University. We spoke yesterday about a project I am doing. I hope you haven't forgotten me!'

Ms Mehta immediately recollected who Simran was. 'Of course I haven't forgotten you! How are you?'

'I'm fine, thank you. I hope I am not disturbing you. Is this a good time for you to talk?' asked Simran.

Ms Mehta looked at her watch and replied, 'Actually, I am just about to go to a meeting.'

'Oh, I'm sorry! I was just calling to see if you had any time to spare today to meet me.'

Ms Mehta remembered she had told Simran yesterday that she could maybe meet her today. She was very busy, but the young girl sounded so enthusiastic and seemed so polite that Ms Mehta answered, 'You know, today is quite busy for me. But, I can try and squeeze you in during the late afternoon. Why don't you come to my office around five? You might have to wait though.'

Simran was relieved. 'Oh, that's no problem! Thanks so much for your time and I really look forward to meeting you.'

'Me too, Simran. See you at five.'

In the second conversation, Ms Mehta made time to meet Simran because Simran was polite, professional and energetic. Let's examine the difference between the two conversations and learn the rules behind good telephone etiquette.

27.3 THE RULES OF PHONE ETIQUETTE

Rule 1: Timing

Be careful with your timing. If you are calling a business executive you don't know too well on their cellphone, don't call before 9 a.m. or after 7 p.m. It might be considered rude if you call after business hours. If you must call someone before or after these times, be sure to apologize for it: 'I am so sorry to disturb you so early/late.'

Rule 2: Don't call from a noisy place

If you are in a noisy place—a train, a crowded building, outside—don't make a professional phone call. Find a quiet place. Also, if you are calling from your cellphone, make sure you have a clear signal.

Rule 3: Know how to pronounce the person's name

When you call someone make sure you know the correct pronunciation of their name. If you don't know how to pronounce a particular name, ask someone for help in advance. Then, before making the phone call, practice saying the name out loud once or twice to get used to it.

Rule 4: Introduce yourself

Don't assume that just because you spoke to someone once they will remember who you are. Always state your full name, where you are calling from, and how the person knows you. Remember Simran's introduction? The first time she said: 'Hi, this is Simran. What time can we meet today?'

Simran *assumed* that Ms Mehta remembered her name and who she was. Let's look at Simran's improved introduction from her second conversation: 'Hi Ms Mehta, this is Simran Shah from Delhi University. We spoke yesterday about a project I am doing. I hope you haven't forgotten me!'

This time, Simran mentioned her first and last name, where she was from, and how Ms Mehta knew her. Also, she said very politely, 'I hope you haven't forgotten me!' Adding a friendly phrase like this can break the ice and make the rest of the conversation much easier for you.

Rule 5: People are busy—respect their time

Just because someone answers the phone does not mean they have the time to talk to you. Especially when you call someone on their cellphone you have no idea what they might be doing. They could be in a meeting, they could be having an argument with someone, or they could be at the hospital visiting someone. You must ask if it is a convenient time to talk. Simran did not do this the first time. The second time, she said: 'I hope I am not disturbing you. Is this a good time for you to talk?' A question like this will make the other person feel that you are polite and respectful of their time.

Rule 6: What if they *are* busy?

If someone tells you they are busy, apologize immediately and then quickly get to the point. For example, in the second conversation when Ms Mehta told Simran she was busy, Simran quickly said: 'Oh, I'm sorry! I just was calling to see if you had any time to spare today to meet me.'

Notice how Simran apologized first to Ms Mehta for disturbing her *before* asking to meet her. This is what we refer to as *etiquette*: being polite and gracious.

After this, Simran immediately got to the point and asked if Ms Mehta would have time to meet her. Keep in mind, though, that if you don't have a direct question and the person tells you they are busy, just ask what is a good time for you to call back. Only continue to ask your question if it is a short, direct, yes/no type question. In Simran's case her question was a quick, yes/no question. Also, because she had been so polite, Ms Mehta ended up saying yes.

Rule 7: Closing the call

No matter what the outcome of your phone call is, you must say goodbye politely. In Simran's first conversation, she ended the call with: 'Uh, okay. Bye.'

In the first conversation, Simran did not get the answer she was looking for, as Ms Mehta said she couldn't meet with her. In spite of this, Simran should have stayed positive and given Ms Mehta a polite response. One way Simran could have said this is: 'Okay, I will call you later this week to see if you have some time to meet. Sorry once again to have disturbed you, and I do hope we can meet soon!'

Here, Simran ended the call on a positive note. She told Ms Mehta she would follow up, she apologized, and she showed a genuine interest in meeting Ms Mehta in the future. This creates a favourable impression of Simran in Ms Mehta's mind. When Simran follows up later in the week, Ms Mehta is more likely to meet her.

Now let's look back at Simran's second conversation with Ms Mehta. In this conversation, Simran got the answer she was looking for, as Ms Mehta agreed to meet with her. Simran ended this call by saying: 'Thanks so much for your time and I really look forward to meeting you.'

In this case, Simran thanked Ms Mehta for her time and showed a genuine interest in meeting her later that day.

There are many ways to end a call politely. These two examples should give you a basic framework to use. Every call is different, and you must use your own judgment. Keep in mind that showing respect for people and their time will never go unnoticed.

CHAPTER 28

How do I follow up with a company executive for a job?

Telephone etiquette (Part 2): Following up with a company executive after sending your CV

We learnt over how to put together a professional email when sending a CV out to company recruiters in the grammar section.

In this chapter, we will learn the next step in this process—actually being called for an interview. Just because you have sent someone a professional email and a great CV does not mean they will call you back. Company HR representatives receive many CVs and are very busy. Thus, it is up to you to follow up and stand out from everyone else.

Following up after you have emailed your CV is a delicate matter. You want to come across as proactive and enthusiastic about the job, but if you say the wrong things or call at the wrong time, you might come across as pushy and annoying. This chapter will give you a framework to fall back upon when making important phone calls.

What will I learn in this chapter?

28.1 The first follow-up phone call.

28.2 The second, third and fourth time you follow up on the phone.

28.3 How to take rejection positively.

28.1 THE FIRST FOLLOW-UP PHONE CALL

Before learning what to say when you follow up with company executives, let's read the email from chapter 14 that Rohini sent to Ms Patel once again. Pay close attention to the last sentence.

> Dear Ms Patel,
>
> My name is Rohini Gupta and I obtained your contact information from your company website. I am interested in applying for a position in your research department. Currently, I have over two years of experience in this area. Please find attached to this email a copy of my CV that details my past work experience.
>
> I will follow up with you during the week to confirm you have received this email. I look forward to speaking with you.
>
> Regards,
> Rohini Gupta
> 981-122-3456

In the final paragraph of this email, Rohini gave herself permission to follow up with Ms Patel. Now when Rohini actually calls, it is justified and she won't seem pushy.

When calling an executive for the first time, you really need to put your best foot forward. This is your chance to make a good impression and win an interview. These three rules will help you make your follow up strategies more professional.

When should you first follow up?

First, you need to find the direct telephone number of the person you sent the CV to. If you don't have the direct number, and the company operator will not give it to you, then have the operator transfer you to him/her. I recommend waiting three days before you make your first follow-up phone call.

What should you say?

The point of the first phone call is to make sure the person received your email. When you make your first call, try saying something along these lines:

```
'Hi, my name is Rohini Gupta. I emailed my CV to
you this Monday regarding a possible position in
your research department. I just wanted to confirm
that you received it.'
```

If the person says yes, she did receive it, then you can respond:

```
'Great! Have you had a chance to look at it yet?'
```

If she says no, she has not had a chance to look at it, you could say:

> 'That's okay; I know you must be very busy. I *am* very interested in working for your company so I *do hope* you will be able to look at it soon.'

Do not say:

✗ 'I want to work for your company so please look at it soon.'

This sounds too pushy. Remember, it never helps to sound pushy and annoying. Saying something like 'please look at it soon' is just too forceful and commanding. Saying 'I do hope you will be able to look at it soon' is polite, professional and friendly.

Before you hang up, make sure to say:

✓ 'I will give you a call next week to see if you have had a chance to look at my CV. Thanks a lot for your time and have a nice day!'

By informing the other person that you will call again next week, you are once again giving yourself permission to call. Don't ask:

✗ 'Is it okay if I call you next week?'

If the person says 'no', then your options are limited. You must never call someone if they tell you not to. That is why it is always safer not to actually ask for permission to call. Instead, just politely tell the person that you will call them.

Leaving a message

It is possible that you might not get the person on the phone at all, and will have to leave a voicemail message. I would recommend calling a few times first, just to see if you can catch them by chance. If after the third or the fourth time you still get their voicemail, then leave a message which sounds like this:

> 'Hello Ms Patel, my name is Rohini Gupta. I am calling regarding my CV that I emailed to you on Monday, for a position in your research department. I just wanted to make sure you received my email. My name, once again, is Rohini Gupta, and my phone number is 981-122-3456. I look forward to hearing from you.'

Make sure you repeat your name at the end of the message, and leave your phone number. Also, try and make your voice sound friendly, positive and professional during the phone call. Try to not sound drab, boring or too casual.

28.2 THE SECOND, THIRD AND FOURTH TIME YOU FOLLOW UP ON THE PHONE

Even after following up with a company executive, your call may not be returned. Usually, you will have to follow up and call the person several times before you get an interview. If they don't return your call, do not feel defeated and think they don't like you. Most company executives are so busy that they really do need to be reminded of things many times.

The second phone call

After the first follow up phone call, I recommend waiting another week or so before calling again. This time, you can say:

> 'Hi Ms Patel, this is Rohini Gupta again. I emailed you my CV last week for a position in your research department. I am sorry if I am bothering you, but

```
I just wanted to know if you have had a chance to
look at my CV.'
```

It is very important that you remind the person who you are and when you sent your CV. Do not just say your name without a context. People are busy and might not remember your name. If you are unable to contact the person and have to leave a voicemail message, you can say the same thing. Just remember to say your phone number clearly at the end of the message, and repeat your name.

Now, if you do happen to get the person on the phone and they say they have not had a chance to look through your CV, you should reply:

```
'Okay, I understand. Since it has been a while
since I sent it, would you like me to send it
again?'
```

If they say yes and tell you to resend your CV, you can say:

```
'Great! I will go ahead and email you my CV again
today. I look forward to hearing from you, and
have a nice day.'
```

If they say no, don't resend the CV, you should simply say:

```
'Thanks, I look forward to hearing from you and
have a nice day.'
```

The third phone call

I would wait about two weeks before following up and calling the same person again. Now, it is possible that the person will tell you that if they are interested in you, and that they will call you. This does not mean you should not call and follow up with them. Remember, you need to stand out from all the other people who also sent in their CVs for the same position. You must keep calling so that the person realizes that you are truly interested, and agrees to give you an interview. Only if the person directly tells you not to call, do you stop calling. Never call someone who tells you not to call them.

When you call for the third time, say something along these lines:

> 'Hello, Ms Patel. This is Rohini Gupta again. I sent you my CV a few weeks ago. I apologize for calling you so many times; it is just that I am really interested in meeting you. Have you had a chance to look at my CV?'

If the person says they have not had a chance to look at it, you could say something like:

> 'Okay. Is it possible for me to come to your office and meet you, even for just five minutes? I am really interested in working for your company and would really appreciate just five minutes of your time.'

If they say yes, that's great! You have got yourself an interview! If they say no, they are busy and it's not possible to meet, you can say:

> 'What about next week? Can you spare some time then?'

If they say they're not sure about next week, you could say:

> 'I understand. I will give you a call early next week to see if you have any time. I really appreciate you taking the time to talk to me, and again, I am sorry for calling so often.'

Then, go ahead and call the person next week and see if they are free to meet. Your goal is to get an interview, and that is what you should aim for without coming across as pushy and annoying.

28.3 HOW TO TAKE REJECTION POSITIVELY

When you call to follow up, the person might tell you that they have looked at your CV and are not interested in hiring you. If this happens, don't get upset. Instead, politely say:

```
'Thanks very much for taking the time to look at my CV. Please do keep it on file so that you can contact me if anything comes up.'
```

Always leave things on a good note, as you never know what might happen in the future. Also, remember to stay positive during the process of looking for a job. Most successful people have had to work very hard to get their first few jobs. You may have to send your CV and follow up with many different companies. Take each rejection as a learning experience, and think of how you can do better the next time. Getting upset will only make things more difficult for you. Remember, it takes a lot of effort and patience to get a good job!

CHAPTER 29

I got an interview! Now what?

How to conduct yourself at interviews

We have learnt how to speak and dress well, how to behave in a professional manner and how to secure an interview from HR executives. In this chapter, we will learn what to do once you actually get to the interview. We will go over basic questions that people are asked across a range of industries. Additionally, we will cover a few BPO-specific questions.

What will I learn in this chapter?

29.1 General tips for interviews.
29.2 How to answer specific interview questions.
29.3 How to answer BPO specific interview questions.
29.4 Dealing with stress interviews.

29.1 GENERAL TIPS FOR INTERVIEWS

1. Dress well and look good. (See chapter 25 for tips on dressing and grooming.)
2. Shake hands confidently. (See chapter 26 for more tips.)
3. Take an extra copy of your CV with you.
4. Do your homework and be prepared: no matter how confident you are, no one can ever be fully prepared for an interview. Go over your answers to possible questions. Have hard facts to talk about. Ask a friend or family member to do a mock interview with you. If that is not possible, try saying your answers out loud while looking at a mirror.

5. Look confident even if you don't feel it. There are two ways to reduce nervousness before interviews. One, prepare well so you are confident before you go in there. Two, realize that not getting a particular job is not the end of the world. If you can do this, you will begin to enjoy your interviews. The more you look forward to going to an interview, the better you will perform.
6. Learn from your interviews: Look at each interview as an opportunity to learn. It is no big deal if you are not selected for a few jobs, instead analyse what went wrong in each failed interview. If you don't get a certain job, call the person who interviewed you. Ask them if they have any suggestions for you so that you can improve before your next interview.

   You can learn a lot from your interviewer. Observe how they dress, how they talk, and really try to learn what you can. Interviews are great opportunities to gain knowledge on how professional environments operate. The more interviews you go to, the better you will become at answering interview questions.

29.2 HOW TO ANSWER SPECIFIC INTERVIEW QUESTIONS

Let's go over some common interview questions and how you can best answer them.

Q. Can you tell us about yourself?

This is a very, very important question. Although it seems easy and straightforward, most people mess up the interview at this very question. This question gives you the opportunity to quickly differentiate yourself from the other candidates. No interviewer wants to hear you list your academic or other qualifications. But at the same time it is important that you talk about yourself in relation to the things mentioned in your resumé. How do you do this? Here is a trick that usually works. Say something interesting about yourself: 'I am an assertive and ambitious person.' Then, link this quality to a work or academic experience. Make sure the example is a quick one:

```
'For instance, when I was at university I was
doing a summer project for a communications company.
I realized that my team was not heading in the
right direction, so I took the lead and came up
with an entirely new approach to the problem. This
resulted in a big improvement in sales, and the
company head personally congratulated me.'
```

As you can see, you have accomplished two things. One, you have given the interviewer an insight into your personality. Two, you have talked about something on your resumé—but in a way that your interviewer will remember.

It is very important that you make sure the example you give is quick and to the point. Don't go on narrating a long story about yourself. You need to have crisp, concise examples prepared before walking into an interview.

If you can't think of an example for a certain quality, you need to pick another quality. No interviewer will remember what you said unless you give them an example. Hard evidence will make you stand out from other people.

This process can be tiring. It is difficult to introspect and come up with actual examples. It is very easy to say, 'I am a giving person.' But it is when you have to think of actual experiences to back up this statement that things can get difficult. However, introspecting and learning about yourself is an important part of this process. Sit down and seriously analyse your past actions, your accomplishments, or the skills that you have developed.

Q. What are your strengths and weaknesses?

This is another question that looks easy, but can actually be quite tricky. The key is to make your strengths and weaknesses link together and make your weaknesses really sound like strengths. For instance, let's say you tell your interviewer that your strengths are that you are hardworking and friendly.

First, you must give a quick one-sentence example to back up these strengths with facts.

```
'For instance, if I have an assignment due, I will not sleep until it is completed. Also, I get along very well with people I work with. I have lots of friends and enjoy interacting with others.'
```

Next, you have to state your weaknesses. Your weaknesses should relate to these strengths. In this case then, you could say, 'I am a workaholic and I am easily trusting.'

Notice how being a workaholic is the flip side to being hardworking, and trusting people easily can be a side effect of being friendly. So, while you have listed attributes that are in fact weaknesses, they do not actually make you look bad! Instead, they make your strengths sound even stronger.

Next, you must give brief examples to explain your weaknesses:

```
'For example, I sometimes work too hard and ignore my family. Also, when I trust people too easily I get taken advantage of. Once, a colleague got me to do his work, telling me that he was very sick. I later found out he was not sick, but instead had gone out of town!'
```

It is very important that when you state your strengths and weaknesses, you give actual examples to justify them. That will make it clear to your interviewer that you are not exaggerating, and that you have really thought deeply in order to come to these conclusions.

Q. Why do you want to work for this company?

This is another question that you should not take lightly. First, you should research the company you are interviewing with. You can find information by going to the company website, by looking up press releases or news articles on the internet, by looking up annual reports, or by researching trade sites like NASSCOM or CII. You will be amazed at how much you can find on the internet on any given company (public or private). A simple online search with the company's name, or the name of the company's CEO can result in all kinds of useful information. You can also ask around to see if you know anyone who works for the company.

Second, you should know background information about the job you are interviewing for. You should know what the job entails, and be able to talk about why you will be good at it. You should bring up why you will be a good fit for the position during the interview, and be able to give a well-thought out answer like:

> 'After researching your company's website, I noticed you have a commercial banking process. I studied commerce and am very interested in consumer financial markets, which is why I want to work for a BPO focussed in this area.'

HR managers are concerned with attrition and want to make sure you will not 'jump ship' if lured by extra money. If you are honest about the reasons you want to work in the company, it will be evident that you won't be tempted to leave quickly.

Q. Why do you want to leave your current job?
It is always best to be positive about the place where you work, even if you are unhappy there. Explain what you have learned in your current job, how you have grown (stick to the positives), and then talk about why you are looking for a change. It is perfectly okay to want to change jobs or careers. You only need to think of positive reasons for doing this. Some examples are wanting to learn more, wanting to grow intellectually, looking to take on greater responsibilities, etc. Do not start talking about issues you have with your boss or colleagues. No one likes people who complain.

Q. Where do you see yourself in 5/10/15 years?
The interviewer is asking you to really think and visualize your future goals. Stick to talking about your professional goals. It is important that you have some sort of goal to talk about, so that you don't

seem unmotivated. At the same time, you don't want to come across as overly ambitious as it may sound fake and egoistic. Also, it may make some companies refrain from hiring you as they might think you will leave if lured by a better offer.

The best response is to talk about how you want to grow as a person, and what value you want to add to the world. A good example of how to answer this question is:

> 'In the next ten years I want to be in a management position where I have serious responsibilities, and where I am challenged intellectually. I want to be in a position where I can add value, affect people's lives, and create a positive change in whatever I am doing.'

29.3 HOW TO ANSWER BPO SPECIFIC INTERVIEW QUESTIONS

Q. Why do you want to work in a BPO?

To answer this question, you need to ask yourself why you really want to join the BPO industry. Many young people make the mistake of taking jobs only for the money without thinking of their long-term career goals. When you are just starting out in your career, it is important that you are in a place where you will learn the skills you lack. So think about what (other than money) you will gain from working in a BPO. It could be learning to communicate with international customers to improve your communication and interpersonal skills. Also, ask yourself what excites you about working in a BPO. Perhaps it's something as simple as your desire to be a part of a gowing, fast paced industry.

Q. Why do you want to work in this company?

As we discussed, you need to research the BPO you are interviewing with. Figure out what their processes are (finance, accounting, etc.). Also, find out what type of work you might be doing (customer service, sales, etc). Then talk about how your skill set is in line with what the BPO is offering. For example:

> 'I noticed from your website that you are heavily involved in international sales. I am very good at communicating with people, but I also want to learn how to become more persuasive. I believe working in this company will help me improve my skills. I also believe I will be very good at international sales.'

Also, keep in mind that HR managers in BPO are extremely concerned with attrition (even more than in other industries), and really want to make sure you will not leave if lured with extra money. Here, it is important to convey that you are interested in staying in the company for an extended period of time rather than many different ones for short durations. You may want to point out that you are trying to build your resumé, and it looks better to have been with one company for a steady amount of time. You will also learn more (and certainly gain more in-depth knowledge) if you stick with one company.

Remember—the more honest you are, the more believable you will sound. Lastly, focus on letting your interviewer know what you want to learn, and how you think you will grow in the position.

29.4 DEALING WITH STRESS INTERVIEWS

In a stress interview you will receive rapid-fire questions in a possibly rude tone. Everything you say will be scrutinized and criticized. You may have a panel of people watching you, which is likely to make you feel even more nervous.

The best way to handle these interviews is to not get defensive or scared. Remember, this is just a show. When you are criticized, don't take offense—take a deep breath and answer the criticism as best you can. Do not at any time try to argue back or match your interviewers' tone. Do not get defensive. Remember, the interviewers are just doing their job—they are not attacking you personally.

Next, try and stay confident. Make sure your posture is straight, and no matter how difficult you feel the question is try and answer it as best you can. Being nervous, stammering and looking away from the panel will not help you.

The point of these rather awful interviews is to see how well you will handle difficult clients or customers. So, you can see how important it is that you do not get defensive or scared!

ANSWER KEY

SECTION ONE

Chapter 1

Exercise 1.1

1. I am a software developer.
2. Sahil is at home.
3. Mr Gupta has four children.
4. The monkey ate my sandwich.
5. The Indian team won the cricket match.

Exercise 1.2

1. I am a software developer.
2. Sahil is at home.
3. Mr Gupta has four children.
4. The monkey ate my sandwich.
5. The Indian team won the cricket match.

Exercise 1.3

1. I am a software developer.
2. Sahil is at home.
3. Mr Gupta has four children.
4. The monkey ate my sandwich.
5. The Indian team won the cricket match.

Exercise 1.4

1. Correct.
2. Correct.
3. Fragment—who is currently working? The subject is missing.
4. Fragment—what is the basic criteria for the job? The verb and object are missing.
5. Correct.
6. Fragment—who is lacking confidence? The subject is missing.

Exercise 1.5

3. I am currently working in a company in Bangalore.
   or
   Sunita is currently working in a company in Bangalore. (You can use any name in the place of 'Sunita'.)
4. The basic criteria for a job in a call centre is good customer service experience.
6. I am even lacking confidence in myself.

Exercise 1.6

1. Rahul is going to the gym today.
   Rahul → subject
   Is going → verb
2. Pooja is going to the beauty parlour to pamper herself.
   Pooja → subject
   Is going → verb
3. Tennis is such a boring game.
   Tennis → subject
   Is → verb
4. I asked a girl at work for her phone number.
   I → subject
   Asked → verb
5. I suggest you call the police.
   I → subject
   Suggest → verb

Exercise 1.7

1. My English is quite good, but I don't get the chance to practise speaking English. Can you tell me how I can improve?
2. I want to improve my grammar and English. What should I do?
3. I have a Bachelor's degree in computer applications. I have good typing skills and a good command of English. Are these things desirable for a job with a multinational?
4. I am interested in getting a job with a software company. I am a graduate in computer science. I have had a few interviews with BPOs, but did not get a job.
5. I want to work in a BPO. Can you please tell me how I should prepare myself for an interview?

Exercise 1.8

1. Fragment.
   ✓ Can you give me some steps to improve my communication skills?
2. Run-on sentence.
   ✓ How can I prepare myself for a marketing interview? What are the qualifications I need to be hired? I am also familiar with MS Office.
3. This sentence is correct.
4. Incorrect word order.
   ✓ Where is she?
5. Run-on sentence.
   ✓ I am a software developer. I am working for a medium-size software company.
6. Fragment.
   ✓ I was capturing data for HCA this morning.
7. Run-on sentence.
   ✓ This is a good job where I am a sales executive. I have to make calls to convince people from the textile industry to be members of our portal.

Chapter 2

Exercise 2.1

1. computer (common)
2. ocean (common)
3. love (abstract)
4. director (common)
5. man (common)
6. marriage (abstract)
7. death (abstract)
8. **F**atima (proper)
9. book (common)
10. **S**pain (proper)
11. president (common)
12. sadness (common)
13. **M**umbai (proper)
14. tree (common)

Exercise 2.2

1. India (country)
2. New Delhi (city)
3. Pepsi (soft drink)
4. Microsoft (company)
5. Marine Drive (street)
6. *Times of India* (newspaper)

Exercise 2.3

Dear **K**etan,

Yesterday I went to an **a**nniversary **p**arty for my **m**other and **f**ather. It was a real blast. We held it at the **S**tarwood hall in **A**ndheri. My brother brought a DJ and he played all kinds of good **m**usic. The **p**resident of the hall also came to the **p**arty. Wish you could have been there.

Regards,
Joshi

Exercise 2.4

1. Files
2. BPO**s**
3. Compan**ies**
4. Equipment (irregular noun)

5. **Teeth** (irregular noun)
6. Keys
7. Cities
8. Trees
9. Wolves
10. Lunches
11. **Children** (irregular noun)
12. **Feedback** (irregular noun)

Exercise 2.5

1. Do you have any **ideas** for me?
2. I have a **degree** in computer applications.
3. They are very successful **people** in their company.
4. What are the **qualifications** I need for the job?
5. One of my **friends** asked me why I am joining a call centre instead of the corporate industry.
6. What should the answer to this question and other related **questions** be?
7. Thank you for the **advice** you gave me.
8. My voice sounds totally different on **calls** and my colleagues make fun of it.
9. The **children** have come with the other **people**.
10. He had given me great **help** when I installed my **software**.

Exercise 2.6

1. The **company's** file.
2. The **boss's** desk.
3. My **mother's** table.
4. Her **sister's** wedding.
5. **Karishma's** computer.

Exercise 2.7

1. The **driver's** phone.
2. The company's transportation (correct).
3. The world's highest mountains (correct).

4. **India's** achievements.
5. **India's** population.

Exercise 2.8

1. **Indians'** lifestyle.
2. The **call centres'** interviews.
3. The **candidates'** qualifications.
4. The **employees'** computers.
5. The **companies'** files.
6. The **women's** books.
7. The **people's** votes.

Exercise 2.9

1. Singular noun: girl
   a. Plural noun: **girls**
   b. Singular possessive: The **girl's** lipstick.
   c. Plural possessive: The **girls'** hairbrushes.
2. Singular noun: person
   a. Plural noun: **people**
   b. Singular possessive: The **person's** resumé.
   c. Plural possessive: The **people's** resumés.
3. Singular noun: foot
   a. Plural noun: **feet**
   b. Singular possessive: Her left **foot's** fungus problem.
   c. Plural possessive: Her **feet's** fungus problem.

Exercise 2.10

1. It is one of the most beautiful **monuments** in the world.
2. The **people** were waiting at the bus station.
3. Those **women** are very noisy when they engage in small **talk**.
4. I put the files on **Paresh's** desk.
5. That **restaurant's** food is very good.
6. Those **companies'** workers are very well paid.
7. I cleared the first and second **rounds** but could not get through the last round.

8. I am a postgraduate in M.Sc. computer **science** and I had given a few **interviews** in BPO**s**.
9. I cannot pronounce **words** correctly.
10. Please give me some **suggestions** regarding these.
11. My **position** is **b**usiness development manager.
12. I have these **problems**.
13. I like all Abhishek Bachchan's **movies**.
14. It is a small valley surrounded by hills on all **sides**.
15. I have read many **biographies**. However, the most important one is **Nehru's** biography.
16. I love flowers. Every time I see **flowers** I stop and smell them.
17. I have a lot of **problems** in my life.
18. She should realize that she is going to be **someone's** wife.

Chapter 3

Exercise 3.1

1. **The** USA is a nice place. ~~The~~ America is a really good place to study.
   - 'USA' stands for 'United States of America'. The word 'states' implies that we are talking about a group of states that make up a country. Thus, it is considered a plural proper noun and we must add the article 'the' before it. However, if we just say 'America', we must not include an article as then we are referring to a *singular* country named America.
2. I am going home with ~~the~~ Jagpreet.
   - 'Jagpreet' is a singular proper noun, thus we don't include an article before it.
3. **The** Himalayas are beautiful.
   - 'Himalayas' is a plural proper noun, as we are referring to a group of mountains that form a mountain range. Thus, we need the article 'the'.
4. When I was on vacation I went sailing on **the** Caribbean Sea.
   - 'The Caribbean Sea' is a singular proper noun and should technically not need an article before it. But, as we learned, oceans and seas are exceptions to this rule.

5. I saw a movie about ~~the~~ Mount Everest.
    - 'Mount Everest' is a singular proper noun and thus we do not require an article before it.

Exercise 3.2

Jay: I want to buy **a** car.

- You don't need the article 'the' as it is unclear at this point which car Jay wants to buy.

Car Dealer: What type of car are you looking for?

Jay: I am looking for **a** red Maruti.

- You don't need the article 'the' as there are many types of red Maruti cars in the world. It is still unclear which car exactly Jay wants to buy.

Car Dealer: Great! take a look at this one here. What do you think of **the** car?

- We need the article 'the' in this sentence as it is now clear which car Jay and car dealer are referring to. This car has now become *specific.*

Exercise 3.3

Person 1: Would you like to buy **a** cake?

- You don't need the article 'the' as it is unclear which cake the person is referring to at this point.

Person 2: Yes, I like **the** chocolate cake. It looks yummy!

- You need the article 'the' as it is now clear which cake we are referring to. The cake has now become *specific.*

Exercise 3.4

Proper nouns are in bold. Specific nouns have been circled.

Reporting to the (CEO) of the (company) is difficult. **Sonia** had a big responsibility with her new job. She would be in charge of the (purchasing and inventory departments) and she would have to ensure that all clients get the best service possible. Also, she would have to lead the **Maharashtrian team** during the company's meetings.

Exercise 3.5

My attitude towards ~~the~~[a] life is that I want to help ~~the~~[b] mankind. I believe that ~~the~~[c] rural India is not well governed. The roads are not good and ~~the~~[d] money is not spent well. ~~The~~[e] Both the things need lots of attention. I hope that ~~the~~[f] help will come quickly to the poor people there.

(a) 'Life' is an unspecific/general noun.
(b) 'Mankind' is an unspecific/general noun.
(c) 'Rural India' is a singular, proper noun.
(d) 'Money' in this case is unspecific. You may be confused as to why 'the roads' is acceptable. This is because we know we are talking specifically about roads in rural India. But we don't know what, or whose, 'money' we are referring to. We are talking about money unspecifically.
(e) 'Both' is unspecific. Also, the article 'the' should fall before 'things' only and it is unnecessary to use it before 'both'.
(f) 'Help' is unspecific. Where is the help coming from? Who will be helping?

Exercise 3.6

1. She is involved in **the** murder case.
2. **The** government should take care of **the** areas surrounding **the** Taj because this year is its 350th anniversary.
3. They will be taking me out to see **the** city where they live.
4. I appeared for an interview at **the** company's headquarters.
5. I'm going to **the** hospital where *nani* is.
6. If you had seen me with another girl at **the** theatre you would have been angry.

Chapter 4

Exercise 4.1

1. ✗ I am looking for sports shoes. ('Sport shoes' is plural, so we do not need the article 'a'.)

2. ✓ She was a happy girl.
3. ✗ My favourite hobby is planting flowers in the garden. ('Flowers' is plural, so we cannot use the article 'a').
4. ✓ I gave her a bouquet of flowers for her birthday. (Even though there is more than one flower, we are referring to one bouquet, or one *group* of flowers.)
5. ✓ I saw a glass on the table.
6. ✓ There was a stack of newspapers on the ground. (Even though there is more than one newspaper, we are referring to one single stack, or one *group* of newspapers.)

Exercise 4.2

1. I saw **a** park when I was driving.
    - Avoid using 'one' before a singular noun.
2. Her hair is wet and she wants **a** towel.
    - 'Some' should only be used if the noun is plural. 'Towel' is a general, singular noun, so you need to add the article 'a'.
3. I saw **a** tiger when I went to Kanha National Park.
    - 'Tiger' is a general, singular noun so you need to add the article 'a'.
4. I am working as **a** software engineer in the company.
    - 'Software engineer' is a general, singular noun so you need to add the article 'a'.
5. I want to work in **a** BPO.
    - 'BPO' is a general, singular noun so you need to add the article 'a'.

Exercise 4.3

1. Table—Countable
2. Detail—Countable
3. Hour—Countable
4. Air—Non-Countable
5. Mankind—Non-Countable
6. Holiday—Countable
7. Information—Non-Countable
8. Love—Non-Countable

Exercise 4.4

1. I need advice from you.
   - 'A' was removed because 'advice' is a non-countable noun.
2. What should I wear when I go for interviews?
   - 'A' was removed because 'interviews' is a plural noun.
3. I am **a** student in my final year of college and want to sit for the CAT.
   - 'A' was added because 'student' is a general, singular noun.
4. Every morning when I wake up, I give them water.
   - 'A' was removed because 'water' is a non-countable noun.
5. She had information on the issue.
   - 'A' was removed because 'information' is a non-countable noun.
6. She had **a** party for her sister.
   - 'A' was added because 'party' is a general, singular noun.
7. I am not good at math.
   - 'A' was removed because 'math' is a non-countable noun.
8. They need to do work in the office.
   - 'A' was removed because 'work' is a non-countable noun.
9. She needs to get **some** shirts ironed.
   - 'A' was removed and 'some' added because 'shirts' is a plural noun.
10. I want to specialize in marketing.
    - 'A' was removed because 'marketing' is a non-countable noun.

Exercise 4.5

1. **A** call centre
2. **An** international call centre
3. **A** software programme
4. **A** BPO
5. **A** multinational
6. **A** process
7. **An** application process
8. **An** interview
9. **A** human resource manager (We pronounce the consonant sound 'h' in this word.)

10. **An** HR manager (We don't pronounce the consonant sound 'h' in this word. It sounds like 'aich'.)

Exercise 4.6

1. Mr Patel is **an** unrealistic person.
2. Teresa is **a** bright woman.
3. Phil has **an** eraser.
4. Ali is **an** adventurous man.
5. Jatin is **an** irresponsible boy.
6. I don't think I need **a** pen for the meeting.
7. Can you believe she didn't take **a** gift for the birthday girl?
8. I think he is such **an** arrogant person!

Exercise 4.7

1. This is a **unique** painting.
2. My mother has a **green** purse.
3. We want to live in a **quiet area**.
4. They are going to join an **exciting club**.
5. What a **beautiful** dress that is!
6. I am about an **hour** away from finishing.
7. The book has an **interesting** theory.
8. I feel like eating a **meal**.

Exercise 4.8

1. I was eyeing **the** food on the table. ('Food' is specific here because 'the table' that 'the food' is on has been specified. Also, 'food' is non-countable and thus you cannot use the article 'a'.)
2. I saw a beautiful girl. **The** beautiful girl told me her name was Manjeet. ('Girl' is specific here as 'a beautiful girl' was previously mentioned in the first sentence.)
3. Sophia is looking for **an** interesting book. ('Interesting' starts with a vowel sound.)
4. I want to make **a** few points. (The clause 'few points' is collective and singular. Thus, you can't use the word 'some' and need the singular article 'a'.)
5. I want to find **a** solution to the problem. ('Solution' is singular.)

6. I have **the** very latest model. (The 'model' being described is specific because it is the 'very latest'.)
7. Let's have **a** drink. ('Drink' is singular.)
8. She didn't have **an** affair. ('Any' is not an article and is used incorrectly here. 'Affair' is singular.)
9. You've got **the** wrong information. (Both speaker and listener are aware of the 'information' that is being discussed—thus making it specific. Also, 'information' is non-countable and thus you must never use the article 'a'.)

Exercise 4.9

1. I am just **a** graduate in commerce. ('Graduate' is general and singular.)
2. It has **an** audio recording capacity of five hours. ('Audio recording' is the adjective describing 'capacity'. It starts with the vowel sound 'a'.)
3. India is a beautiful country. ('India' is a singular proper noun.)
4. Please provide me with **the** details of **the** tuition classes. *or* Please provide me with details of **the** tuition classes. ('Details' and 'tuition classes' can both be made specific in this sentence as the speaker is asking someone for exact information. The second option, to take out the article 'the' before 'details', also works as then we are talking about general details in regards to specific tuition classes.)
5. She is **a** hardworking secretary. ('Hardworking' is the adjective describing 'secretary'. It starts with consonant sound 'h'.)
6. There is paint on the floor. Please wipe it. ('Paint' is not specific at the time the speaker says this sentence. Once the receiver of this statement looks at the paint the speaker is referring to, *then* the paint becomes specific.)
7. Q: Is he a manager?
   A: He is not exactly **a** manager.
   ('Manager' is general and singular.)
8. She is putting on **a** negative attitude. ('Negative attitude' is general and singular.)
9. I have **a** job at Hindustan Lever. ('Job' is general and singular.)

10. I'm **a** nature-loving person. ('Nature-loving person' is general and singular. As a note, 'nature' is a non-countable noun, but in this sentence, the word 'nature' is a part of the adjective 'nature-loving', which is describing the noun 'person.' We base the article on the noun—'person' is general and singular.)
11. I sit in front of **the** computer all day. (We are talking about a specific 'computer'.)
12. I am working for **a** BPO as **a** business development associate. ('BPO' and 'business development associate' both start with consonant sound 'b'.)
13. What is the difference between **a** call centre and **a** BPO? I am interested in joining **a** BPO. ('Call centre' and 'BPO' are both general and singular.)
14. I am working as **a** project leader in **a** software company. ('Project leader' and 'software company' are both general and singular. It is not specific which software company we are referring to, so we cannot use 'the'.)
15. I am a student at NIIT in Delhi and I am currently doing research in **a** BPO. ('Research' is a non-countable noun. 'BPO' is general and singular.)
16. The city is located in the north-eastern part of India. ('India' is a singular, proper noun.)
17. Can you do me **a** favour? (We don't use 'one' before general, singular nouns—we use 'a'.)
18. I keep asking genuine questions but no one answers me. ('Genuine questions' is plural.)

Exercise 4.10

Dear Kartik,
We need forty items for a back order analysis. Contrary to **the**(1) earlier discussion, we have decided to carry out **the**(2) back order analysis for all forty items. **An**(3) earlier mail from Mr Gupta has already intimated **the**(4) change.

After **an**(5) internal discussion, we have divided these forty items between **the**(6) four of us.

```
In case you feel that we need to change anything
about the(7) above matter, please let us know.

Thanks,
Sharique
```

(1) 'Earlier discussion' is specific, as by using the word 'contrary' it is clear that the discussion is one both Sharique and Kartik are aware of—and most likely one they were both a part of.
(2) In the first sentence, we have already said '*a* back order analysis'. In this sentence, we are referring to that same analysis that is needed on the forty items. Because we have identified 'back order analysis' before, in this sentence it becomes specific—both Sharique and Kartik know which back order analysis Sharique is referring to.
(3) 'Earlier mail' is general and singular. It is not clear from the email if Kartik is aware of the mail Sharique is referring to the mail from Mr Gupta. Thus, we don't use the specific article 'the'.
(4) We need the article 'the' because after reading the previous sentence, we know the specific 'change' Sharique is referring to.
(5) 'Internal discussion' is general and singular. It is not clear from the email if Kartik is aware of the internal discussion Sharique is referring to.
(6) Because Sharique writes 'four of us', it looks like he assumes Kartik knows which four people he is referring to. Otherwise, he would have probably listed their names or given more information. Thus, Sharique should use the specific article 'the'.
(7) Both Kartik and Sharique know what the 'above matter' is, as Sharique wrote the email and Kartik read it. Thus, this phrase is specific and needs the specific article 'the'.

Chapter 5

Exercise 5.1

1. **I** will give her the message.
   - 'I' is the subject of the verb will 'give'.

2. If you see **her**, please give **her** the message.
    - 'Her' is the object of the verb 'see' and also the object of the verb 'give'.
3. It was **I** on the phone.
    - The formal way to say this sentence is by using 'I'—the 'it' refers to 'I', so both subject and object are the same.
4. My mother asked my sister and **me** to finish getting ready.
    - 'Me' is the object of the verb 'asked'.
5. Samir, Tarun and **I** went to the movies.
    - 'I' is the subject of the verb 'went'.
6. **I** told **them** that the show was over.
    - 'I' is the subject of the verb 'told'. 'Them' is the object of the verb 'told'.
7. **They** were unhappy with **her** work.
    - 'They' is the subject of verb 'were'. 'Her' is the object of the verb 'were'.
8. Will **we** apply for the job?
    - 'We' is the subject of the verb apply.

Exercise 5.2

1. **I** am the eldest.
    - The verb 'am' needs a subject pronoun before it. 'Me' is an object pronoun and thus cannot be used here.
2. I want to work in a call centre because **I** will have better prospects.
    - The pronoun 'it' does not match the subject of the sentence 'I'.
3. My younger brother and **I** started a small software development centre in Bangalore.
    - Both the person speaking and his/her younger brother are subjects of the verb 'started'. 'Me' is an object pronoun and thus cannot be used here.
4. Please give Dev and **me** your address.
    - Both Dev and the person speaking are objects of the verb 'give'. Thus the subject pronoun 'I' cannot be used here.

5. Krish ordered filet of fish. **It** was delicious.
   - The plural pronoun 'they' does not match the singular subject of the sentence, 'filet of fish'.
6. Kemaya and **I** want to join the debate club.
   - Both Kemaya and the person speaking are subjects of the verb 'want'. 'Me' is an object pronoun and thus docannot be used here.
7. I asked **them** to finish the gardening. They refused.
   - 'Them' is the object of the verb 'asked'. 'They' is a subject pronoun and thus cannot be used here.
8. She assisted me once, so now I will help **her**.
   - This sentence could seem tricky as the subject 'she' in the beginning of the sentence turns into object 'her' at the end. But the end 'her' is the object of verb 'will help'. Thus, the subject pronoun 'she' cannot be used there.

Exercise 5.3

1. During the discussion I had with the client, **I** introduced our products and other relevant information.
2. Last week on Wednesday when I went to the site, **I** spoke to Mr Shah regarding the disadvantages of water-based adhesives.
3. I am a final year student and **I** am going to write the CAT this year.
4. I am Christie and **I** have completed my MBA.
5. We are rejecting this order and **we** are sending **it** back to you. We will send **our** accounts representative to your office to collect our money.
6. They are telling **me** that this is not a safe career because **it** may collapse at anytime and I should not get into it.
7. I collect flowers from various places and plant **them** in my garden.
8. Dear Mr Srinavasan,
   I spoke to Mr Patil yesterday about the merchandise we need. He informed **me** that presently they have quantity in stock but **it** may be required in the next month depending on the job schedule. He asked **me** to contact Mr Mulki this week for further

discussion. He further informed **me** that the quality may not be as good as the last stock. I told him **I** wanted to inspect **it** myself.

Exercise 5.4

1. I live in Nagpur. ('Itself' taken out)
2. She hurt herself on the door.—Correct
3. I will call him today. ('Itself' taken out)
4. He accidentally bit himself.—Correct
5. I did it yesterday. ('Itself' taken out)
6. **My name is** Piyush.
7. The desk closed in on itself.—Correct
8. They drove themselves there.—Correct

Exercise 5.5

1. It belongs to **me**.
   - Here, the subject and object are different and so you can't use the reflexive pronoun 'myself'. 'Me' is the correct object pronoun that fits this sentence.
2. **They** were discussing the assignment.
   - Here subject and object are not the same, so you can't use the reflexive pronoun 'themselves'. 'They' is the correct subject that agrees with the helping verb 'were'.
3. Roxanne was giving **herself** a manicure.
   - The subject is performing an action that is reflected back on the subject. Thus, you should use a reflexive pronoun. 'Herself' agrees with the noun 'Roxanne'.
4. It is up to **us** to win the game.
   - First, 'ourself' is not a proper word—the correct reflexive pronoun would be 'ourselves'. Second, subject and object are not the same so you can't use the reflexive pronoun 'ourselves'. 'Us' is the correct object pronoun that fits this sentence.
5. I have to train and teach people all the qualities and skills which I have developed in **myself** as a leader.
   - Here the subject is performing an action that is reflected back on the subject. Thus, you should use a reflexive pronoun. 'Myself' agrees with the pronoun 'I'.

6. It's no one else's fault, they brought the punishment on **themselves**.
   - Here the subject is performing an action that is reflected back on the subject. Thus, you should use a reflexive pronoun. But, 'themself' is not a word. Instead you should use 'themselves'.
7. It was given to **her**.
   - Here the subject and the object are not the same so you can't use the reflexive pronoun 'herself'. 'Her' is the correct object pronoun that fits this sentence.
8. The pizza had many toppings on **it**.
   - We can only use reflexive pronoun 'itself' when the subject is reflecting an action back on the same subject. A pizza is not a living thing, and thus cannot perform this reflexive action.

Exercise 5.6

1. For a man: This is **his** car. It is **his**.
2. For a woman: This is **her** purse. It is **hers**.
3. For a friend and his family: This is **their** home. It is **theirs**.
4. For me: This is **my** book. It is **mine**.
5. For me and my friends: These are **our** coffees. They are **ours**.
6. For you: This is **your** gift. It is **yours**.

Exercise 5.7

1. Our house is larger than **hers**.
   - 'Hers' is the possessive pronoun that is replacing the possessive adjective 'her house'. Since we already stated the word 'house' in the beginning of the sentence, we should not repeat it again at the end.
2. It's **your** file.
   - Here we are trying to describe whose file it is. Thus, we need to use the possessive adjective 'your' and not the possessive pronoun 'yours'.
3. Her drawing is like **yours**.
   - 'Yours' is the possessive pronoun that is replacing the possessive adjective 'your drawing'. It is incorrect to use the word 'one' after possessive pronouns.

4. That company does not treat **its** employees well.
   - 'Its' is a pronoun that is replacing the noun 'company'. 'It's' stands for 'it is'.
5. The money is not mine, it is **yours**.
   - 'Yours' is the possessive pronoun replacing the possessive adjective 'your money'. Remember, the word 'your' must always be followed by a noun. If it is not, remember to use 'yours'.
6. The black cat is **mine**.
   - 'Mine' is the possessive pronoun replacing the possessive adjective 'my cat'. Since we have already used the word 'cat' in the beginning of the sentence, we should not repeat it at the end.
7. The baby drank **its** milk.
   - 'Its' is a pronoun that is replacing the noun 'baby'. 'It's' stands for 'it is'.
8. It is **his** car you are looking at.
   - There is no such word as 'hims'. The correct male possessive pronoun to use is 'his'.

Exercise 5.8

Jyoti:	Namita did you take my brown skirt from **my** closet? I need it and I can't find **it**.
Namita:	No, I didn't take **your** skirt! You always blame **me** when you can't find something.
Jyoti:	Well, usually when I can't find something it is because **you** took it! You always take my things when you can't find **your** own things.
Namita:	Instead of blaming me, you should ask Tina. Tina and **her** sister always take **your** things without asking.
Jyoti:	Yes, **they** always do that. I am tired of **their** carelessness with my things!
Namita:	Jyoti, don't get so angry. **We** all make mistakes.

Exercise 5.9

1. Hi, **my name is** Raj.
   - 'I am Raj' is too harsh.
2. Recently, I have appeared for four job interviews and **I** failed to get any one of the jobs. The problem is I get very nervous and subsequently **I am** unable to pronounce words correctly. I can pronounce the same words correctly with **my** friends.
   - Remember to add pronouns after the word 'and' in long sentences. The last correction deals with possessive adjectives. 'The friends' makes no sense—we can only use 'the' if we know the specific noun we are referring to (see chapter 3). We need to add the possessive adjective 'my' before 'friends' to describe *whose* friends we are talking about.
3. Hi, **my name is** Gopika.
   - There is no reflexive action taking place so the use of 'myself' is incorrect. Also, you must never use this as a form of introduction.
4. My mother and **I** are yoga teachers.
   - Both 'mother' and 'I' are the separate subjects of verb 'are'.
5. **My** question is will you help me?
   - Possessive pronouns should not be followed by a noun. Remember, possessive pronouns replace possessive adjectives *and* nouns. Here, we are simply trying to describe *whose* question it is and thus you must use the possessive adjective 'my'.

Chapter 6

Exercise 6.1

1. Shorter than
2. Busier than
3. Prettier than
4. More gorgeous than
5. More amazing than
6. Lazier than
7. More wonderful than
8. Nicer than
9. Fatter than
10. More respectful than

Exercise 6.2

1. 'Sweet' is a one-syllable word, so use Formula 1.
   - Why are you **sweeter** than your sister?
2. Formula 1 is 'er' + 'than'. The use of 'to' is incorrect.
   - Naan is better **than** chapatti.
3. Tall is a one-syllable word, so use Formula 1.
   - Between the two girls, Payal is **taller** than Perveen.
4. Use Formula 1.
   - She is **better** than him.
5. 'Beautiful' is a three-syllable word, so use Formula 3.
   - My girlfriend is **more beautiful** than yours.
6. 'Smart' is a one-syllable word, so use Formula 1.
   - After many years I realized I am **smarter** than my wife.
7. Formula 1 is 'er' + 'than'. The use of 'to' is incorrect.
   - My brother thinks that working in a call centre is better **than** working anywhere else.
8. 'Angry' is a two-syllable word ending in 'y', so use Formula 2.
   - Geeta is **angrier** today than she was yesterday.
9. 'Hungry' is a two-syllable word ending in 'y', so use Formula 2.
   - Ali was **hungrier** than Shaheen when they went to the restaurant.

Exercise 6.3

1. The shortest
2. The busiest
3. The prettiest
4. The most gorgeous
5. The most amazing
6. The laziest
7. The most wonderful
8. The nicest
9. The fattest
10. The most respectful

Exercise 6.4

1. I went to Lonavla with my brother and had the **happiest** time!
2. She is **the** most interesting of all the friends.

3. My math teacher is the **most boring** of all.
4. Why are we sitting in the **coolest** area of the entire theatre?
5. I keep falling in love with the **weirdest** girls.
6. The business requires the **largest** investment.
7. She speaks the **most fluent** English of all the students in the class.
8. Why are you always trying to get **the** best deal with every shopkeeper?
9. The people who talk the fastest are always the ones hiding the **most critical** details.
10. I want to be **the** best person in the world.

Exercise 6.5

1. Comparative; 'nicer than'.
2. Superlative; 'the happiest' and 'out of'.
3. Comparative; 'earlier than'.
4. Comparative; 'fatter than'.
5. Superlative; 'the most'.

Exercise 6.6

1. the most intelligent; superlative.
2. the tallest; superlative.
3. sweeter; comparative.
4. better; comparative.
5. the fastest; superlative.
6. the most; superlative.

Exercise 6.7

1. Delhi roads are **broader** than Mumbai roads.
2. Why can't Avinash be **the nicest** out of his brothers? OR Why can't Avinash be nicer **than** his brothers?
3. Pratima works **the hardest** and is a good candidate for the job.
4. She is **better** than him.
5. I cleared my final rounds **faster** than anyone in my group. OR I cleared my final rounds **the fastest** in my group
6. My accent is not **nicer** than hers.
7. I am the **oldest** in the family.

8. I have worked there for three years and I am **the best** in terms of work quality.
9. When I go for an interview, I always do **the worst** at extempore rounds.
10. I panic **more than my friends** when going for interviews.

Chapter 7

Exercise 7.1

1. My friends **visit** me.
2. Yasmin **calls** for her food.
3. These things **belong** to my mother's friend.
4. Jehangir **asks** us every day if we want to eat with him.
5. I **clean** my office all the time.
6. Sushmita Sen has a very nice smile and her height **makes** her different from other heroines.
7. He **looks** like his father.

Exercise 7.2

1. The people **have** made up their minds.
2. The table **is** on sale.
3. He **doesn't** speak English very well.
4. Even if the actor **doesn't** do the best, he is my favourite.
5. My trousers **are** on the bed.

Exercise 7.3

1. She never **watches** TV in the evenings.
2. She **doesn't** know what she **is** talking about.
3. They **go** to the badminton club every day.
4. Rahul **forgets** the way to the office all the time.
5. I am looking for a company that **has** good opportunities and that **is** close to my home.
6. The driver **knows** the way to the airport.
7. This activity **is** very boring.

8. The people **have** to leave because they **are** bothering everyone.
9. Good things **are** hard to find.
10. I love her because she **understands** and **respects** my family.

Exercise 7.4

1. I **am** not going to the interview.
2. They **do** not (**don't**) want to give us the forms.
3. The unemployment rate **is** going up.
4. Some good offers **are** also available.
5. She **does** not (**doesn't**) really want to work in a call centre.

Exercise 7.5

1. What books **does** Dinesh read?
2. Insurance companies **do** give people a safety net if something bad happen**s**.
3. The audience **is** not enjoying the movie because the script **is** boring. (Remember, 'audience' is a collective noun and thus singular. One collective group of people is being referred to. See chapter 2 on nouns.)
4. It **does** not matter if the movie **is** bad.
5. These tourists **have** to go and **get** their tickets.
6. I want to **be** different from others.
7. We **are** just not getting enough sleep.
8. You all **were** sitting there.
9. I **belong** to a traditional family.
10. Some apples **were** good and some **were** bad. (Remember, 'some' is an indicator of plural nouns. See chapter 7 on nouns.)
11. I **am** looking for a girl who understand**s** me.
12. She **runs** away because she **is** such a shy person.
13. I **do** not want that.
14. I want to **be** independent.
15. Some fake companies **are** also there in the market.
16. That **is** (**that's**) right.
17. You **seem** to be very smart.

Exercise 7.6

1. The boss and her staff **are** attending the work get-together. (Remember, 'and' is telling you that the noun is plural.)
2. Both Maria and Manoj **attend** cricket games.
3. Pratima **has** a beautiful baby.
4. The latest information the Congress party received **was** wrong.
5. Sayed and his wife **do go** to parties together.
6. The software engineers **weren't** able to leave work early.
7. Theatre halls that **don't have** nice chairs are hard for people to like.
8. My mother likes to **cook** every day.

Chapter 8

Exercise 8.1

1. Tigers **live** on land.
    - It is a fact that tigers live on land, so we use the present simple tense.
2. Rehanna **is watching** TV right now.
    - The verb 'to watch' needs to be in the present continuous tense because it is an ongoing action. Rehanna is doing it *right now* and the action is not yet complete.
3. I **eat** bread every day.
    - For everyday, regular actions we use the present simple tense.
4. She does **look** very nice.
    - If using the helping verb 'does', the following main verb should be in the present simple tense.
5. Because she is cooking alone, I **am helping** her.
    - The verb 'to help' needs to be in the present continuous tense as the 'helping' is going on at the same time as the 'cooking'. And, the 'cooking' is ongoing and not yet complete.
6. I am planning on **implementing** the report's recommendations.
    - The verb 'to implement' needs to be in the present continuous tense because it is an ongoing action. Also, planning and

implementing are two actions occurring at the same time—since planning is in the present continuous tense, implementing needs to be in the present continuous tense too.

7. Q: What are your hobbies?
   A: I **like** to paint.
   - Since it is a fact, we use the present simple tense.
8. I always **watch** Amir Khan's movies.
   - For habits (we know this is a habit because of the word 'always') we use the present simple tense.
9. I do **want** to go to Delhi.
   - If using helping verb 'to do', the following main verb should be in the present simple tense.
10. They **are looking** at the sky because the airplane show is going on.
    - The verb 'to look' needs to be in the present continuous tense because the airplane show is an ongoing action and is not yet complete.
11. Akshay **is going** to the park tonight.
    - The verb 'to go' needs to be in the present continuous tense as the action will take place in the future.
12. We **watch** the World Cup every day.
    - For everyday, regular actions use the present simple tense.

Exercise 8.2

1. I **know** your girlfriend.
2. She does not **remember** my name.
3. I **love** my dog.
4. I **have** certain questions to ask you.
5. Presently, she **is** depending on others.
6. We **are** partying at my friend's house.
7. I don't like movies which **have** little emotion.
8. I **have** a day off from work on Saturday.
9. My elder brother **is** working as a software engineer in Dubai.
10. I **have** strong values and am a romantic at heart.

11. I would like to know if you **are** going to accept this offer.
12. I completed my education at India's premier institute, and now I **am** working with a major company in Bangalore.

Exercise 8.3

1. I **don't understand.**
2. ✓ They are chewing gum.
3. I **can't hear** you.
4. He **does not want** tea.
5. We **like** this music.
6. ✓ She is smoking a cigarette.
7. I **know** your girlfriend.
8. She **does not remember** how to do it.
9. ✓ I am having my reception on Tuesday. (See exceptions to Present Continuous Rule 4.)
10. I **love** my dog.
11. They don't need me.
12. I **see** your files on my screen.
13. ✓ I am concentrating on the assignment.
14. I **mean** that I did it.
15. I **have** a small red car.
16. ✓ Rekha is not thinking very clearly. (See exceptions to Present Continuous Rule 4.)
17. I **don't own** my apartment.
18. ✓ James is driving.
19. I **belong** to a large family.
20. ✓ You are eating chicken.
21. We **have** offices in five cities.
22. I want to work in a finance company because it **has** growth prospects.
23. I **did not know** there would be such high security.
24. I see myself running the organization and **managing** lots of people.

Exercise 8.4

Customer:	Hi, I (need) to update my information for your files.
Agent:	Just give me a second, sir. I (am looking) for your information.
Customer:	My computer information (is) not updated.
Agent:	I will update that for you now. I (need) the serial number on the back of your computer.
Customer:	It (is) 548291. How long will it take you to (update) the system?
Agent:	I also (require) the warranty information.
Customer:	I (don't have) a warranty.
Agent:	I (see) from your previous account that you had a warranty before?
Customer:	Yes, (I believe) so.
Agent:	You (are) right. Okay, that is all the information I need.

Exercise 8.5

1. Yes, I speak English well.
2. I am watching a movie.
3. I watch movies.
4. He lives in Hyderabad.
5. Because she is sleeping.
6. Because I did not get the last job.
7. She has a very tough job.
8. I am going to play tennis.
9. I don't want you there.
10. They are leaving tomorrow.

Chapter 9

Exercise 9.1

1. One second, I **have** some urgent work to do first.
2. We went to a restaurant to **have** lunch and all my colleagues **introduced** themselves.
   Or
   We went to a restaurant **and had** lunch and all my colleagues **introduced** themselves.
3. On my first day we **had** an induction programmme. Our programmme **was** at 10 a.m.
4. I **need** your help.
5. Yes, I have **made** the new entries.
6. My elder sister, my mother and I **live** together in Mumbai.
7. I **feel** much better now.

Exercise 9.2

1. I **forgot** her name.
2. I **knew** her father and mother.
3. She **wore** red shoes.
4. I **didn't** see her.
5. She **swept** the floor.
6. She never **told** a lie.
7. I **didn't** eat meat.
8. He **spent** his time working.

Exercise 9.3

I really love my hometown because it is away from the city. Whenever I **go** outside my home, I can only **see** natural beauty. Also, I really **miss** my relatives. It is also very safe there; there **are** no problems in going out alone. Now I live in Delhi and here if I go out at night, people **tell** me that it is not safe. Whenever I have these problems I **miss** my hometown.

These errors are a result of Sunil incorrectly placing verbs in the past tense. The past tense is used for actions that are *over.* Here, Sunil is telling Tanvi about why he *still* loves his hometown. Sunil is talking about a current fact. Thus, all the verbs should be kept in the present tense.

Exercise 9.4

1. How did you **do** that?
2. We did not **make** any food today.
3. We didn't **get** the error message this time.
4. ✓ Did you get that computer replaced?
5. We didn't **have** that on the monitor.
6. Where did you **buy** the original computer from?

Exercise 9.5

1. They told me that if I get my diploma quickly they will give me a promotion. So now I **prefer** to get it quickly.
2. In college I used to be very independent. I never **bothered** about anything in life.
3. I didn't **take** a typing test.
4. Just as my company **changed** my future, I want to help others.
5. I **was** eliminated in the fourth round.
6. My friends have interviewed with Tata but they didn't **get** the job. (Verb following 'did' must be in the present simple tense.)
7. The boy **kicked** the ball.
8. It was **built** in memory of love.
9. In the end we **were** just happy to be home.
10. I have two sisters and both of them **got** married and are settled.
11. I will call you in case your cheque **gets** bounced.
    Or: I will call you in case your cheque **bounces**.
12. Whenever I get **stuck** she helps me.
13. Did you **click** on anything?
14. She **hit** the ball really hard.

Chapter 10

Exercise 10.1

1. She called me while I **was watching** the news.
   - The helping verb 'was', not 'were', agrees with the subject 'I'.
2. Last year Tricia **was working** in a call centre.
   - You must place a helping verb (like *was* or *were*) before the main verb to form the past continuous tense.
3. I **had** a Maruti car.
   - Avoid using 'having' in the past continuous tense except in certain contexts.
4. We **did not know** what to do.
   - Avoid using 'knowing' in the past continuous tense except in certain contexts.
5. That **belonged** to me.
   - Avoid using 'belonging' in the past continuous tense except in certain contexts.
6. Pradeep **was running** when he suddenly fell on the ground.
   - 'Running' was the longer action that happened first, so it should be in the past continuous form.
7. They **had** an off day yesterday.
   - Avoid using 'having' in the past continuous tense except in certain contexts.
8. I **was talking** last month to the class.
   - You must place a helping verb (like *was* or *were*) before the main verb to form the past continuous tense.
9. Sorry, we **needed** you to send your CV yesterday.
   - Avoid using 'needing' in the past continuous tense except in certain contexts.
10. My senior finally **agreed** to let us go after four hours of overtime.
    - Use the past continuous tense for actions that happened over time. 'To agree' is a quick action—not one that takes a long time to happen. Thus, you should place the verb in the simple past.

11. I **was dancing** when they cut me off.
    - 'Dancing' is the longer action that happened first, so it should be in the past continuous form.
12. **Were** you working last year?
    - Because of the words 'last year', we know this sentence refers to an action that happened in the past. Thus, you must use the past tense helping verb 'were' instead of the present tense helping verb 'are'.
13. I **knew** you were coming.
    - Avoid using 'knowing' in the past continuous tense except in certain contexts.
14. She **was helping** me with my studies.
    - The helping verb 'was', not 'were', agrees with the subject 'she'.
15. I **liked** her when I met her.
    - Avoid using 'liking' in the past continuous tense except in certain contexts.

Exercise 10.2

1. I **have** gone through different situations in my life.
    - You must add 'have' or 'has' before the past participle of the verb. 'Gone' is the past participle form of the verb 'to go'.
2. I **have** never hurt anyone before.
    - If using the word 'before', it is better to use the present perfect tense and not the past simple.
3. I can speak English fluently without fear, but I **have** not yet completed my graduation because of my family circumstances.
    - The fact that this person's graduation did not happen is something of the past *and* of the present (the graduation has still not happened). Thus, we need to use the present perfect tense and not the past simple.
4. Last week, I **went** to see my uncle in Nagpur.
    - We are stating the exact time (last week) when the action happened. Thus, we need to use the past simple tense and not the present perfect.

5. Everything **has** gone in vain.
   - You must add 'have' or 'has' before the past participle form of the verb.
6. I **have** worked as a software professional for the last one year.
   - This person was (in the past), and still *is* (in the present) working as a software professional. Thus, it is better to use the present perfect tense rather than the past simple. Also, the word 'for' in the sentence should have given you a hint.
7. **Have** you gone crazy?
   - You must add 'have' or 'has' before the past participle form of the verb. 'Gone' is the past participle here.
8. Everyone **has** been to the temple today.
   - You must add a 'have' or 'has' before the past participle of the verb.
9. My younger sister who **has gotten** married in the last year is coming with us. OR My younger sister who **got** married in the last year is coming with us.
   - If you use 'have' or 'has', you need to use the past participle of the verb 'to get'. If you do not use 'have' or 'has' then use the past simple tense 'got'. As a note, 'gotten' is more commonly used in the USA, while 'got' is used more in the UK.
10. I **called** you just yesterday.
    - We are stating the exact time (yesterday) when the action happened. Thus, we need to use the past simple tense and not the present perfect.
11. How long **have** you **been** in Delhi?
    - This person is asking how long you were (in the past), and still are (in the present) in Delhi. Thus, we need to use the present perfect tense and not the past simple.
12. My family **has** never **gone** outside of our hometown.
    - This is an 'ever' or 'never' statement where the time phrase is left vague. Thus, we use the present perfect tense and not the past simple.
13. I **have** worked for the last four years.
    - This person is asking how long you were (in the past), and still are (in the present) working. Thus, we need to use the present perfect tense and not the past simple.

Exercise 10.3

1. I **had gone** there before we met.
2. We had not **enjoyed** any luxuries until my father became a manager.
3. I had **worked** as an independent designer prior to joining this firm.
4. Jagpreet **had gone** to Ahmedabad recently, so I called him to learn more about the city.
5. We enjoyed the delicious food my sister had **cooked**.
6. The rain **had stopped** before we found our umbrella.
7. When I woke up this morning, my brother **had** already left.
8. I went to the office after I **had** eaten my food.

Exercises 10.4

1. Because I have been there for over three years and I still have not received a raise.
   - The raise was not received in the past and is still not received in the present, so we must use the present perfect tense.
2. I enjoyed the freedom to make my own choices.
   - This person's university days are over—we are talking about freedom that was enjoyed in the past and is now over. Also, we are referring to a specific point in time. Thus, we should use the past simple tense.
3. I went there on Tuesday.
   - Because we are stating the exact time (Tuesday) of the visit we should use the past simple tense.
4. I was working on a project for my company.
   - Hearing the good news is a quick action; this action interrupted the longer action of working on a project. Thus, we use the past continuous tense here.
5. I had completed the entire proposal and kept it ready.
   I completed the entire proposal and kept it ready.
   - The proposal was completed before another action—in this case the boss arriving. Thus, we use the past perfect tense. (The second choice using the past simple tense is also correct.)

6. I have worked here since last September.
   - This person was working here (in the past) and continues to work here (in the present). So, we use the present perfect tense. Also, words like 'since' are giveaways to use this tense.

Exercises 10.5

1. Maria **has** already **completed** the tenth standard
   OR
   Maria already **completed** the tenth standard.
   - You can't use the present continuous tense verb 'completing' along with the verb 'has'. Also, this sentence is talking about something that ended in the past, so use either the past simple tense or the present perfect tense.
2. We **were waiting** at the terminal for our bags to arrive when we saw Sapna Aunty.
   - The action of 'waiting' happened first and is longer than the action of 'seeing' someone. Thus, you must place the longer action in the past continuous tense.
3. Jehangir **has enrolled** in a university.
   OR
   Jehangir **enrolled** in a university.
   - Both the present perfect and past simple tenses will work fine here.
4. Tinaz **had applied** for several jobs.
   OR
   Tinaz **applied** for several jobs.
   - Both the past perfect and past simple tenses will work here.
5. I **have** seen some interesting advertisements.
   OR
   I **had** seen some interesting advertisements.
   OR
   I **saw** some interesting advertisements.
   - All three of the above past tenses will work as they all imply an action that ended in the past. Remember that the verb 'to see' is irregular, so its past tense 'saw' is different from its past participle 'seen'.

6. Sanya was talking on the phone when her boss **came** into the office.
   - The action of 'talking' happened first and is longer than the action of 'coming' into the office. Thus, you must place the shorter action in the past simple tense.
7. Gurjot **has** decided to work in a hospital.
   OR
   Gurjot **decided** to work in a hospital.
   - The verb 'have' does not agree with the subject 'Gurjot'. The past simple tense will do as well.
8. They **were running** along the beach when a bicycle cut across their path.
   - The action of 'running' happened first and is longer than the action of being 'cut' by the bicycle. Thus, you must place the longer action in the past continuous tense.
9. For the last week, she **has** definitely not been in a good mood.
   - Because of the phrase 'for the last week', we know this action happened in the past but still continues to happen in the present. Thus, we need to use the present perfect tense.
10. The magazine **had written** that our school won the prize.
    OR
    The magazine **has written** that our school won the prize.
    OR
    The magazine **wrote** that our school won the prize.
    - All three past tenses will work as they all imply an action that ended in the past. Remember that the verb 'to write' is irregular so its past tense 'wrote' is different from its past participle 'written'.
11. Everyone is ecstatic that Rashid **got** a raise and is now our head of finance.
    - 'Gets' is a present tense verb and must be changed to its past simple tense form 'got'.
12. The price of oil **has fallen** and this is affecting many people.
    - Because it is unclear when the price of oil fell, and the effects of the fall are continuing in the present, using the present perfect tense is the best choice. If you used the past simple tense you are not completely wrong, but it is not the best

choice. Remember that the verb 'to fall' is irregular and its past tense 'fell' is different from its past participle 'fallen'.

13. I **was shopping** at the mall last week when I met Riyaz.
    - The action of 'shopping' happened first and is longer than the action of 'meeting' Riyaz. Thus, you must place the longer action in the past continuous tense.

Chapter 11

Exercise 11.1

1. Mr and Mrs Gopaldas **will be** visiting Bombay next year.
2. I **will** go to the show at 7 p.m. tomorrow.
3. I **will** do my work when I want!
4. I **will be** interviewing at ten offices this week.
5. The HR manager **will** call me if they like me after my interview.
6. My parents **will be** watching the cricket match in an hour.
7. Your inputs **will** help us greatly.

Exercise 11.2

1. Because we have lots of good teachers.
    - This is asking why you like college in the *present*, not the future. Thus, you can't use the future tense.
2. I like to take photographs of people.
    - This is asking what you do for fun in the *present*, not the future. Thus, you can't use the future tense.
3. I will live in Bandra.
    - This is asking where you will live in the future. Thus, the choice using the future tense 'will' is correct.
4. Yes, I'll help her.
    - It is obvious that helping Kishori aunty has not been discussed in the past. The person agreeing to the plan is doing so at the time of speaking and thus 'will' should be used. (Exception 1.)
5. I will be playing tennis with my friends.
    - This is asking what you will be doing in the future. Thus, the future continuous tense 'will be playing' (and not the present tense 'play') is the correct choice.

6. Yes, I'll catch it.
   - To 'catch' a ball is not an action that happens over time. Thus, you can't use the future continuous tense 'will be catching'.
7. I'll be meeting her tomorrow.
   I am going to meet her tomorrow.
   - Both answers work as this is a future plan that will happen over time. (You can use the future simple tense 'am going to meet' and future continuous tense 'will be meeting' for future plans that will happen over time.)
8. I'll go at 4 p.m.
   I am going to go at 4 p.m.
   - You can't use 'will' when talking about future plans that were decided in the past.
9. Yes, I'll walk you there.
   - It is fairly obvious that the plan to walk the person to the floor has not been discussed in the past. This plan was made at the time of speaking and thus 'will' should be used.
10. No, sorry I can't. I am going to go to my dance class.
    - You can't use 'will' when talking about future plans that were generally decided in the past.
11. I will go in the afternoon.
    - This is asking when you will go to the park in the future. Thus, the option using the future tense 'will' is correct.

Exercise 11.3

1. I will **be** grateful as I am lacking in self confidence.
   - You need to add the base form of a verb after the word 'will' while forming this future simple tense.
2. When I **improve** myself I **will** come and take classes from you.
   - Because of the word 'when', we know that this is an 'if' statement. Thus, the verb must be kept in the present tense. You must also use the verb 'come' in the future tense because this person will 'come' to take classes only *after* he improves himself.
3. Please provide me with your valuable suggestions which **will help** me improve my English.

- The speaker is describing what will happen in the future if he gets the suggestions. Thus, 'help' needs to be placed in the future tense.

4. Don't worry, Suman **will** be coming to the party!
   - You cannot use the word 'would' before verbs ending in 'ing'.
5. I will **like** her if she gets a haircut.
   - 'Like' is a not an action verb and it can't be placed in the continuous tense in this context.
6. Since we have already forwarded our technical data to them, we **will be visiting/will visit/are going to visit** their Nasik plant next week.
   - Here, the helping verb before 'visiting' was forgotten. Since we are referring to a future continuous action, we need to use the helping verb 'will be'. Since we are speaking about a plan that will happen over a period of time in the future, the two simple tenses are also acceptable.
7. How long **will** you be staying?
   - This question is in the future continuous form. But, the word 'will' was forgotten.
8. She **will** be going there in the evening.
   - Avoid using the word 'would' before verbs with endings in 'ing'.
9. We **will not understand** the movie.
   - 'Understand' is not an action verb and it can't be placed in the continuous tense in this context.
10. I **will buy** her a thank you gift next week if she gives me the job offer!
    - To 'buy' something is not an action that happens over time. To 'shop' happens over time, but 'buying' only takes a moment. Thus, you cannot use the future continuous tense.
11. We **will** be joining/**will** join/**are going to** join you there.
    - Don't use the word 'would' before verbs ending in 'ing'.
12. I **am** going to apply for a job in a multinational.
    - You need to add 'am' while forming this future simple tense.

13. I **will take** care of the whole process.
    OR
    I **will be taking** care of the whole process.
    - When forming the future simple tense, leave out the 'be'. If forming the future continuous tense, add an 'ing' to the base form of the verb.
14. I am going to call him after I **go** there.
    - The use of the word 'after' indicates that this is an 'if' statement. Thus, the verb following the 'if' word should be kept in the present tense.

Chapter 12

Exercise 12.1

1. Why **do/did** you want to join a call centre?
   - You can't place a pronoun ('you') after a question word ('why').
2. What **are** you looking out for?
   - You can't place a pronoun ('you') after a question word ('what'). You can only place a *noun* or a verb after the question word 'what'.
3. How **will she** get time to reply to my mail?
   - After the question word 'how', the helping verb 'will' needs to come first.
4. When **does/did** she want to come?
   - You can't place a pronoun (like 'she') after the question word 'when'.
5. What **does** the word 'soft skills' really mean?
   - You have forgotten to place a verb before the subject.
6. What could **my answer be**?
   - The question word 'what' + verb 'could' needs to be followed by a subject noun or pronoun, and not the verb 'be'.
7. What time **should** I get back to you?
   - The question word 'what' + noun 'time' needs to be followed by a verb and not pronoun 'I'.

8. Which model **are** you using?
   - The question word 'which' + noun 'model' needs to be followed by a verb and not the pronoun 'you'.
9. Why **will she** reply?
   - The helping verb 'will' needs to come first after the question word 'why'.
10. What **did you do**?
    - You can't place a pronoun ('you') after the question word 'what'. If following Formula 1, then you need to place the verb 'did' after the question word 'what'.
11. What language **are you** speaking in?
    - The question word 'what' + noun 'language' needs to be followed by a verb, and not the pronoun 'you'.

Exercise 12.2

1. **Is** Mr Gupta in his office?
2. **Did** you get all the data you needed for your project?
3. **Are** you going to the interview?
4. **Has** she eaten yet?
   - Remember, if you are using the past participle 'eaten' you must use 'has' and not 'did'. (See chapter 10)
5. **Did** she eat yet?

Exercise 12.3

1. **Are you** going to the movies?
   - The verb 'are' needs to come before the pronoun 'you'.
2. **Didn't they** enjoy it?
   - The verb 'didn't' needs to come before the pronoun 'they'.
3. **May I** come in for an interview tomorrow?
   - The verb 'may' needs to come before the pronoun 'I'.
4. **Are** they dancing in the sangeet?
   - The verb 'is' does not agree with the pronoun 'they'.
5. **Could she** help me?
   - The verb 'could' needs to come before the pronoun 'she'.
6. **Will she** be there?
   - The verb 'will' needs to come before the pronoun 'she'. Also, don't add 'no' to the end of the question.

7. **Has** she gone to get her waxing done?
   - The verb 'have' does not complement the pronoun 'she'.
8. **Is Ketan** not going to be able to help?
   - The verb 'is' needs to come before the noun 'Ketan'.
9. **Can I** go now?
   - The verb 'can' needs to come before the pronoun 'I'. Also, don't add 'no' to the end of the question.
10. Are **you** going to help me?
    - You must place a noun or pronoun after the helping verb 'are' and not a verb (going). The pronoun 'you' agrees with the verb 'are'.

Exercise 12.4

1. **What** is your name?
2. **Where/When** is your interview?
3. **When/Why** did you leave the meeting?
4. **What/Which** project are you working on?
5. **How** do I get a job in a software engineering company?
6. **Where** is the new mall?

Exercise 12.5

1. What time is your flight? Or, When is your flight?
2. How did you get here?
3. Which airline did you fly? Or, What airline did you fly?
4. Why did you leave your old job?
5. Where are Shiraz and Kartik going?

Exercise 12.6

1. **Can/Could** you hand me the remote control? Or, **Would** you hand me the remote control?
2. I need his advice. **Should** I call him again?
3. Thank you for looking at my CV. **Can/Could** I meet you sometime to discuss job opportunities? Or, **May** I meet you sometime to discuss job opportunities?
4. **Would** you be interested in tutoring me in math?
5. **Can** you hear what I am saying?

6. **Would** you read my report for me? Or, **Can/Could** you read my report for me?
7. **Can/Could** I see the minutes from the last meeting? Or, **May** I see the minutes from the last meeting?
8. **Could** you do the work if you needed to? Or **Would** you do the work if you needed to?

Exercise 12.7

1. **Would you** like to come for shopping with me?
2. Why **are** you looking for a change?
3. **Have you** been to other interviews?
4. **Why are you** in America? Or, **What is** the reason **you are** in America?
5. How can I improve my English skills**?**
    - You must always end questions with a question mark.
6. What else **do** you want?
7. Will it be hard to qualify for the job**?**
    - You must always end questions with a question mark.
8. What **did you do**?
9. **Which standard is** he in?
10. How **will he** come on his own?
11. How **can I** get rid of this panic at interviews and at group discussions**?**
    - You must always end questions with a question mark.
12. **Are you** suggesting something to me?
13. Where **are you** going?
14. How **do** you like your bread?
15. What movie **are you** watching?

Exercise 12.8

1. Incorrect. Questions should start with question words.
   Possible answer: Will there be any improvements in my English?
2. Correct.
3. Correct.
4. Correct.
5. Incorrect. Questions should not start with pronouns.

Possible answer: Can you give me some advice about my problem?

6. Incorrect. Don't place a pronoun after the question word 'what'. You need to place either a noun or a verb.
   Possible answer: What did you do?
7. Correct.
8. Incorrect. The question word 'how' needs to be followed by a verb.
   Possible answer: How can I learn to work more effectively?
9. Correct.

Exercise 12.9

Big Boss:	Why **do** you want this job?
Kartik:	**I** believe getting this job is good for me.
Big Boss:	What **do** you want to get out of it?
Kartik:	**I want** to learn more.
Big Boss:	**Have** you been to other interviews?
Kartik:	**I have gone to** many interviews.
Big Boss:	So why **aren't you** taking up other jobs?
Kartik:	**I have not found any other jobs** to be interesting.
Big Boss:	Where **do** you live?
Kartik:	**I** live in Borivali.
Big Boss:	So, what **are you** doing now?
Kartik:	**I am** working with my dad.
Big Boss:	**Can you** start next week?

Exercise 12.10

1. My problem is that I am confident when I speak one on one, but if I have to speak in front of a crowd I get nervous and stammer. What can I do to solve this problem?
2. I am asked about my strengths and weaknesses in interviews. How do I explain my weaknesses so that the interviewer is satisfied?

3. I am a commerce student and I have just completed my second year of college. Do I stand any chance of getting a job in the banking industry?
4. I am only moderately fluent in English. Is it advisable for me to look for a career in counselling?
5. The interviewer might ask me why I want to shift from the BPO industry to the software services industry. What answer should I give him?
   OR
   If the interviewer asks me why I want to shift from the BPO industry to the software services industry, what answer should I give him?
6. I would like to be a flight steward. I have one year of experience in the hospitality industry. Could you suggest any courses for me?
7. I have been working in a medical transcription company for the last six years. I would like to switch to a sales job because I have reached the top level, and there is no growth for me going forward. Do you think I will be able to make the shift to a sales job? What growth opportunities will I have?
8. Your articles are in the Marathi language. Did you write in Marathi or did the newspaper translate the articles into Marathi?
9. I am completing my B.Com. final year and I want to be an MBA. I am currently preparing for the CE. Can you please give me some information about the MBA entrance exam?

Chapter 13

Exercise 13.1

1. I think he will be here.
2. She came to meet me eight days **ago**.
3. She is **really** looking forward to it.
4. She always **makes** mistakes in class.
5. How **many** people will come to the party?
6. I **live** in Belapur and commute to work every day by train.
7. She can **say** these things to me because we are best friends.
   OR, She can tell me these things because we are best friends.
8. The **lady** will call you in two hours.

9. There is **a lot** of food on my plate. Or, There is **so much** food on my plate.
10. She always **explains things to** me when I don't understand. Or, She always **explains it to** me when I don't understand.

Exercise 13.2

Executive: Thank you for calling Bank of Baroda. **How may I** help you? (When asking a question, a question word must come first. Thus, 'may' should be first in this case.)

Client: Yes, I am calling to find out why my mutual fund account is doing so poorly.

Executive: Let me pull up your account, sir. What is **your name?**

Client: My name is Tarun Khan.

Executive: I am sorry, I did not **understand** you.

Client: I said my name is Tarun Khan.

Executive: Thank you. There are a few stocks in your mutual fund whose prices dropped a few days **ago**.

Client: Well, will you guys do anything about this?

Executive: **Can I** put you on hold for one moment to check this? (When asking a question, a question word must come first. Thus, 'Can' should come first.)

Client: Sure.

Executive: Thank you for staying on the line. I found out that these particular auto stocks have dropped because of the budget that just came out. But we **think** that they will bounce back in a few days.

Client: I have not been happy with this mutual fund for some time now.

Executive:	Why **don't** you see if there are other mutual funds you would rather invest in?
Client:	Can I speak to someone about this matter?
Executive:	You can **speak to** our investment manager.
Client:	Fine.
Executive:	Okay, I will transfer your call to **him now**.
Client:	Thank you.
Executive:	**You are welcome.** Or, **Don't mention it**.

Exercise 13.3

Natasha:	Rohan, I am **very** upset with you.
Rohan:	Why?
Natasha:	I don't want to be your girlfriend anymore.
Rohan:	But what have I done?
Natasha:	Weren't you supposed to meet me today at the store in Bandra? (Incorrect use of reflexive/intensive pronoun 'itself'.)
Rohan:	I did go to the store, but I couldn't find you. Your cellphone wasn't working so I couldn't even call you. I should be the one who is upset!
Natasha:	I was there. ('Only' removed.) You should have **been more careful when looking for me.**
Rohan:	Well, I am sorry. But it is no reason for you to be so upset.
Natasha:	I **think** you are being very rude. You are not speaking **nicely**.
Rohan:	Natasha, I am sorry.

Natasha:	I was even going to **give** you a shirt **as a gift** when I saw you.
Rohan:	Can I come and meet you right now?
Natasha:	No, that's **all** I wanted to talk about with you. I have to go out now.
Rohan:	Natasha, I am really sorry and I want to meet you today.
Natasha:	Okay. I will **be back later**. I will call you then.

Exercise 13.4

Hi, **my name is Arjun**. I will be **staying** at your guest house **this** evening. My sister stayed at your guest house a few months **ago**. She told me a lot about your place. But she forgot to **tell** me your address. **Can you please send me your** address?

Also, I hope that your guest house is quiet as I have to study for an exam that I am **taking** in a few weeks. Please let me know if it will be noisy. That's **all** I wanted to know. **Please do let me know soon**.

I look forward to meeting you and **becoming friends.**

Exercise 13.5

Customer:	I am having a lot of trouble with the cellphone I just bought from your company. I am unable to send text messages.
Company agent:	I am sorry you are having **so many** problems with your phone. What is your **cellphone** number so I can look your account up?
Customer:	My number is 98-777-43341.

Company agent:	I am sorry but we don't have that number listed. Do you have **another** number?
Customer:	No! This is my only number!
Company agent:	Okay, let me repeat the number. Nine, eight, **seven, seven, seven, four, four,** three, four, one.
Customer:	That is wrong! I said 43341 not 44341.
Company agent:	I am sorry **about** that. Yes, I see **your information** listed on my computer screen. It seems that you have no balance on your phone. That is why you are unable to send any **text messages.**
Customer:	I just paid for more credit on my phone. I should have a positive balance on this phone!
Company agent:	Would you like to speak to our accounts department? You can **let them know** the details. They will be able to help you.
Customer:	Fine. Please transfer the call.

Exercise 13.6

1. Those guards are **saying** that I cannot come into the building.
2. I have a group of people **in my office** who are working along with me.
3. I went to meet **someone who can help me with my problem in your office**.
4. **What do you think** about Delhi?
5. I am **staying** at the hotel for one night.
6. I'll try to reply **to** you.
7. I am going to **take** my exam on 11 April.
8. I was capturing data for the project **this** morning.
9. I am **in** college.

10. I like to **make friends** with different types of people.
11. Is there **another** manager I can talk to **in this company**?
12. What is your name?
13. I don't like this sari! Do you have **another** sari I can wear?
14. My sister is smart, she will learn to drive herself.
15. She **told** me that she will come at 10 p.m.
16. Did she **let you know** what was happening?

Exercise 13.7

1. Please confirm receipt.
2. I don't think it is a good idea.
3. He told me that the class was on Sunday.
4. When will **you tell me** about the plans for Saturday?
5. That **lady/woman** from the bank called for you in the afternoon.
6. Wait for me, I'll **be back soon**.
7. Q: Do you have anything else to say?
   A: No, that's **all** I wanted to talk about.
8. I have been **living** in Mumbai for the last ten years.
9. You can **tell the HR manager your thoughts**.
10. She is **the very** best at work.
11. We were not able to **understand** what he said.
12. Can you please explain the math problem **to** me?
13. Will you say **hello** to her?
14. I need help bringing my things from the car. Can you **help me**?
15. I used to live in Mumbai five years **ago**.
16. When we see them, they always have **a lot of** advice for us.

Exercise 13.8

1. What **do** you need for your trip?
2. How **many** glasses of water are there on the table?
3. Q: Why didn't you call me last night?
   A: I'm sorry **about** that but I was very busy.
4. She is **very** pretty.
5. I **found out** about the problem after my senior told me about it.
6. Sameer came to my house some time **ago**.
7. She **gave** Ranvir a book **as a gift** for Diwali.

8. I can **say** this to you because I trust you. OR I can **tell you** this because I trust you.
9. Can I know your name, ma'am?
10. I **live** in Borivali.
11. I will explain **to** you the Pythagorean Theory.
12. What is your **cellphone** number?
13. Please call me. I will **let you know** about the plan.
14. Why **don't** you take a look at my CV?
15. I am very happy with the food.
16. I **think** the interview will be very hard.
17. She speaks very **nicely** to me.

Chapter 14

Exercise 14.1

1. **Please** tell me why **you** want to join this company.
2. If an interviewer asks, 'why **are you changing your** job,' what do **I** tell him?
3. **My name is Kousik**. Please tell me **if you are** interviewing in town **next week**.
4. I was looking at **your** website today.
5. **Am I** ready to interview for a job?
6. It's **because** of her that **I am** here today.
7. **I am** a graduate in computer science.
8. I was asked, 'Why do **you want** to work in an IT services company?'
9. **Please** advise me on how to get a job in a BPO.
10. **I am working** in a multinational company and I would like to improve my communication skills.

Exercise 14.2

1. Could you please tell me the basic job profile of a team leader**?**
2. I want to grow in my profession. **I** know that is only possible if you have good communication skills. Am I right**?**
3. Do **you** have any idea what I should do**?**

4. My name is Vibha and I **have** recently joined a manufacturing company. **I am** really happy with this company.
5. What are they looking for in a telephonic interview?
6. **C**an **you** tell me what offshore outsourcing is all **about**? **I am** interested in learning more **about** this field. **Thanks** for your help.
7. I **have** a couple of questions. **A**fter my BCA I think **I am** proficient in English, but I sometimes get confused. **I am** confident in writing but **have** some doubts speaking.
8. Does the speed at which you talk matter?
9. **My name is** Prakash **and I am** from Chennai. I worked as a software professional, **but I couldn't** cope with the java technology and coding.
10. How are you?
11. If an interviewer asks me why I changed from the software field to the BPO field, what answer should I give him?
12. I have completed my SSC in Marathi medium, **and** I have just joined a new job.
13. I am planning to join a training class to improve my English. **Can** I come meet you? Also, how do **I** rate my vocabulary skills? Do you have any online tests?

Exercise 14.3

1.

```
Dear Madam,

I've looked at your website. I would like to know
if you are offering training in Delhi. I am working
in an accounting firm and would like to improve
my communication skills. If possible, please send
me details about the training course.

Regards,
Sanjay Desai
982-098-2664
```

2.

Dear Sir or Madam, (or, To whom it may concern:)

I am working in a telecom company as a team leader and want to advance in my job. Could you send me the schedule of new course**s** that are starting in September or November? I **want to** start early. **Please** let me know the fees for the programmmes offered.

Regards,
Vikram Patel
932-244-6789

3.

Dear Ms Khiantani,

I want to improve my communication skills**. Please** help me with this. Are **you** offering any communication courses? Do you have courses in Mumbai? **Please** send me **the** course details.

Thanks,
Lalit Joshi
222-3556-754

Exercise 14.4

Step One—Cleaning up spelling and sentence structure problems.

Dear **Sir or Madam,**

I am Ramesh Desai from Bangalore**. I am** a **c**ommerce **g**raduate from Pune University.

I have spent the last five years working as an **a**ccountant for a software **c**ompany in Bangalore. I saw **your** ad for an accountant. I **would** like to **work** for **your** company.

```
I have attached my CV.
I'll be expecting a call or a linc from you.
Regards,
Ramesh Desai
983-454-3567
```

Step 2—Rewrite the email in a professional way using the guidelines learned in this chapter.

```
Dear Sir or Madam,

My name is Ramesh Desai and I obtained your contact information from your company's website. I would like to apply for the position of accountant that you have listed on your website. I have been working as an accountant for a software company in Bangalore for the last five years.

Please find attached to this email my CV, which details my past work experience.

I will follow up with you during the week to confirm you have received this email. I look forward to speaking with you.

Regards,
Ramesh Desai
983-454-3567
```

SECTION 2

Chapter 15

Exercise 15.1

1. The way in which people pronounce their vowel sounds.
2. People in India tend to pronounce consonant sounds differently from people who speak English in other parts of the world.
3. No. Each letter of the alphabet can have multiple sounds. Sounds can be different than letters.

4. An aspirated sound is the sound created by forcefully expelling air from the mouth in a 'kah' sound. Aspirated sounds are also known as 'air sounds' or 'plosive sounds' (technical term).
5. A throat sound. 'Kah' is an aspirated sound—its opposite is 'Ba'—a throat sound. The technical term for throat sounds is 'voiced sounds'.
6. A sound defined by the 'friction' caused by the air that escapes from the narrow gap created by the placement of our teeth.

Chapter 16

Exercise 16.1

1. They are strong, aspirated, air sounds.
2. Your tongue should be pointy and placed on the roof of your mouth, where the skin touches the teeth.

Exercise 16.2

1. **P**in**k**y is a **p**oli**t**e **p**erson with **p**olishe**d (tah)** English, nice **p**urses and lo**t**s of li**p**s**t**i**ck**s.
2. I**t** is **c**us**t**omary **t**o **c**arry a **c**on**t**ainer when **c**oas**t**ing through **c**us**t**oms.
3. **T**a**k**e a **c**oo**k**ie from the **c**abine**t** and **pack** the **c**a**k**e from the **t**able.
4. **T**ell me **t**onigh**t** wha**t** **t**o **t**a**k**e on the hun**t**ing **t**ri**p**.

Exercise 16.3

Kar**t**i**k** wan**t**ed **t**o join **C**a**p**i**t**a, a **C**all Cen**t**re[1] for the **p**osition[2] of agen**t**. Bu**t**, during his in**t**erview, his s**p**eech[3] was un**c**lear and he made many mis**t**a**k**es. His in**t**erviewer, **T**anvi, **t**old him **t**o go home and **p**ra**ct**ise s**p**ea**k**ing English **c**learly. A**t** firs**t** **K**ar**t**i**k** was disa**pp**oin**t**ed. Af**t**er a few days, though, he decided[4] **t**o **t**a**k**e **T**anvi's advice[5] and s**t**ar**t**ed **p**ra**ct**ising. He bough**t** a grammar boo**k**. He also s**t**ar**t**ed watching[6] **T**V shows in English. **K**ar**t**i**k** s**p**en**t** nigh**t** af**t**er nigh**t** wor**k**ing **t**o im**p**rove his English. Af**t**er **t**wo months, he wen**t** ba**ck** **t**o **C**a**p**i**t**a. **T**anvi was im**p**resse**d**[7] with him and his de**t**ermination[8] **t**o improve his s**k**ill-se**t**. **K**ar**t**i**k** go**t** the job and also learned a very im**p**or**t**an**t** lesson–hard wor**k** is the se**c**re**t** **t**o su**c**cess[9]!

To note:

(1) Cen**tr**e—the letter 'c' has not been marked as it is a 'sah' sound.
(2) **P**osition—the letter 't' has not been marked as it is a 'shah' sound.
(3) S**p**eech—the letter 'c' has not been marked as when followed by the letter 'h' it produces a 'cha' sound.
(4) Decided—the letter 'c' has not been marked as it is a 'sah' sound.
(5) Advice—the letter 'c' has not been marked as it is a 'sah' sound.
(6) Watching—the letter 't' has not been marked as it is not pronounced. (It is silent.)
(7) Im**p**resse**d**—the letter 'd' has been marked as it is actually a 'tah' sound.
(8) De**t**ermination—the second letter 't' has not been marked as it is a 'shah' sound.
(9) Su**c**cess—the second letter 'c' has not been marked as it is a 'sah' sound.

Chapter 17

Exercise 17.1

1. **Th**ink about the **th**eory of **th**ermal **th**under.
2. The grow**th** of **th**orns is any**th**ing but ear**thy**.
3. 'Have fai**th**,' said the father to the **th**ief.
4. Dea**th** is no**th**ing but a pa**th** to take.

Exercise 17.2

'THah' sounds are in bold and weak 'th' sounds are circled.

```
The theory that Theodore thought of was nothing
but wrong math. Thus, Theodore's father paid a
wealthy sum to Cathy to further think through
the theory.
```

Exercise 17.3

'THah' sounds are in bold and 'tah' sounds are circled.

```
Tonight is Martha's birthday party¹. I have not
gotten her anything yet. I think I will take her
a tennis racket as she has a thing for sports².
On Thursday I am taking her, Thelma, and my three
brothers to a tennis tournament.
```

1. The letter 't' in 'party' can also be pronounced as a soft 'da' sound.
2. Because of the strong 'sah' sound that follows the 'tah' sound in 'sports', the 'tah' sound is not as prominent. (Much air does not come out.)

Exercise 17.4

1. The tip of your tongue should be jutting out between your top and bottom teeth.
2. Strong, friction, aspirated, 'air' sound.
3. The weak 'th' sound does not require your tongue to come out of your mouth. Also, little air should leave your mouth. The normal 'THah' requires your tongue out and lots of air to escape through the gap between your tongue and teeth.
4. The 'tah' sound requires your tongue to be placed on the roof of your mouth where skin touches teeth, whereas the 'THah' sound requires your tongue to be sticking out of your mouth. Both sounds are aspirated and require lots of air.

Chapter 18

Exercise 18.1

'Tah' sounds have been marked in bold and 'da' sounds have been circled.

1. I wan**t** **t**o ea**t** dinner downs**t**airs **t**onigh**t**.
2. Madonna is a music s**t**ar with lo**t**s of beau**t**y, diamonds and dollars.
3. I had **t**ears **t**onigh**t** when I dream**t** of dancing with Dev Anand.
4. Dwarnik submi**tt**ed the **t**ax deposi**t** **t**en days after i**t** was due.

Exercise 18.2

'Tah' sounds have been put in bold and 'da' sounds have been circled.

Tarun **t**ook **t**oo much **t**ime **t**o s**t**udy and **t**urn in his presen**t**ation[1]. I**t** was due on **T**uesday bu**t** **T**arun finishe**d**[2] i**t** on Wednesday[3]. His **t**eacher, Mrs Jadhav, was impatien**t**[4] and upse**t**. **T**arun fel**t** **t**errible and though**t**, 'Wha**t**'s the ma**tt**er with me?' **T**arun promise**d**[5] **t**o do a be**tt**er[6] job nex**t** **t**ime around and during the week was ex**t**ra poli**t**e **t**o Mrs Jadhav.

To note:

(1) Presen**t**ation—the second letter 't' has not been marked as it is a 'shah' sound.

(2) Finishe**d**—the letter 'd' has been marked because it is in fact pronounced as a 'tah' sound.

(3) Wednesday—the first letter 'd' has not been circled as the word is pronounced 'Wensday'.

(4) Impatien**t**—the first letter 't' has not been marked as it is a 'shah' sound.

(5) Promise**d**—the letter 'd' is marked because it is in fact pronounced as a 'tah' sound.

(6) Be**tt**er—the bold letter 't's can also be pronounced as a soft 'da' sound.

Exercise 18.3

'Tah' sounds have been marked in bold and 'da' and 'na' sounds have been circled.

> The house tha**t** Anand and **T**inaz lived in was divided in**t**o nine sections[1]. Anand never felt the need **t**o hang[2] ou**t** in the **t**op **t**wo sections[1]. He ins**t**ead spen**t** **t**ime during[3] the day in the drawing[4] room and **t**ime a**t** nigh**t** in the mas**t**er bedroom. **T**eresa on the other hand, did something differen**t**. She spen**t** her **t**ime in the **t**yping[5] room, nursery room and dining[6] area.

To note:

(1) Sections—the letter 't' is not marked as it is a 'shah' sound.
(2) Hang—the letter 'n' is not circled as there is no 'na' sound.
(3) During—the letter 'n' is not circled as there is no 'na' sound.
(4) Drawing—the letter 'n' is not circled as there is no 'na' sound.
(5) **T**yping—the letter 'n' is not circled as there is no 'na' sound.
(6) Dining—the last letter 'n' is not circled as there is no 'na' sound.

Exercise 18.4

'Ra' sounds have been marked in bold.

> The a**rr**ow b**r**oke in th**r**ee pa**r**ts. **R**uki **r**idiculously **r**otated it and then **r**ipped he**r** d**r**ess. She then **r**ode he**r** ho**r**se to **R**ajasthan while making he**r** poo**r** dog **r**un with he**r**. What a te**rr**ible pe**r**son she is!

Exercise 18.5

1. When your tongue is too far back in your mouth, or when not enough air is used for certain sounds.
2. They share the same tongue placement—right behind the teeth where the skin touches the teeth on the roof of the mouth.
3. 'Tah' is aspirated and requires lots of air; 'da' is a throat sound and requires almost no air and lots of vibration in the throat.
4. It shares the same tongue placement.
5. You should avoid your tongue touching the roof of your mouth.

Chapter 19

Exercise 19.1

'Fah' sounds have been marked in bold and 'pah' sounds have been circled.

1. Praful put on his **f**lip-flops and **f**lew to Paris.
2. Pu**ff**ing away, Piyush appeared in **f**ront of[1] the **f**ort.
3. The party **f**or **F**arukh was **f**un and was **f**illed with **f**amily, **f**riends and people **f**rom the o**ff**ice.
4. I support pro**f**it and will **f**ight those who oppose sel**f**-made people.

(1) Of—the letter "f" has not been marked because it is pronounced as a 'va' sound.

Exercise 19.2

'Fah' sounds have been marked in bold and 'pah' sounds have been circled.

Payal and **F**iroze were pondering over their problem. They **f**ound that **f**illing out **f**orms was purposeless and **f**elt they should **f**ocus on **f**iner things. **F**iroze loved opera and painting pictures of[1] **f**lapping **f**ire**f**lies. Payal instead loved parties **f**illed with **f**ood and **f**un people.

Note:

1. Of—the letter 'f' has not been underlined because it is pronounced as a 'va' sound.

Exercise 19.3

'Va' sounds have been marked in bold and 'wa' sounds have been circled.

1. (W)hy (w)onder about **v**ery useless e**v**ents?
2. **V**ertigo makes you (w)a**v**y and une**v**en.
3. (W)ednesday is a (w)onderful day to **v**isit acti**v**e (w)omen.
4. (W)acky, (w)ild **v**isitors are al(w)ays (w)elcome in my (w)inter ta**v**ern.

Exercise 19.4

'Va' sounds have been marked in bold and 'wa' sounds have been circled.

(O)ne[1] day **V**inaya (w)as (w)alking to(w)ards her **v**aluable **V**olks(w)agen (w)hen she saw[2] a (w)oman she kne(w) (w)aiting near a **v**eranda. **V**inaya (w)ondered (w)hat her name (w)as. She q(u)estioned[3] the (w)oman who[4] re**v**ealed she had met **V**inaya se**v**eral (w)eeks ago. Her name (w)as (W)anda; she was t(w)enty-two[5] years old and had a lo**v**ely wrist(w)atch[6] on.

To note:

(1) One—the letter 'o' has been circled because it is in fact pronounced as a 'wa' sound.

(2) Saw—the letter 'w' has not been circled because it is not pronounced.

(3) Questioned—the letter 'u' has been circled because it is in fact pronounced as a 'wa' sound.

(4) Who—the letter w has not been circled because it is not a 'wa' sound.

(5) Two—the letter 'w' has not been circled because it is not pronounced.

(6) Wristwatch—the first letter 'w' has not been circled because it is not a 'wa' sound.

Exercise 19.5

1. The 'fah' and 'pah' sounds are similar as they are both strong sounds that require lots of air. They are different as the 'fah' sound requires you to bite your upper teeth down to your lower lip whereas the 'pah' sound requires you to simply join your lips.
2. The 'fah' and 'va' sounds are similar as they both share the same teeth and lower lip placement. They are different as 'fah' requires air and 'va' does not ('va' is a throat sound).
3. 'Bite your Vs and Kiss your Ws'.

Chapter 20

Exercise 20.1

Strong: 'Fah', 'Kah', 'Pah', 'Sah', 'Tah',
Weak: 'Ba', 'Da', 'Ga', 'Ja', 'La', 'Ma', 'Na', 'Ra', 'Va', 'Wa', 'Ya', 'Za'

Exercise 20.2

1. They are cut short.
2. They are stretched and become longer.

SECTION 3

Chapter 21

Exercise 21.1

Agent: 'Okay, someone will call you back in two days.'

Customer: 'No, I won't have time in two days; I'd like to speak to someone now.'

Agent: **'Ma'am someone will surely call you in two days.'** (*The agent did not listen when the customer said that she wouldn't have time in two days. A better response could have been, 'I am sorry but no one is available now.*

	Since you won't have time in two days, when will you be free?')
Customer:	'Did you not hear me? I won't have time in two days! I'd like to speak to someone now.'
Agent:	'Sorry ma'am, but **someone will call you in two days surely.'** (*Again, it is a bad idea to repeat that someone will call in two days when clearly the customer has already said she won't have time then.*)
Customer:	'Are you telling me no one is available in the entire bank to speak with me? And why does it take two days to return customers' calls?'
Agent:	**'Yes, sorry ma'am it takes two days.** But don't worry, someone will surely call you.' (*The customer asked* **why** *it takes two days to return calls. The agent did not answer this question. Also, the agent ignored the customer's first question about no one being available in the entire bank. Ignoring difficult questions does not make them go away!*)
Customer:	'This is so frustrating. You aren't even answering my questions. Fine, have someone call me in two days.'
Agent:	**'Thank you ma'am, goodbye.'** (*The agent once again ignored the accusation that he/she did not answer any of the customer's questions. It is almost like the agent is just listening to what he/she wants to.*)

Customer:	'Wait! You haven't taken down my contact information...' (*The agent has already ended the call. He/she did not wait for the customer to say goodbye.*)

Exercise 21.2

1. Extraordinary listener
2. Bad listener
3. Average listener

Chapter 22

Exercise 22.1

Five possible thoughtful questions:

1. How are you preparing for the race?
2. Why have you decided to enter the marathon?
3. Do you believe only athletes can finish marathons?
4. Why does participating in a marathon excite you?
5. Do you believe that marathons should only be for non-profit causes?

Five possible shallow questions:

1. What time does the marathon start?
2. Where is the marathon taking place?
3. When is the marathon taking place?
4. Are you running in the marathon with anyone?
5. Which part of the marathon are you running in?

The key difference between the thoughtful and shallow questions listed above is that the former allow for more open-ended responses. They also allow for more interesting and unique responses. To answer those questions, the person you are speaking to would have to think critically and share personal details.

Exercise 22.2

Nitin:	Hi Anand, did you hear about Anu's party?
Anand:	Yes, I did but I won't be able to make it.
Nitin:	Oh really? Well that is too bad. **How is your girlfriend doing?**

(Here, Nitin did not ask Anand why he won't be able to make the party. Instead he switched to an unrelated topic.)

Anand:	She's doing okay. She's really busy on a new project right now.
Nitin:	Well that is exciting! **Hey, are you guys attending Rohan's wedding later this month?**

(Here, Nitin did not ask what the new project is. Instead he switched to an unrelated topic.)

Anand:	Yes, both of us are going to his wedding.

Chapter 23

Exercise 23.1

Interviewer:	You do seem though to have a lot of experience in the finance field.

Explanation: Because Rohan is interviewing for an advertising job, the above comment means that the interviewer doubts whether Rohan has enough *advertising experience* for the job. What Rohan could have said to assure the interviewer was:

Rohan:	Yes, I do have quite a bit of finance experience but I also have years of advertising experience. Also, my

advertising experience was hands-on, where I was working directly with client companies on their campaigns.

Exercise 23.2

Gurjot: But why?

(This is too broad a question. Instead, Gurjot could have said:)

Gurjot: I am sorry to hear that. Are there any parts of the project in particular you are not happy with?

(Gurjot again fails to probe effectively when he asks:)

Gurjot: Okay, I apologize on behalf of my team, but what are you unhappy with?

(This is again too broad a question and slightly confrontational. Instead, Gurjot could have asked:)

Gurjot: I apologize on behalf of my team. Was it the overall writing you didn't like? Did you feel the report wasn't detailed enough or did it lack the information you were looking for?

Chapter 24

Exercise 24.1

1) Step 1: WHAT—Diwali
2) Step 1: WHY Reason #1—I love firecrackers; WHY Reason #2—having my entire family together
3) Step 2: Backup for WHY Reason #1: When we burst firecrackers in the air the entire sky lights up and it seems as if the whole world is happy.
   Backup for WHY Reason #2: Before my family goes out to play with firecrackers, we have a large meal where we laugh together,

talk to one another and in general catch up with each other's busy lives.

4) Step 3: Concluding sentence: All in all, Diwali, through lights, laughter and fun, brings my family together.

Exercise 24.2

Rajal's introductory sentence is: 'I forgot to call you because I was studying and looking after my little brother.'
Part I (WHO, WHAT, WHERE, WHERE) = I forgot to call
Why Reason #1 = studying
Why Reason #2 = looking after little brother

Now, instead of supporting these two reasons with examples, Rajal starts stating *additional.* Why reasons:
-pick up something for mother
-cleaning room

Rajal also does not give a concluding sentence that restates her introduction .

An example of a correct, concise response utilizing the format we learned is:
I forgot to call you because I was studying and looking after my little brother. I have exams next week so I was really trying to concentrate on my books. Also, my little brother is very demanding of my time as he runs around pulling things off the shelves and breaking stuff. I'm so sorry that I forgot to call you, but it just slipped my mind as I was completely preoccupied with my studying and my little brother.

Exercise 24.3

Vipasha's introductory sentence is: 'Ms Badani I was unable to find the necessary data because my computer was not working properly and I was unsure whether I was supposed to concentrate only on the client's marketing plan.'
Part I (WHO, WHAT, WHERE, WHERE)—I was unable to find the necessary data
Why Reason #1—computer was not working properly.
Why Reason #2—unsure about concentrating only on the client's marketing plan.

Now, instead of supporting these two reasons with examples, Vipasha starts giving completely different Why reasons: 'While I was going through the client records, I found that their in-house information was not properly stated. Their product figures did not match their sales figures and thus I decided not to include any financials.'

These are good examples, but they do not explain why her computer was not working properly or why she didn't know if the assignment was only about the client's marketing plan. Vipasha also does not restate her introductory sentence during her concluding sentence.

Let's look at two responses Vipasha could have given. The why responses have been underlined (both in the introductory sentence and the concluding sentence) and their correlating supporting reasons given.

Using the same introductory sentence:
Ms Badani I was unable to find the necessary data <u>because my computer was not working properly</u> and <u>I was unsure whether I was supposed to concentrate only on the client's marketing plan</u>. My computer did not have access to the company folders and our technician has not been able to fix my problem all week, thus making it impossible for me to access the necessary data. Also, the brief I received included both finance and marketing, and when I asked Mr Joshi which I should concentrate on, he was unable to give me a proper answer. Thus, I did not have the <u>direction I needed</u> or the <u>technical support necessary</u> to complete this project properly.

Support for Why reason #1: computer was not working properly
My computer did not have access to the company folders and our technician has not been able to fix my problem all week, thus making it impossible for me to access the necessary data.

Support for Why reason #2: unsure about concentrating only on the client's marketing plan
Also, the brief I received included both finance and marketing, and when I asked Mr Joshi which I should concentrate on, he was unable to give me a proper answer.

Using the same Body:
Ms Badani I was unable to find the necessary data because the client information was unclear and seemed misstated. While I was going through the client records, I found that their in-house information was not properly stated. Their product figures did not match their sales figures and thus I decided not to include any financials. Thus, because I felt the client had misrepresented their figures and not presented the material clearly, I did not complete the report properly.

Support for Why reason #1: client information was unclear
While I was going through the client records, I found that their in-house information was not properly stated.

Support for Why reason #2: seemed misstated
Their product figures did not match their sales figures and thus I decided to not include any financials.